Rape on Prime Time

Feminist Cultural Studies, the Media, and Political Culture

Series Editors
Mary Ellen Brown
Andrea Press

A complete list of books in the series is available from the publisher.

Rape on Prime Time

Television, Masculinity, and
Sexual Violence

Lisa M. Cuklanz

PENN

University of Pennsylvania Press

Philadelphia

10 9 8 7 6 5 4 3 2 1

Published by
University of Pennsylvania Press
Philadelphia, Pennsylvania 19104-4011

Library of Congress Cataloging-in-Publication Data
Cuklanz, Lisa M.
    Rape on prime time : television, masculinity, and sexual violence
/ Lisa M. Cuklanz.
        p.   cm. — (Feminist cultural studies, the media, and
political culture)
      Includes bibliographical references and index.
      ISBN 0-8122-3522-3 (alk. paper). —
    ISBN 0-8122-1710-1 (pbk. : alk. paper)
        1. Women — Crimes against.   2. Rape in mass media.   3. Sex in mass
    media.   4. Feminist theory.   I. Title.   II. Series.
    HV6250.4.W65C85   1999
    306.7 — dc21   99-38729
                                                                         CIP

Contents

1. Introduction: Rape and Prime Time Episodic TV   1

2. What Is Rape? Prime Time's Changing Portrayals   28

3. Hegemonic Masculinity and Prime Time Rape   62

4. Representations of Victims and Rape Reform Ideas   99

5. Unusual and Groundbreaking Episodes   128

6. Conclusion   154

Appendix 1: Program Descriptions and Episode List   161

Appendix 2: Timeline of Rape Reform and Related Events   170

Notes   171

References   175

Index   183

Acknowledgments   189

Chapter 1
Introduction
Rape and Prime Time Episodic TV

The relationship between prime time television and social change is complex, historically significant, and as yet only partially understood. As one contemporary analysis notes, "few commentators would question that television has become more open about treating political issues and social controversies as the stuff of entertainment. But the substance and implications of its treatment are hotly disputed."[1] Although we know that prime time drama frequently depicts controversial issues and political debates, it is also generally accepted that prime time texts are constructed so as to avoid offending potential audience members. Thus the issues and ranges of opinion depicted are usually somewhat "safe," either because the passage of time has made the issue less emotional and less controversial, or because prime time treatment of it is mild and nonthreatening.[2] Although some episodes of prime time dramatic programs have depicted hot-button issues (such as *Maude*'s well-publicized decision on abortion and *Designing Women*'s "Hill-Thomas" episode), prime time more often simply incorporates subtle changes into its themes and dialogues. The broad patterns of this incorporation of the new and different over time require further examination if we are to understand the important relationship between the mass media and social change. Yet studies of television seldom focus on evolving depictions of important contemporary issues, tending instead to focus on a particular program or genre, or to examine many programs within a fixed time period. Longitudinal studies of issue-oriented or issue-based dramatic programming will be necessary in order to delineate the complex historical process that links public issue advocacy with fictional dramatic programming on prime time. The subject of rape provides a unique and important opportunity for the study of relationships between television programming and social change, because the movement for rape reform has been long-lived, well publicized, and successful on many fronts, resulting in drastic changes in law, courtroom procedure, evidence gathering, crisis counseling, and victim care.[3] More important, the movement proposed a model for understanding rape that directly and purposely opposed the traditional conception, thus clearly challenging dominant ideology with a coherent alternative. Thus analysis of the ways prime time has altered its representation of rape can provide important information about how television negotiates positions on difficult and prominent issues and can offer evidence as to how fully or marginally the ideas of rape reformers have been accepted in the mainstream.

This introductory chapter explicates the rationale and historical framework for the study of prime time episodic portrayals of rape during the key historical period from 1976 through 1990, discussing feminist challenges to traditional notions about rape that were widely circulated during these years. It examines previous scholarship on rape representations in the mass media, on the relationship between television and social change, and on the definition and significance of the concept of hegemonic masculinity. Finally, it outlines the central argument of the book, that prime time episodic portrayals of rape during this period provided a discourse of masculinity, helping to construct and define a version of hegemonic masculinity in the face of feminist challenges to the traditional construction. This emphasis on masculinity was maintained throughout the fifteen-year period in question, even though the content of rape representation changed dramatically during the same time period. This chapter introduces the basic themes that are later used to elaborate both this central argument and the historical progression of rape portrayals. Central here are the identification of a basic rape formula in the early years from which later programs deviated, and the observation that shifts in the genre most regularly representing rape had implications for the specific ways in which the crime, its perpetrators and victims, were portrayed over time.

Why 1976–1990?

The pace, manner, and implications of prime time television's treatment of the issues of rape and rape reform are the subject of this book. By examining a collection of more than 100 prime time dramatic episodes aired on U.S. television from 1976 through 1990, it traces the development of television's portrayal of rape during and immediately following the period when the rape reform movement in this country was most active and most effective. Through this examination, the book offers clear evidence that prime time programming does change in response to issue-advocacy movements, but that it does so in ways that are severely constrained by the limitations of genre, medium, and precedent. Furthermore, patterns of change in prime time's discourse on rape have consistently reinforced key elements of dominant ideology. By examining fifteen years of rape-centered dramatic episodic programs, this book shows how prime time adjusted early to some rape reform claims, yet incorporated others quite slowly, reluctantly, and/or infrequently. The fifteen-year time frame under examination here allows for a long view of the development of prime time's dominant conception of rape, and it encompasses significant changes in genre, character interactions, and themes in prime time episodic programming.

This book focuses specifically on the years from 1976 through 1990 because this period coincides with the most important era of development of the feminist rape reform movement. This movement began in the early 1970s and gained its first formal recognition with the passage of the reformed Michigan Statute in 1974. It continued to develop momentum and recognition in the following years, as evidenced by the volume of publications in fields like sociology, psychology, and women's studies. Prime time's response to the public promotion of a reformed view of rape clearly started after 1976 and had undergone substantial change by 1990. The starting years, 1976–1977, represent a "time when feminist activism for rape reform was well under way, however not yet widely publicized outside scholarly and legal circles" (Sanday 1996, 184). The fifteen-year period under examination here is crucial for the understanding of rape outside of television representations because "starting in the 1970s research on acquaintance rape conducted by psychologists, sociologists, and medical researchers began, and by the

1990s a significant body of knowledge on all aspects of sexual assault and abuse had been established" (185).

As we reach the millennium, it is important to take a historical look at the pace and trajectory of change that has taken place in television programming in response to social change movements including the struggle for rape reform. From the vantage point of the present, it is clear that the key period of change in prime time's representations of rape was during the late 1970s through 1990, during which time such representations experienced notable patterns of transformation. Although television portrayals certainly continued to change in some ways, these years represent the primary adjustment in prime time's content in response to the rape reform movement. By 1990, prime time episodes were offering complex depictions of date/acquaintance rape and other issues more often than the highly formulaic depictions of violent stranger rape commonly found in the earlier years. Thus this fifteen-year period encompasses a remarkable adaptation in television's treatments of rape. This book examines these transformations in detail, tracing prime time's steps from violent stranger depictions to a predominance of date/acquaintance rape portrayals. Although subtle changes can be observed in prime time's more recent depictions, the years 1976–1990 represent the most intense, rapid, and obvious changes in response to feminist reformulations of rape. Together, these changes can be characterized as a clear transformation of prime time episodic television's typical portrayal of rape. However, this transformation took place over many years, and remnants of earlier representations remained visible even in the latest programming examined here.

Prime Time Rape Episodes

The preliminary data for this book were gathered at the Annenberg Television Script Archive at the University of Pennsylvania. This archive has an extensive collection of scripts of prime-time (8–11 P.M.) television programs from 1976 to the present.[4] The archive maintains a computer database that catalogues scripts according to subject and includes "sexual assault" as one of the key terms according to which scripts are catalogued. The archive provided an initial database of 94 scripts of sexual assault-related episodes.[5]

Eighteen episodes were eliminated from this group because the subject matter was sexual assault other than rape, such as child molestation or child prostitution. The remaining 76 scripts were supplemented through examination of episode guides from numerous programs, and some additional scripts were obtained from other sources. These sources yielded 25 additional episodes. Rape episodes from all these sources were collected on videotape. Although not all episodes could be obtained on tape (especially for older and more obscure programs that were never in syndication), over half the total number of episodes were collected in this form. Thus the analysis here is based on script and/or broadcast versions of the approximately 100 episodes under discussion.[6] Appendix 1 lists the programs and specific episodes represented.

Initially, I examined all hundred episodes for their depictions of the basic elements of victim/survivor and rapist characterization and treatment of the crime itself, to ascertain where key elements of rape law reform ideology and language had infiltrated into TV programming and where they had been rejected or effectively resisted. Almost immediately a clear pattern emerged among the majority of early episodes, which presented rape almost exclusively as violent stranger attacks that featured severe brutality and trauma to the victim. This early formula is discussed in detail in "The Masculine Ideal: Rape on Prime-Time Television, 1976–1978" (Cuklanz 1998). Most of the episodes exhibiting these strikingly formulaic characteristics took place on detective programs classified as some variation of "police drama" or "crime drama," such as *Baretta*, *Spenser: For Hire*, *Starsky and Hutch*, *The Rockford Files*, and *Quincy*.[7] Programs that did not so clearly exhibit this formulaic quality included a variety of types: situation comedy (such as *Barney Miller*, *The Facts of Life*, and *Welcome Back, Kotter*), western (e.g., *Little House on the Prairie*, *Oregon Trail*, *The Quest*), and evening soap (*Dallas*). The unusual and unique (such as a *Barney Miller* episode featuring marital rape) will be examined in Chapter 5; the unmistakable pattern of representation in the majority of early episodes forms the starting point of this book. I argue that this pattern clearly establishes that the primary function of rape on prime time episodic television, from 1976 through 1990, was to provide material for the demonstration of ideal masculinity in terms that worked to contain feminist arguments.

The Formula Plot

The formula established in the earliest episodes examined here remained the most prominent type of rape representation on prime time through the early 1980s. I call this formula the "basic plot" throughout this book, which traces the development of prime time representations of rape, beginning with this basic plot formula and moving toward more complex, varied, and ambiguous portrayals. In the majority of the episodes through the early 1980s, the victim is attacked by an unseen rapist who clamps a hand over her mouth, grabs her forcefully or throws her to the ground, and speaks lines filled with threats, sexist stereotypes, and outmoded ideas about women and sexuality. Brutal violence is often suggested by the use of weapons, through the post-rape appearance of the victim, or through the inclusion of an unusual "MO" that involves restraints, weapons, or strange marks on the victim's body. The beginning of the attack often emphasizes the rapist's intense depravity, which is condemned by the (male) protagonist and contrasted with his own actions, beliefs, and character. The hospital or other post-attack scene emphasizes the helplessness of the victim and the severe psychological and physical damage done to her. Rapists are depicted as identifiably outside the mainstream through their language, clothing, habits, or attitudes. Each of these plot elements works to reinforce sensitivity and desire for justice on the part of the male protagonist. In most episodes it is the male detective/main character who provides the primary comfort and support for the victim. The stories end when the detective protagonist has completed his work, that is, when the rapist is caught or killed. The detective's sense of morality, and often his need for revenge on the criminal, thus culminate in a successful triumph of the "good guy," which is often accomplished through violence against the rapist. However, the further plight of the victim through the course of counseling or a trial are not included.

In short, these plots are about the male avengers of rape rather than about the problem or crime of rape or the experiences and feelings of the victim. And the narratives tend to require repeated rapes to provide both suspense and enough evidence for the criminal to be apprehended.

Despite the predictability of most prime time rape episodes, it would be inaccurate to say that these episodes all feature the same characteristic elements. Rather, the basic plot episodes illustrate what could be called a pattern of limited variation. They follow a predictable pattern consisting of a number of recognizable and often-repeated elements, and seldom break out of these established conventions in any substantial way. A single episode very seldom includes all the characteristic elements; each episode includes almost all but omits one or two. Nearly every episode includes some unique element that, however small, makes it different from a simple standard template. If the standard version features a victim/survivor who is passive and silent after the rape, one or two episodes include a defiant or violent victim. If the standard version features the use of sexist language and weapons on the part of the rapist, one or two episodes will feature rapists who do not express outmoded attitudes about gender or do not coerce their victims with weapons. The basic plot pattern was the predominant form of rape representation in the prime time episodes through the early 1980s. In later years, new forms of representation, new versions of rape, and new types of characters were included as the genres in which rape episodes were depicted themselves evolved.

The Rape Reform Movement

Some background on the rape reform movement in the United States and on previous scholarship on mass media representations of rape will establish the terms and themes that have been important to the movement, and to media writers and scholars, since the early 1970s. These elements will be used in the analysis of prime time episodes as one means of assessing the manner and degree of change in prime time's construction of rape. A timeline of rape reform and related events is included for reference in Appendix 2.

Feminist activists have been working on the issue of rape for over thirty years. Feminist analyses of the causes of rape vary from those that attribute the crime to male and female socialization to those that assert that rape is a fundamental part of the patriarchal domination of women, or that it is merely a logical extension of a sexual system that depends on violence and subordination. More recent feminist work also varies widely in attitudes toward the relationship among rape, sex, and violence. The early feminist notion that rape is violence rather than sex has been called into doubt in recent radical feminist work. In general, though, feminist efforts surrounding this important issue have centered on redefining the crime, its perpetrators, and its victims and on bringing contemporary notions of rape in line with contemporary social realities. According to Davis (1991) and others,[8] the movement began when groups of women gathered in the early 1970s to discuss their rape experiences. The 1971 Speak Out on Rape, organized by the New York Radical Feminists, was a defining event for early activists. They quickly realized that rape victims faced considerable obstacles in obtaining justice because

The police were often indifferent or didn't believe the woman, especially if the man wasn't a total stranger . . . they sometimes implied that she was sex-starved and that her story was wishful thinking. Then again, some forced the victim to describe the attack in such minute detail that it was clear they were enjoying themselves. (Davis 1991, 311)

The New York Radical Feminists also organized a conference on rape in 1971, during which several key points were agreed on that would form the core of feminist thinking about rape, such as the idea that victims of rape were unfairly made to feel guilty and responsible, the observation that victims were often accused of lying or exaggerating their claims of rape, the assertion that rape was treated differently from other felony crimes with respect to standards of proof and assumptions about victim behavior, and the conclusion that current law reinforced shame and secrecy (Sanday 1996, 174). The previous year had marked the publication of Kate Millet's *Sexual Politics*, in which a "feminist understanding of rape was first articulated" (172). The book linked socialization, sexuality, sexual violence, and the social construction of gender and politics and presented a challenge to the biological explanation of observable gender differences.

Early activists were appalled by the abysmal conviction rate for rape and the process of attrition whereby rape cases were dropped or weakened as they moved through the system. Susan Brownmiller's *Against Our Will* (1975) showed that approximately 85 percent of rape claimants were believed by the police. Of these 51 percent of perpetrators were caught. Of these 76 percent were brought to trial, and of these only 53 percent were convicted (175). Davis (1991) reports similarly depressing statistics from New York, noting that

In 1971 there were 2,415 rape complaints that the police considered "founded" and worth pursuing; they made 1085 arrests; 100 cases were held to be solid enough to present to the grand jury; the grand jury subsequently handed down 34 indictments. In the end, there were 18 convictions—less than 1 percent of all complaints. (311)

In jurisdictions where proof of penetration was required to establish rape, even lower rates were recorded (see Connell and Wilson 1974, 128). The rate of reported rape was also climbing rapidly: "In 1969 the rape rate surged ahead of all other crimes against the person, and in the early 1970s it again increased markedly" (Sanday 1996, 163).

Survivors shared individual stories of rape and rape trials (see Griffin 1979) and began to understand that experiences of rape were determined by systems beyond the control of the individual victim: from police attitudes toward rape claimants to courtroom procedures and standards of evidence and proof, to comments and attitudes of friends and family, victims noted that they had met with suspicion, distrust, and blame as they attempted to discuss their rape experiences. They soon realized that powerful historical, legal, and ideological forces contributed to the uniform negativity of these experiences. Beyond their consciousness-raising efforts, feminist anti-rape activists began to construct a coherent counterformulation of rape, and they began to circulate their critique of the traditional view of rape to the general public. A wave of publications in the mid-1970s document a rapidly emerging feminist viewpoint on the subject of rape. This coherent counterformulation was advanced broadly in a range of fields including sociology, psychology, and law.[9] These works differed in their attribution of the causes and purposes of rape (Brownmiller's *Against Our Will* was controversial for its claim that rape was an integral part of the patriarchal control of women throughout history), but they nonetheless expressed remarkable unity in their assertions both on how rape had traditionally been viewed and on how this traditional view should be rejected in favor of a feminist understanding that directly opposed and critiqued this widely accepted understanding of rape, its causes and implications.

Prior to these feminist efforts in the 1960s and 1970s, attitudes toward rape in the United States were drawn from traditional notions perhaps most clearly articulated in British Common Law and in U.S. legal literature that borrowed assumptions from this traditional British code. Cultural and legal understandings of rape held that the crime was uniquely characterized by lying victims and false accusation (because of the supposed "revenge" or "covering shame" motives); feminists asserted that actual rates of false accusation were no greater for rape than for other violent crimes. The traditional view understood rape as a brutal crime involving a rapist and victim unknown to each other; feminists observed that most instances of nonconsensual intercourse involved people who knew each other, often as friends, dates, partners, or spouses. The traditional view often held victims responsible for their own attacks (because of dress, seductive behavior, drug or alcohol use, subconscious desire, and other factors); the feminist reformulation asserted that it was simply absurd to claim that people would "ask for" sexually violent treatment and that this self-harm notion was unique for rape among all other violent crimes.[10] The traditional view held that rapists were abnormal, depraved, or marginal men; feminists countered that many men who might be considered normal in other ways, and who might not commit other violent crimes, committed rape. Feminists argued that the traditional understanding of rape, written into legal codes and judicial practice, fostered a context in which victims rather than defendants were placed on trial and forced to demonstrate moral purity while the defendant's sexual history was deemed irrelevant. Finally, while the traditional view of rape held that black men were more likely to be rapists than white men and were more likely to choose white victims, feminists and others used statistics to prove that the opposite assertions were true. In fact, intra-racial rape was most common, and a black attacker raping a white victim was the less common form of interracial rape (LaFree 1992).

The belief that rape was a "special crime" because of its interpersonal and sexual nature legitimated extraordinary legal practices such as jury warnings as to the questionable credibility of victims, virtually unattainable standards of evidence such as proof of "utmost resistance," and the requirement of corroborative testimony and/or physical evidence to prove nonconsent. Activists asserted that women were unlikely to fabricate claims of rape that would ultimately mean they were stigmatized, accused of contributing to the incident, and scrutinized for amoral behavior, all in order to watch the rapist go free.[11] Feminist activists worked to help survivors of rape, setting up counseling networks and crisis lines, and working to educate police and hospital staff on evidence collection and victim treatment (Matthews 1994). Activists fought to alter public consciousness and legal statutes regarding rape in hopes of improving reporting and conviction in cases of rape. They wanted to make their understanding of rape known to the mainstream culture, and argued that their view matched contemporary social conditions much better than the traditional view, handed down from a time when a woman's survival depended on her ability credibly to claim chastity before marriage and fidelity afterward (see Craik 1984). In addition, they referred to the work of Ida B. Wells-Barnett and others documenting the racist use of rape claims as a means of maintaining racial separation and domination, demonstrating that, historically, black men were falsely accused of rape as a means of legitimizing their brutal murder by lynching, while white men raped black women with impunity (see Thompson 1990). Feminists have generally agreed that rape is a result of gender inequality in economic, political, and social terms, but have differed in their formulations of how these inequalities variously contribute to the problem of rape and the likelihood of meaningful change within a patriarchal and capitalist system.

As Sanday documents, several early studies of rape made distinctions between "jump-from-the-bushes stranger rape and rape involving people who know one another" (186). Sanday traces this distinction back to the 1950s and locates it in important studies from subsequent decades including those of Amir (1971), Russell (1975), and Brownmiller (1975). Sanday attributes the first use of the phrase "date rape" to Brownmiller in *Against Our Will*. Later, researchers such as Dianna E. H. Russell used the phrase "acquaintance rape" as "an umbrella term to distinguish rapes involving people who know one another from rapes involving strangers" (Sanday 1996, 189). Susan Estrich in *Real Rape* (1987) has emphasized the recalcitrance of public opinion in accepting feminist ideas about rape. Estrich focuses on the remaining dichotomy in the public mind between what she calls "real rape," a violent and unexpected attack by a stranger, and what the legal system calls "simple rape," which involves a rapist and victim known to each other. She argues that a decade after the initial wave of publications on the subject our culture as a whole was still willing to treat only violent stranger rape as a real crime. Other attacks that did not fit this profile (because victim and rapist knew each other, were dating, or were married to each other; because the attacker did not use a weapon or beat the victim; because the victim used alcohol or drugs; or because the victim did not show utmost resistance) have continued to be considered borderline cases in which it is too difficult to judge whether rape has been committed. Gregory Matoesian makes almost the same point in his summary of the feminist structural analysis of rape: noting that conviction is more likely

when the perpetrator and victim are strangers, and some type of extrinsic force is used; when consent, intimacy, and prior sexual history are not introduced as issues in the case; and when the victim is a "nice girl" or a virgin, and has not been drinking, using drugs, "partying," or otherwise violating traditional female gender role behavior. (1993, 15)

These observations suggest that the traditional view is still with us.

Alongside this social and political context, our popular culture has consistently depicted rape and sexual assault, often graphically, prompting many to inquire about the relationship between popular representation and general attitudes toward rape.[12] The importance of the complex and contested relationship between media representations of rape and social attitudes about it cannot be underestimated. This book examines the extent to which the feminist movement, with its successes in changing public perceptions of rape, and in rape law reform, was influential in creating change in an important area of mass mediated portrayal of rape.

Prime Time Television and Social Change

John Fiske (1987) has argued that "hegemony characterizes social relations as a series of struggles for power" and that "cultural studies views texts similarly, as the site of a series of struggles for meaning" (41). Hegemony theorists examining television are interested in understanding this give-and-take between televisual representation and events in the realm of social change politics. Studies examining this relationship have shown that prime time content does reflect both contemporary social issues and the results of interest group advocacy for and against specific subject matter. Taylor notes that "the urbanity and social-problem orientation that developed in the first half of the 1970s remained a feature of prime-time programming and established themselves as core characteristics of television entertainment in the 1980s" (1989, 55). Prime time programs increasingly portrayed socially relevant issues, including rape. A copious body of work examines the content, production, and/or reception of 1970s television. The most helpful with regard to this analysis is Todd Gitlin's *Inside Prime Time* ([1983] 1985), which investigates factors that affected the writing, selection, and scheduling of prime time series programming from the late 1970s through 1982. Gitlin argues that television, rather than practicing or representing a severe or frightening "cultural tyranny," instead exercises at best only a "soft tyranny, operating through stripped-down formulas that the networks selectively abstract, via other media, from mass sentiments" themselves formed by "the immense weight of mass culture's formulas as they have accumulated over the years (203). Gitlin's observation is similar to that articulated by Fiske (1987): "social change does occur, ideological values do shift, and television is part of this movement. It is wrong to see it as an originator of social change, or even to claim that it ought to be so" (45). Gitlin further notes that television executives are more interested in repeating and copying successful programming than in carrying out any particular plan of ideological coherence: "executives like to say they are constantly looking for something new, but their intuition tells them to hunt up pre-packaged trends and then recognize the new as a variant of the old" (63). While *Inside Prime Time* focuses primarily on how this phenomenon of minimal ingenuity functions from show to show (such that *St. Elsewhere* is conceived as "*Hill Street* in the hospital" 76), Gitlin suggests that it can also function on a much smaller scale, with individual episodes mimicking each other. Episode writing proceeds primarily by imitation, with writers copying what others have written.

The episodes analyzed here show that copying or formula writing occurred frequently with respect to plots centering on rape, particularly in the late 1970s and early 1980s: the majority of episodes were part of the detective/cop genre and followed a specific pattern of characterization of rapist, victim, crime, and detective. The patterned representation of rape persisted through the early 1980s, even though changes in programs and shifts in genres might have predicted otherwise. Thus an important method of studying television may be to examine similar plots or themes across series or across genres to investigate how specific issues, problems, and elements of social change are treated. This book illustrates that political issues and social problems that exist in the world outside television can be constructed with a great deal of uniformity within a given time period across programs and even across genres. The 1970s and early 1980s rape episodes examined here show remarkable similarity, as if they were written according to a "rape formula" (rather than simply specific program formulas).

A number of authors have examined 1980s television for its relevance to the real world of politics and social life. The most important of these in relation to this project is Bonnie Dow's 1996 work *Prime-Time Feminism: Television, Media Culture, and the Women's Movement Since 1970.* Dow traces the inclusion of feminism in selected prime time programs that have centered on women characters and have been considered feminist by audiences and analysts. She discusses the different formulations of feminism on these prime time shows, as well as their different narrative means of containing their feminist potential. Dow's work is notable in its examination of several prime time programs in historical relation to each other and its discussion of how these programs have incorporated elements of social change into their representations of women's lives while omitting others. Dow's shows were selected because of their potential for depicting and standing for feminist social change, and most of them are situation comedies, because "the programming form representing feminism that has been the most long-lived on television historically has been the situation comedy" (103). This is because "comedy offers a space for representing social controversy and social change that might be too threatening when encoded as realist drama" (103). Dow's work offers an important precursor to the analysis in this book, which also traces the incorporation of feminist social change ideas into prime time programming since the 1970s. However, because Dow's work examines the "best case" programs, chosen especially for their inclusion of feminism, it leaves open the question of what other genres of prime time have done. In one sense, this examination presents the flip side of Dow's analysis, examining episodes aired primarily on the least feminist of genres, the police/detective drama.

Rape in the Mass Media

The relationship between the mass media and the rape reform movement has been examined by numerous scholars in recent years. Both Helen Benedict (1992) and I (1996) analyze news coverage of prominent sexual assault and rape cases between 1978 and 1990, and both conclude that mainstream news of these cases has done little to present a coherent view of any feminist-based understanding of rape. Benedict focuses on how reporters' work could be done more responsibly with victim rights and concerns in mind, in contrast to the suspicious, overly dramatized, and sometimes prurient treatment often afforded victims in mainstream news stories. My own work argues that mainstream news coverage of two prominent rape cases included acceptance of isolated rape reform ideas but offered only fragmented depictions of rape reform history and efforts. It also discusses fictionalized treatments of the same cases, noting that movies, including those made for television, have done better than mainstream news in depicting victims sympathetically and offering a coherent understanding of feminist ideas.

Sujata Moorti (1995) also examines the mass media's treatment of rape, focusing on the late 1980s and early 1990s and noting that, with regard to recent highly publicized trials, television talk shows have in general served as a more reliable source of expression of feminist ideas about rape and victim experiences than has mainstream news. Moorti's chapter on late 1980s serial television argues that male protagonists tend to have pro-feminist beliefs, but that they also react violently to rape (266). In addition, she notes that prime time dramas underscore the vulnerability of women and imply that rape is primarily a symbol of failure in fulfilling the norms of masculinity (266). Moorti notes some inclusion of feminist ideas by the late 1980s, but she examines earlier texts only in passing. Thus, Benedict, Moorti, and I have found mainstream news poorly suited to the expression of feminist reformulation of rape and rape reform. Other forms including film, serial prime time television, and television talk shows have been more useful in making rape reform ideas available to a mainstream audience. These findings indicate that prime time serial television may be an important ground on which the tensions between traditional and feminist ideas about rape are played out.

Susan Brinson's work is most closely related to this book. Her 1990 dissertation, *TV Rape: The Representation of Rape in Prime-Time Television*, an examination of rape-centered episodes aired primarily in the fall of 1989, applies a feminist framework to the study of traditional and reformed rape themes within 26 rape episodes. It closely examines characterizations of victim, rapist, and the crime itself and compares uses of traditional "rape myths" and of feminist ideas oppositional to those myths. In both the dissertation and her study entitled "The Use and Opposition of Rape Myths in Prime-Time Television Dramas" (1992), Brinson argues that traditional rape myths are invoked and articulated more frequently than any opposing frameworks or understandings of rape. Brinson's work raises but does not explore the question of how rape was depicted prior to the late 1980s, during the period when rape was in the process of emerging as a social issue in the mass media and public consciousness. She concludes that a clearer understanding of alterations in cultural attitudes over time could be gained through a longitudinal study examining depictions of rape on prime time (1990, 177).

All four researchers have specifically compared depictions of traditional ideas about rape (those inherited from British Common Law and expressed in popular culture and legal statutes prior to the 1970s) to ideas advanced by feminist reformers beginning in the early 1970s. The specific elements labeled "rape myths" or "traditional ideas about rape" vary only slightly and include the following notions: rape claimants are often liars, rapists are marginal or readily identifiable, real rape is violent and committed by a stranger, victims contribute to their own attacks by provoking or asking for rape, and rape is a special crime that warrants unusual legal and judicial procedures. All four authors agree that feminist ideas have found expression in the mainstream mass media in severely limited ways, and that "mythic" (traditional) ideas about rape receive more frequent, more coherent, and more legitimate expression.

Additional insights into television's representation of rape are briefly included in Lichter, Lichter, and Rothman's *Prime Time: How TV Portrays American Culture* (1994), which observes that rape is "a crime ideally suited to television. It is violent and therefore action packed. The sexual nature of the crime can easily be presented as the act of a violent, mentally unbalanced madman" (280). The authors note that prime time portrayals of rape differ significantly from the fact patterns of rape in the real world. They find that, while real world rapes tend to be perpetrated by acquaintances and relatives of victims, television rape is "the last refuge of the sadistic, irrational criminal" (1994, 279). Berman also emphasizes this point in noting that police programs present a view of crime and police work that is "completely mythological" (1987, 82). These observations match the basic argument made here regarding programming through the early 1980s, but not the late 1980s examples.

The way television portrayals of rape reverse real-life statistical truths is also discussed in Schlesinger et al.'s (1992) analysis of female audience responses to media violence in Great Britain. Their focus is on the way TV suggests that most rapes are brutal surprise attacks by strangers. They examine various audience types in relation to rape content and conclude that the one area of violence in which differences of class and race do not affect women's reaction is when the violent act is rape. They find it "puzzling" that the women in their study were more afraid of stranger rape than of domestic violence or acquaintance rape, and they observe that "The fact that males are more likely to be physically violent to other males and that they are more likely to be physically or sexually violent to wives, lovers, or girlfriends than to total strangers is either ignored or relatively unstressed in the popular culture" (1992, 166–67). They note that rape is the only violent crime to be a matter of universal concern among women of all class and ethnic backgrounds and suggest that media content is in part responsible for the pervasiveness and universality of women's fear of stranger rape.

The findings of these authors are supported here. Prime time episodes aired during the first decade examined routinely depicted stranger rape as overpowering (the victims could not effectively fight back or escape), brutal, and devastating. They also provided visual images of rape occurring in virtually every location where women might routinely spend time — homes, back yards, hospitals, parking garages, cars, and public transportation. These elements combined to depict rape as something devastating to and out of the control of victims. However, prime time episodic television also included a range of representational elements that worked together to place primary focus on the role of male figures, especially protagonist detectives, in defining, condemning, avenging, and repairing the evils of rape. Most central characters in rape episodes were males, and female characters, including victims, played peripheral roles until the latest years under examination. The reasons for this can in part be explained through the insights of scholars who have identified and explicated the concept of hegemonic masculinity in relation to mass media content.

Hegemonic Masculinity

Several researchers have examined the role of television in defining, reproducing, and shifting the mainstream definition of masculinity. Much of this work focuses on the genres of police and detective fiction in film and television. In his important chapter on masculine gendered television, Fiske (1987) argues that cop/detective shows represent the primary masculine television genre. Using Fiske's observation as a starting point, Robert Hanke (1992) argues that television plays a key role in reproducing "hegemonic masculinity," which he defines as "the social ascendancy of a particular version or model of masculinity . . . that defines 'what it means to be a man'" (190). Hanke finds the operation of hegemonic masculinity in the mass media complex, and he notes that

apparently modifications of hegemonic masculinity may represent some shift in the cultural meanings of masculinity without an accompanying shift in dominant social structural arrangements, thereby recuperating patriarchal ideology and making it more adaptable to contemporary social conditions and more able to accommodate counter-hegemonic forces such as liberal-feminist ideology. (197)

Hanke further explains that "one way in which conflicts in gender relations may be handled and defused is through the construction of a social definition of masculinity (sensitive, nurturing, emotionally expressive) that is more . . . accommodating of traditionally feminine connotations and values" (196). Hegemonic masculinity is a construct that takes into account feminist critiques of traditional masculinity, incorporating them into a new hybrid version but leaving the traditional version intact and simply overlaying new traits. Thus detectives on these rape episodes are caring and sympathetic to rape victims and even demonstrate reformed or enlightened views about rape as compared with other characters, but they still establish their masculinity in part by demonstrating volatility and routinely resorting to violence to solve problems and avenge the victims of rape. As Mary Eaton observes in her work on television crime dramas in Britain and the United States, hegemonic masculinity is necessarily defined only in relation to other less favored masculinities, to the extent that the "interplay" among these various forms is key to the functioning of patriarchy. Hegemonic masculinity "marginalises other masculinities [and] defines as 'other' all femininities" (1995, 169). These features can be seen clearly as common elements of police and detective dramas, and hegemonic masculinity and crime dramas are often discussed together. Male characters who do not fit the traditional parameters of masculinity and do not use violence to solve problems are contrasted to the heroic protagonists, illustrating imperfect versions of masculinity that help define and delimit the parameters of the hegemonic ideal.

The Detective Genre on Prime Time

Fiske (1987) treats cop/detective shows, which account for the preponderance of rape episodes in the database for this book, as the primary masculine television genre, with a predominantly male audience. Thus the frequency with which rape plots appeared on detective/police dramas is significant because it suggests that prime time's treatment of rape has had more to say about masculinity and male characters than about rape as a social issue or as a problem for victims and/or activists. Fiske also notes that detective shows, which cater to mostly male audiences, "have less need to produce a [text] that allows for oppositional or resistive meanings" and that, thus, these texts "are structured to produce greater narrative and ideological closure" (198). Programs in this genre are not as complex and open to interpretation as those of many other genres. Detective programs tend to depict clear contrasts between bad and good, and tend to have central protagonists around whom the action takes place. Fiske outlines the major components of masculinity in masculine gendered television programming, asserting that "most masculine texts" eliminate "the most significant cultural producers of the masculine identity — women, work, and marriage" (202), thus avoiding basic contradictions of male existence within the contemporary ideological and social structure and producing an untroubled version of masculinity.

Masculine television programming displays male achievement and performance, using the role of male as savior (rescuer) to distract attention from the ideologically problematic role of male as privileged oppressor. As the evidence from these rape plots shows, the genre serves important functions with regard to masculinity: it deflects criticism that condemns the mainstream construction of masculinity as macho; it objectifies women; it perhaps contributes to serious social problems such as pornography and rape, by offering a subtle redefinition that frames masculinity as the means through which women are protected and avenged rather than brutalized and demeaned. At the same time, protagonist males can engage in violence within certain parameters, such as when they become so morally outraged at criminals that they can no longer contain their anger. Masculine volatility is harnessed for acceptable purposes and never used against women. In traditional masculine programs, "sensitivity is seen as a threat to masculinity and women are victims in need of succor. In later programs sensitivity and caring are incorporated into the traditional masculine profile to create a hybrid" (Fiske 1987, 220). Fiske summarizes the relationship between narrative structure and gender by noting that masculine narratives provide a clear oppositional structure of gender difference, in which masculinity is characterized as tough, professional, public, outdoor, and strong, whereas femininity is sensitive, domestic, private, indoor, and weak (221). Rape provides a subject matter for which these stereotypes are easy to maintain. Not only are victims clearly deserving of protection and care, but the extreme evil and brutality of rape also serve as a clear contrast to the detective's behavior and legitimize his use of force. In most episodes rapists are shot to death, verbally condemned, or physically beaten by outraged detectives. Although such violence is not always condoned by other characters, it is presented as understandable and is common enough to be considered a basic element of hegemonic masculinity as constructed in these programs.

Police and detective dramas have been both popular and long-lasting. Ronald Berman (1987) describes the basic parameters of the classic crime/police drama as including focus on "deduction, pursuit, and capture" (80) as well as a reluctance to deal with "the social costs of crime." Accordingly, these programs "go as far as, but no further than, describing the psychological effect of crimes on victims" (81). Thus early rape plots follow the norms of detective drama in devoting very little attention to rape victims and their post-rape experiences. Police and detective dramas focus on crime and often present audiences with clear-cut moral oppositions. This dimension of moral clarity is emphasized by David Buxton in a discussion of *Starsky and Hutch*: "as in most American action series since, criminals are generally portrayed as mad dogs that have to be put down, so avoiding the 'sociological' problems posed by a criminal underclass" (1990, 133). A part of that moral response is related to the type of person we admire as opposed to the type we despise, and rape plots give us both in the form of male characters. Rape plots with few exceptions maintain Fiske's oppositional structure in their definitions of gender. However, they also allow male characters to show sensitivity by depicting extreme situations in which it is appropriate for the male protagonist to show sympathy and caring.

Buxton documents an evolution of detective programs, from depicting almost no personal life for protagonist detectives, to great detail in the personal lives of several members of the new ensemble casts. He argues that

> The inability to portray police work consistently in terms of a wider social context—which would be fascinating but also deeply disturbing—led the realist police series increasingly on to the terrain of private life. In later series . . . (*Cagney and Lacey*, *Hill Street Blues*), the effect of realism is obtained by foregrounding private life over police method. (139)

In the context of Buxton's observation, prime time's treatment of rape can be seen as fitting into its overall approach to the issue of crime as a social problem. As Buxton notes, because of their ideological functions, these programs could not openly face the tragic fact of endemic crime caused by broad social problems such as poverty, drug abuse, sexism, and poor education. Instead, because detectives in these series had "no interest in addressing the crime and corruption of an unregulated free enterprise system as political or even moral issues," crime stories from the early 1970s depicted conflicts between humanized detectives and "criminals of a somewhat psychopathic disposition" (132). My analysis of episodic rape representations argues that the evolution of the detective genre, with the increasing humanization and privatization of the detective characters, also constituted a shift in its construction of hegemonic masculinity, because in nearly every case the protagonist detective or team was male and male responses and reactions to rape formed the central subject matter of the episode. (Several detective programs have featured female protagonist detectives, and these will be discussed where relevant, that is, where rape episodes were aired on these programs.) It is worth noting that, even in the later-developed ensemble programs such as *Hill Street Blues* and *21 Jump Street*, it is usual to see only one woman in a group of as many as ten officers working together. Thus even in the later stories focus is on masculine reactions to rape.

Rape episodes on prime time television through the early 1980s reveal a discourse that is far more about masculinity than about rape: protagonist males are sensitive, nurturing, and emotionally expressive at the same time that they are competent, effective, volatile, and aggressive. These rape episodes can be seen as providing the circumstances in which dominant males can demonstrate their newly adapted masculinity in interaction mostly with other less reformed males, including rapists. Male detectives and police officers are determined, volatile, and prone to rush out and brutally beat rapists, but they are easily able to show a softer side in dealing with women, particularly victims of rape who clearly need to be handled with sensitivity after their traumatic experiences. In later episodes they effectively "train" husbands and boyfriends of victims in the proper attitude toward, and care of, the rape victim. The subject matter of rape is thus often used to enable the interplay among various conceptions of masculinity, with the detective's version almost always firmly legitimized. Detectives are likely to maintain the traditional masculine element of violence, threatening to "go after" (and many times actually beating up) suspected rapists. They express their anger in tirades against elements of "the system" that prevent prosecution or conviction, and sometimes these elements include unreformed rape laws. Detective characters thus often express views sympathetic to the ideas of feminist rape law reform, but they seldom openly endorse such ideas or attribute them to a social change movement.

The new characteristics of nurturance and caring should be seen as a response to the critiques of feminist analysis, and they should further be seen as means of maintaining the hegemonic power of patriarchal ideology and male dominance. Indeed, in the early years this shift in prime time's construction of masculinity corresponds with a failure to include rape reform discourse, feminist dialogue or characters, female protagonists, or even victim-centered treatments of the subject of rape. Later rape episodes, even those that have substantially altered the operative definition of rape within them, can still be seen to actively negotiate the meaning of hegemonic masculinity. These episodes demonstrate a variety of masculine positionings with respect to rape and clearly select the most preferable mode, usually that demonstrated by the detective or other professional or institutional representative such as a protagonist doctor, judge, or attorney.

Evolution of the Detective Genre and Prime Time Rape Plots

Between 1976 and 1990 television's landscape changed noticeably, such that by 1990 prime time offered very few traditional-formula detective dramas. As these programs became less popular, they evolved into hybrid genres and reformulated police programs, but programming through the 1980s proved that rape was still a subject best treated on shows that grew out of the 1970s detective drama. Programs that still involve police and detection account for well over half the rape-related episodes in the 1980s. These include *Strike Force* (1981–82, 2 episodes), *TJ Hooker* (1982–86, 4 episodes), *Hill Street Blues* (1981–87, 8 episodes), *Cagney and Lacey* (1982–88, 7 episodes), *Miami Vice* (1984–89, 4 episodes), *The Equalizer* (1985–89, 5 episodes), and *In the Heat of the Night* (1988–92, 4 episodes through 1990). Another significant proportion appeared on variations like *21 Jump Street* (1987–91, 6 episodes through 1990) — where undercover cops work in an urban high school.[13] The only non-detective program to air multiple rape episodes during the late 1980s was *L.A. Law* (9 episodes through 1990). Thus, even though the types of rape depicted changed drastically from 1976 to 1990, the type of program that treated rape changed very little. In fact, the evolution of the police/detective genre is responsible for most of the change in the type of program featuring rape. Non-detective programs such as evening soap operas, situation comedies, and family dramas treated rape just as rarely during the late 1980s as they did from 1976 through the early 1980s. Including the nine *L.A. Law* episodes, non-detective programs accounted for about one-fourth of prime time rape narratives in the late 1980s. Non-detective programs other than *L.A. Law* accounted for only 10 percent of the late 80s rape narratives. Overall, non-detective programs, including *L.A. Law*, accounted for about 22 percent of prime time's rape narratives between 1976 and 1990. These are significant percentages of non-detective rape stories, but detective/cop shows clearly represent the majority.

The detective/cop genre itself did experience change, partly in the characterization of protagonist detectives. The central detective's personality became more important as well as more complex, such that "Much of any given program is devoted to intense passages about self-esteem, self-assertion, and emotional rights and wrongs" (Berman 90). During the 1980s protagonist detectives develop fuller personal lives and the personal realm takes up more and more screen time. In effect, detectives become more sensitive and nurturing within limited areas of expression, and even through 1990 it is still mostly detectives who think about, discuss, and deal with the effects of rape. However, an equally noticeable shift concerns the direction of the genre as a whole. In the 1980s the genre became more and more similar to the soap opera, with the aim of attracting a broad-based, mixed-gender audience (Buxton 1990). Using *Miami Vice* as the paradigmatic example, Buxton observes that the ideological dimensions of crime dramas during the years just before 1990 became less and less clear-cut, so that the traditionally simplistic moral opposition between criminal and police officer/detective is no longer central to the functioning of the genre. The trend away from a crime genre that included reliable moral lessons and clear interpretations and toward a more ambiguous and less didactic model may be the most important change in the crime/detective genre during the period under examination here. It is certainly the most relevant to rape representations, as it was accompanied by content shifts that were related to each major area of rape representation: rapist (and cop), the crime itself, and victims.

The study of rape episodes on prime time during this key period in the evolution of the genre confirms that the form and content of crime dramas became increasingly feminized in several observable ways. First, as Chapter 2 demonstrates, protagonist males themselves became increasingly feminine, showing their nurturing and emotional sides more and more in the later years. Second, as discussed in Chapter 3, the form of the genre itself became more ambiguous and open to viewer interpretation. Whereas 1970s plots featured extremely predictable horrific villains and noble, competent detectives, later versions were more open to a multiplicity of readings with regard to the morality and motivation of the characters as well the overall message or position of the program. The increasing ambiguity of the genre emerged as rape plots became more complex and began to include depictions of date and acquaintance rape along with the more familiar image of brutal stranger rape. Third, as Chapter 4 shows, spaces for complex female characters and for female voices were increasingly opened up during the late 1980s, to the extent that competent female police officers and strong rape victims were often included. In spite of all these changes, the crime drama genre remained substantially the same in its focus on male protagonists as central characters and on the performance and negotiation of hegemonic masculinity in relation to other versions of masculinity as the basis for series plots.

Although early plots do not focus on rape reform or even on victim concerns, the context of the rape reform movement is often noted, with rape crisis centers, feminist characters, and post-rape counselors finding an increasingly prominent place in prime time's fictional world. Rape episodes avoid the more difficult and controversial issues (What evidence should be permissible at trial? How should a fair trial be conducted? Are marital rapes as heinous as stranger rapes? How can rapists be convicted when there is little physical evidence to corroborate the victim's story?), but even episodes from the late 1970s reflect a reformed view in their sympathetic treatment of victims. There is never a suggestion that these victims contributed to their own rapes through dress, behavior, or reputation. Few of these episodes question whether a rape has occurred: nearly all depict what Estrich calls "real rape." These episodes depict rapes that would have been considered easy cases with good chances of conviction under the traditional view, so sympathy extends only to victims of unambiguous, often exaggerated brutality. By the late 1980s, prime time included feminist characters, increased dialogue for victims, complex treatments of date and acquaintance rape issues, and thoughtful examinations of multiple perspectives on more difficult rape-related issues.

Race, Masculinity, and Victimization

The emphasis on masculinity in this collection of episodes can also be seen in the ways in which race is included and not included. Although most of the scripts do not include information about the race of their characters, those that do almost always specify that the rapist is Caucasian and/or that the victim is not Caucasian. Racial information is not available for all 100 episodes. Of the 80 or so for which such information is available, only two feature nonwhites in the role of (alleged) attacker, and both are the result of false accusations. In other words, this collection of episodes includes no confirmed plots featuring a nonwhite who is an actual rapist. Most victims of color are African American, but a few are described or portrayed as Hispanic. Thus it is clear that these rape episodes were written with a consciousness of the historical and political context of the relationship between race and rape, as if to attempt a clear contradiction of the traditional racist ideas about rape and race. Beyond this simple symbolic and visual gesture, however, prime time rape episodes have managed to produce very little discourse on the subject of how race and rape are related. Characters do not talk about their feelings about race in relation to their understanding and experience of rape (for instance, detectives do not comment on the racial profiles of the rape cases they have seen), and do not act as persons of a particular race in their dealings with rape (for instance, a black victim is almost never seen discussing her rape experience with black women friends).

Most episodes that feature interracial rape are curiously absent of any dialogue making explicit note of this fact. By the late 1980s, when several programs that dealt with race in an ongoing way aired rape episodes, some more detailed discussion of race is occasionally included, but even their treatment of race and rape is cursory and usually not centered on the most salient issues. On the extremely rare occasions that race and rape are actually discussed or treated as themes, the question of how they are related is carefully avoided. For example, a 1988 episode of *21 Jump Street*, "Fun with Animals," features extended discussion of racism and implies that it may have been the motive for an apparent rape among the students at a high school. However, the episode ends with the revelation that the attack was not actually a rape and that it was not racially motivated. Thus characters take positions against racism early in the episode, but the positions turn out to be irrelevant to the case at hand and no concluding remarks about race and rape are made with reference to the particular case. Even this level of discussion is notable among prime time rape episodes through 1990. It appears that the relationships between these two issues was simply too complex or too politically difficult for prime time to handle.

Preview

The next three chapters examine prime time representations of the crime of rape (Chapter 2), of the masculinity of rapists and detectives (Chapter 3), and of victims (Chapter 4). Chapter 2 argues that the early (basic plot) episodes through the early-1980s portrayed rape graphically, but consistently defined it as "real rape," the surprise violent attack of a victim unknown to the assailant. By the late 1980s they shifted to an emphasis on date and acquaintance rape, as the detective genre itself shifted toward more emotional and ambiguous representations. Chapter 3 argues that masculinity was the central focus of prime time rape episodes in both periods. Rapists were usually depicted as reprehensible characters; detectives through 1990 demonstrated helpful and appropriate reactions to rape victims, at times even teaching other men how to act and think regarding rape and rape victims.

Chapter 4 examines prime time's representations of rape victims, arguing that through the early 1980s the victims were almost incidental to rape programming, serving rather as mute, ineffective, and timid recipients of rapist violence and detective care. The chapter traces the expansion of victim roles through 1990, focusing on changes in amount and quality of victim dialogue, and increasing emphasis on post-rape experiences of the victim and on the support and treatment options available to them. Chapter 4 argues that victims in most episodes through the early 1980s functioned as the objects of detective pity and care, providing detective characters with the material for substantial anti-rape dialogue but themselves remaining mute and passive. Later victims were often stronger, more articulate, more active in pursuing legal remedies and self-healing and more likely to reflect or voice ideas sympathetic to rape reform.

Chapter 5 analyzes unusual and groundbreaking rape episodes, discussing the ways in which these were outstanding and historically notable and focusing on their unique handling of the issues of masculinity, rape, and victimization. This chapter examines exceptions to the general characterization of rape episodes as described in Chapters 2–4, using them to further clarify the elements of the usual prime time rape portrayal. Each of these analytical chapters (2–5) includes detailed examination of selected broadcast episodes to illustrate concepts and arguments from the chapter and to provide more descriptive depth to the discussion of program content.

Chapter 2
What Is Rape?
Prime Time's Changing Portrayals

Television viewers are familiar with the frequency and graphic detail with which rapes have been presented on prime time dramatic programs. This chapter traces the evolution of prime time's portrayals of the crime of rape from 1976 through 1990. It demonstrates a basic change from earlier episodes that mostly depicted "real" stranger rape and followed the basic plot's formula of extreme violence, use of weapons and threats, victim helplessness, and detective effectiveness, to a later phase when most programs began instead to depict date or acquaintance rapes where the victim knew her attacker, no extreme violence or weapons were used, and there was no need for a detective to "solve" the crime by discovering the rapist's identity. Although basic plot episodes are still present in every year through 1990, they become less frequent and the date/acquaintance rape scenario becomes more prominent by the final years. The episodes do not follow a strict historical progression, and date rape episodes can be found as early as 1980. Basic plot episodes in some cases become more violent in the later years, and some brutal and quite formulaic episodes can be found in the late 1980s. A number of episodes aired during the early 1980s are characterized by acquaintance rapes that are presented as almost identical to the presentation of "real rape" in the basic plot episodes. In addition, a number of episodes deal with false accusations of rape. These are discussed at the end of the chapter.

The stranger rape formula through the early 1980s is found primarily on police/detective dramas, where the post-rape narrative follows a detective's efforts to solve the crime and capture the rapist, though many early non-detective episodes also closely follow the parameters of the basic plot. Predictably, basic plot episodes in the late 1980s are found primarily on newer versions of the detective/police drama programs that had first developed the formula, such as *Crime Story*, and *MacGruder and Loud*. Violent stranger rapes receive complex and realistic treatment in newer programs, such as *In the Heat of the Night*, that are adaptations of the police/detective genre. However, these changes take place at the same time that the detective genre is shifting away from the traditional effective male protagonist who works alone or with a partner and toward ensemble casts with complex relationships. The new story line involving date/acquaintance rape emerges in new program formats developing in the mid- to late 1980s such as *L.A. Law* or in situation comedies such as *Different World*. The shift to date/acquaintance rape thus takes place as the detective genre is changing from one that provides unidimensional stories about clear-cut moral opposites (rapist and detective) to one that depicts a more complex and ambiguous world. Because date rapes enter prime time as the programs themselves become more open to interpretation, these scenarios are often more subtly nuanced than earlier basic plot stories. Thus prime time's depictions of date and acquaintance rape are more complex than its earlier portrayals of stranger rape, but they are also more ambiguous in their conclusions.

The story of false accusation was aired often enough to provide an alternative to both the "real" stranger attack and the date/acquaintance versions of rape. Although in most false accusation episodes there is no rape, the stories nonetheless consider the circumstances in which false accusations occur, and some involve actual rapes as well (the accusation is false merely in that it targets the wrong person). As a group, the false accusation episodes are supportive of traditional ideas about rape, illustrating that false accusations are easily believed and very difficult for the accused to disprove. False accusations provide a challenging test of masculinity for the protagonist males who are accused. Most of these episodes involve protagonists as the accused, show the "incident" in question, and feature young and troubled accusers. Thus the stories start from the premise that false accusation occurs, in the context of the certainty that the case depicted is one of false accusation. They then offer reasons it occurs and portray different ways for model males to handle it.

This formula for false accusation stories is difficult to compare with real-world rape statistics. Data from many jurisdictions are tainted by an overly broad definition of "unfounded" (a term used to label claims for which sufficient evidence for prosecution could not be collected). Causes are as wide-ranging as a victim's report to the wrong police jurisdiction, the victim's decision not to press charges, or a simple lack of sufficient physical evidence.[14] Although the "unfounded" rate was very high in some jurisdictions and the term has at times been used synonymously with "false accusation," in reality the data had very little relation to cases in which an accuser fabricated a claim. The idea of easy and frequent false accusation remains with us in the mythic domain. Popular culture representations of rape such as those examined here lend support to fears about the ease of accusers successfully bringing false charges of rape, yet it is not a phenomenon for which statistical measurements can plausibly be kept. Indeed, most of the prime time episodic stories of false accusation would not be documentable as false accusations if they represented real-life scenarios. Only one depicts an actual trial during which the victim admits that she fabricated her claim (and two victims admit mistaken identification to the police). The others are handled informally or do not involve police, so these fact patterns could not enter official statistics on false accusation.

Different Views of Rape: Common Law and Feminist Reform

The question "What is rape?" is one that has been heavily debated over the years since rape law reformers first began to question traditional legal and cultural definitions. Reformers in the early 1970s called into question the British Common Law definition, passed down into American statutes and legal practices, noting that it was narrow and inaccurate. Common law construed rape as a violent attack perpetrated on an unsuspecting victim who was not acquainted with her attacker. The image of an evil criminal leaping out of the bushes with a knife in hand, grabbing a terrified woman by the throat, and forcing her into submission in a dark corner stood as the paradigmatic rape under both British and American law prior to feminist challenge in the early 1970s. In this situation, only a victim who was "respectable" and could show that she did not have a reputation for loose morals or casual sex stood a reasonable chance of seeing the conviction of her attacker. This chance was increased considerably if the woman was white and the attacker black. Before rape law reform, no provision was made for female rapes of male victims, and reformers helped change the legal definition to eliminate gender specificity. The law traditionally understood rape as a spoiling of the chastity and value of a woman by a man who had no legal claim to sex with her. Thus in an important way it was designed to protect men from the destruction of their interests in women's bodies by other men, somewhat like the theft of household objects in a robbery: "rape law regulated women's sexuality and protected male rights to possess women as sexual objects" (Berger et al. 1995, 224). Through the early 1980s, prime time reflected this outmoded view in its focus on masculinity and its portrayal of rape in highly moralistic terms, contrasting good and bad men but failing to offer explanations for rape other than the depraved individual or solutions other than his capture.

Prime time rapes in the years just following the passage of the first reformed rape statute in Michigan in 1974 portrayed only "real rape," going out of their way to show clearly that the attack was a surprise, that the attacker was a marginal character to be despised by others, that the victim was deserving of sympathy not only because of the "violation" but also because of the degree of bodily injury inflicted on her, and that there was no possible way to construe the attack as a consensual encounter. The extreme evil of the rapist and the horror of the attack were often underscored through the serial nature of the crimes committed, the depiction of multiple attackers, or the commission of two attacks on the same victim. There was no real engagement with rape reform ideas because the attack fit the old violent stranger profile that was considered legitimate under the traditional view.

This chapter traces the two-part history of representation of rape as a crime on prime time TV between 1976 and 1990. The first section, focusing on the period from 1976 through the early 1980s, illustrates the ways in which prime time detective dramas employed the basic plot to depict stranger rape. This basic plot formula had very little to do with rape per se. Rape victims, victim experiences, rape law reform, rape trials, and actual public controversies related to these elements of rape were largely omitted. Prime time episodic television during this period avoided overt or explicit treatment of issues related to the definition of rape, treatment of victims at trial, and victim support and recovery systems. Later episodes enhanced many of the predictable and formulaic elements of the basic plot, making rapes ever more violent. Depictions of the crime itself were slow to transform, with most rapes into the mid-1980s following the pattern of the violent, unexpected attack and including elements such as weapons, threats, torture, masks and gloves, and distinctive "MO"s. Developments in rape reform in the world outside television were considerably ahead of prime time's emphasis on traditional constructions of rape and lack of attention to victims' postrape experiences. By the mid-1980s the anti-rape movement in some locations in the United States was already becoming institutionalized through incorporation into governmental structures, and independent crisis lines and other efforts, having proven their usefulness, were folding and being absorbed into existing state-run institutions (Matthews 1994).

The Attack in Basic Plot Episodes

Very few of the early basic rape plot episodes analyzed depict the entire rape, although later episodes are more graphic and tend to prolong the scenes of violence and humiliation of the victim. Basic plot rapes are violent and unexpected. They indicate that a rape is about to take place through the use of brief, frightening scenes of men emerging suddenly out of the darkness, often with weapons or masks, nearly always violently covering the victim's mouth to stifle her terrified screams. Rapes in these episodes are frightening and brutal, emphasizing victim vulnerability and helplessness both during and after the attack. As Schlesinger et al. (1992) note, rape in these early programs is used as a means of portraying a clear polarization between good and evil. The depiction of the attack underscores the extreme evil of the attacker and the vulnerability of the victim.

Typically the attacker pulls the victim off camera and the "rape" scene ends with the sound of screams. In a *Starsky and Hutch* episode ("Rape," 1976) the victim's screams begin as she is attacked and continue as a sound bridge as the scene fades. In "Strange Justice" (1978), Starsky and Hutch investigate a sorority rape in which a large shadowy figure emerges, a hand grabs the victim's throat, and the victim reacts in terror and panic as the attacker threatens to kill her. In *Barnaby Jones*'s "Deadly Sanctuary" (1978) the victim is dragged off camera after a hand clamps over her mouth. Similarly, a *Rafferty* episode has a victim scream when she is shoved violently by an attacker whose gloved hand is all that is shown ("Point of View," 1977). The gloved hand that clamps over the victim's mouth is a staple, and numerous later episodes mimic this means of underscoring the terror of the situation. *Hill Street Blues*'s "Presidential Fever" (1981), *Lou Grant*'s "Rape" (1980) and *MacGruder and Loud*'s "Violation" (1984) depict hands that reach out and stifle the victim's sounds of struggle and cries for help. Even the rape on family drama *Little House on the Prairie*'s "Sylvia" (1980) depicts a surprise attack from the woods and a hand clamped over the victim's mouth by the masked attacker. Ski masks and other disguises also remain standard elements of basic plot episodes into the mid-1980s. *Strike Force*'s "Predator" (1981) features a masked attacker, while *McClain's Law*'s "Time of Peril" (1981) includes a rapist who wears a green trash bag over his head with holes cut out for the eyes. *St. Elsewhere*'s "Drama Center" (1984) involves an attacker wearing a ski mask and terrorizing women who work in the hospital. The emphasis is on victim fear and vulnerability. These are largely stories about women who cannot fight, run, outsmart their attackers, or even yell — they are helpless to resist. Scripts often direct that the victim is thoroughly overpowered, sometimes noting that the victim could never escape the attacker even if he did not have a weapon.

The element of surprise, further enhancing victim vulnerability, is often emphasized. In *Quincy* the unsuspecting victim is attacked by a masked intruder who throws her down and stifles her screams ("Let Me Light the Way," 1977). In one *Baretta* episode the rapist grabs at the victim and she screams and struggles, begging him to stop ("Shoes," 1976). One of the most violent rape episodes, *Lou Grant*'s "Rape" (1980) opens with the victim gathering laundry and making trips back and forth from her apartment to the laundry room. Suddenly, when she returns to her apartment, a knife is held to her throat and she is subjected to hours of verbal and physical abuse. Other programs including *Matt Houston* (1983), *Strike Force*'s "Predator" (1981), *St. Elsewhere*'s "Drama Center" (1984), and *MacGruder and Loud*'s "Violation" (1984) feature surprise attacks on unsuspecting victims in their homes, in parking lots, and at work. In *TJ Hooker*'s "Death on the Line" (1984) two telephone linemen spy on potential victims from their "cherry-picker" truck. When they have identified their victim for the day, they approach stealthily and knock her out with a karate chop. A *Dog and Cat* episode depicts a victim pinned down, immobilized, and silenced by the rapist ("Live Bait," 1977). Basic plot attacks are vicious and frightening. They could not be mistaken for consensual sex and they could not be committed by anyone but a deranged criminal.

When victims of "real rape" are not surprised by masked attackers jumping out of the bushes or sneaking up behind them at home, they are kidnapped, held against their will, and often beaten, tortured, and even killed. This alternative retains the basic character of violent stranger rape, with the focus on the victim's helplessness and fear and the rapist's unmitigated evil. It can be considered a variation on the basic plot formula. The kidnapping theme appears frequently during the early 1980s. In *Strike Force*'s "Lonely Ladies" (1981) a team of rapists takes women to a deserted mansion and slowly tortures them to death. The episode depicts the horrific torture of a kidnapped victim, who shows clear signs of her abuse. One scene depicts her sitting on the floor with hands tied behind her, sobbing and begging for release. A *Tales of the Gold Monkey* scene features the victim lying dead on a bed while men in the foreground adjust their belts ("Sultan of Swat," 1982). In an extremely gruesome post-rape scene, *Hill Street Blues* depicts a "ghetto bar" where several women have been held captive and tortured both psychologically and physically for hours. The techniques used include shooting at them for fun after repeated rape and forced sodomy ("The World According to Freedom," 1982). In the *Vegas* episode "No Way to Treat a Victim" (1981) two men team up, one hiding in the victim's car. An elaborate ruse (one man poses as a kidnapper and pretends to shoot the other) is employed to confuse and frighten the victim, who is then captured and raped. *Walking Tall* (pilot, 1981) depicts a rape/kidnapping perpetrated by a vicious motorcycle gang, whose members drag the victim around and "auction" her off to the highest bidder in the gang in order to buy more beer. The rape is not shown, but gang members rip at the captive woman's clothes and jeer during the "auction." The kidnap variation is often more violent and graphic than the other basic plot episodes because it involves a prolonged interaction between victim and attacker. In these stories, although the rape itself is not a "surprise," the victim is unknown to the attacker, is subjected to extreme violence, and is almost completely helpless and vulnerable.

In addition to victim vulnerability and helplessness, basic plot episodes of both types emphasize brutality in their depictions of the attack. Physical evidence of rape is common. Nearly all post-rape depictions of victims include references to bruises, cuts, swollen eyes, and other signifiers of severe violence. Many episodes underscore the rapist's brutality through the post-rape condition of the victim, as in the *Dog and Cat* episode's portrayal of a second victim who is hospitalized because she is beaten and bruised to the point of being nearly unable to open her cut and swollen eyes. One character notes that she has dealt with over a hundred rapes, and this one is the most violent she has ever handled. Similarly, *Baretta*'s "The Marker" (1978) notes that a rape victim's face is beaten so that she cannot open her eyes at all. A witness leaves out the details, exclaiming only at the severity of the physical damage to the survivor. *Shannon*'s "A Secret Rage" (1981) includes a rapist who wields a knife to cut off phone connections and also to cut the abdomens of his victims. *Starsky and Hutch*'s "Rape" (1976) includes a victim who is raped and so badly beaten that her face is swollen and discolored. Although they do not show the rape itself, all these episodes depict, often with great specificity, the physical effects rapists have perpetrated on their victims, leaving no doubt in the minds of other characters that a rape did occur. In several episodes victims are killed by their attackers. In *Hawaii Five-O* episode "Requiem for a Saddle Bronc Rider" (1977), detectives can tell by looking at the victim's dead body that strangulation was the method used to murder her; because the brutal start of the attack is shown, viewers are left with little doubt that the victim has been raped.

Whether they involve surprise attacks, kidnapping, or a combination of the two, these episodes depict rape as a brutalizing experience that must create sympathy for the victim and could in no way be mistaken for false accusation or consent. Excessive brutality is often further emphasized in the routine mention of the serial nature of the crimes committed. In some episodes, as many as sixteen rapes have been committed in the same way by the same attacker. Under such conditions, consent and provocation are hardly at issue. Although the viewer must sympathize with the victim, in most cases the primary narrative function of the victim's brutalization is not to allow her to speak and tell the story of her attack, but to provide the protagonist detective with an opportunity to vent his rage, righteously pronounce that evil must be eliminated and avenged, and proclaim his intent to protect and care for the damaged victim.

Prime time had not fully abandoned the well-established formula for rape episodes by the 1990 season. Rather, the basic plot remained as a reliable version of television rape representation. Among the late episodes still using an almost unmodified basic plot is *In the Heat of the Night*'s "First Deadly Sin" (1990), which opens with police officers discussing a series of rapes, to which three more are added by the end of the episode. The rapist has an identifiable MO: he chooses blondes in their early thirties and follows them as they enter their homes. To keep from being identified he throws a pillow case over the victim's head. There is little change in this rape story from the early basic plot, although a rape survivor appears briefly to comfort the victim and help her understand that she will eventually recover and feel like herself again. *Crime Story*'s "King in a Cage" (1987) depicts "real rape," the victim is badly beaten as well as raped and ends up in "post-rape shock." Rather than emphasizing revenge for the rape, this episode clearly uses the graphic pre-rape scene at its start to function as a symbol of the extreme evil of the perpetrator, who at the story's end is caught and arrested for a long list of murders. The many other crimes mentioned establish his thoroughly evil character.

Prime Time's Shift Toward Date Rape

By the late 1980s, as Susan Brinson notes (1990), television representations of rape had moved solidly in the direction of date and acquaintance rape. Although it remained a recognizable type of rape narrative, the basic plot receded in frequency and was replaced by more complex treatments, many of which were less violent than those aired earlier. Brinson sums up her findings from the 1989 season, noting that rapists were not drunk or psychologically damaged and their victims were young, middle class white women acquaintances (1990, v). Although Brinson examines only the 1989 season, her findings are consistent with the data from the late 1980s through 1990 examined here. In addition, her conclusions that episodes sometimes favorably portrayed feminist themes and tenets, sometimes favorably or even openly endorsed them, while others supported patriarchal or androcentric interests, are also supported here. The following section traces the evolution of the basic plot formula found commonly in the late 1970s and early 1980s episodes and the shift toward date/acquaintance rape narratives predominant in later narratives.

Date and acquaintance rape have in many ways been the most difficult areas of rape reform, in both the legal realm and in the public imagination. As Sanday (1996), Warshaw (1988), Koss (1992), and others have noted, date and acquaintance rape have remained hidden and underreported crimes in part because people have different definitions of them. These authors have observed that if women are asked questions about penetration by force (questions that use the legal definition of rape without using the word "rape"), they are more likely to answer "yes," meaning that they have had the experience described. When the word "rape" is used, "yes" responses drop. The criminality of the rapist in date and acquaintance rape also seems more ambiguous than when a case involves the surprise violent attack of an unsuspecting stranger. The popular belief has been that if two parties who know each other make opposing claims (rape vs. consent), it is a marginal case that is too difficult for the law to decide. In addition, traditional legal and popular literature promulgated the notion of the frequency of false rape accusations by victims afraid to admit their consent, afraid to take responsibility for pregnancy, or intent on revenge against an innocent man.[15] Date and acquaintance rape will never lend themselves to the moral clarity of violent stranger rape, and critics of the concept continue to claim that these labels might be used to represent almost any physical interaction between women and men (see Sanday 1996).

Stranger rape is clearly nonconsensual; date and acquaintance rape are more ambiguous, especially if weapons and physical violence are not involved. Where "real rape" invites sympathy on the basis of its unexpectedness and randomness, date and acquaintance rape have continued to yield reactions such as blaming the victim and questioning her judgment. "Real rape" usually provides corroborative evidence such as physical marks on the victim's body or even witnesses to the attack, but date and acquaintance rape raise questions about false accusation, possible miscommunication, and female indecision. A victim-oriented perspective based on the evidence of feminist-inspired studies of rape asserts that date rape is at least as common as violent stranger rape, that it is just as real a crime as violent stranger rape, that victims of date or acquaintance rape are less likely to report it to the police, that convictions in cases that are reported are extremely unlikely, that victims of date or acquaintance rape may be as psychologically traumatized as victims of violent stranger rape, that victims of date/acquaintance rape need post-rape counseling and help just like other rape victims, and that structural and institutionalized groups such as fraternities and male sports teams have been among the worst offenders in (gang) acquaintance rape cases.

Research and mainstream press discussions on date and acquaintance rape began to emerge in the early 1980s; lengthy works on the topic began coming out only in the late 1980s and early 1990s. A 1979 *Washington Post* article by Stephanie Mansfield reporting her own experience with date rape was "one of the first journalistic accounts to use the terms acquaintance and date rape" (Sanday 1996, 162). The first widely publicized studies of date rape were just emerging in the middle 1980s, and the first full-length book on the subject, Robin Warshaw's *I Never Called It Rape*, was not released until 1988. Thus the earliest date and acquaintance rape episodes on prime time emerged just as date rape was making its way into the public consciousness through other avenues. Although few in number, these episodes are historically important.

Although the basic plot is represented through 1990, most episodes in the late '80s depict date or acquaintance rape without following any particular formula or pattern. Several episodes depict acquaintance rapes as nearly identical to the violent stranger rapes depicted in earlier prime time episodes. These episodes provide a sort of bridge plot between the "real rape" formula of the early years and the predominance of date/acquaintance plots in the later years. Because episodes from 1984 through 1989 use this combination of elements, the plot represents a thematic, but not strictly chronological bridge. The bridging plot can be seen as an adaptation of the original formula that preserves an emphasis on masculinity and a focus on oppositional morality, while failing to grapple with any of the difficult issues of definition and judgment raised by real-world date and acquaintance rape. *St. Elsewhere*'s "Drama Center" (1984) depicts acquaintance rape that is in almost every way exactly like the violent stranger formula already established. The attack has all the markers of violent stranger rape, including extreme violence, use of a weapon and threats, and disguise of the rapist's identity, but the perpetrator is a doctor in the hospital.

When the mask is finally removed during an attack, it is revealed that the perpetrator is actually a colleague of all his victims. Episodes of this type acknowledge that there is rape between acquaintances but fail to define it as anything significantly different from the old violent stranger rape construction.

This same pattern is used in *MacGruder and Loud*'s "Violation" (1984), in which a self-defense instructor is attacked in a parking lot by one of her students. Although she escapes before the rape is completed, the episode is another example that uses an acquaintance as the perpetrator but otherwise follows the pattern of violent stranger rape. Here the rapist follows his victim, wears a ski mask and carries a knife, and covers the victim's mouth to prevent screaming. For most of the episode his identity is not known, so here even the detective's efforts to solve the crime are similar to the steps followed in the "real" rape episodes. The *Simon and Simon* episode "Outrage" (1987) is similar. It opens with a conversation between a man and woman apparently after the "date" portion of their evening is over. She is telling him that she is not interested in sex, while he insists that he is a mature man who has real "needs" and attempts to bully her into consent. In the next scene, after he has left, the woman is seen preparing for bed, with lightning flashing outside the house. Suddenly the lights in the house are extinguished and a man is inside the house, attacking her. Except for the addition of quite a bit of dialogue about rape victims' responses to their rape experiences, this is really a simple basic plot narrative. The "date rape" theme only enters as a theory about what might have happened. The attack, aftermath, and effects on the victim are all preserved from the original detective / cop formula.

In the Heat of the Night's "Rape" (1989), described in detail in Chapter 3, depicts a rape by an acquaintance that in most ways is exactly like the basic plot "real" rape. It includes extreme violence, surprise attack, severe psychological trauma to the victim, a repeat offender, and a second attempt at rape of the same victim. In this episode, as in the others just described, acquaintances act like strangers in their commission of rape: rather than trapping the victim in an intimate setting such as at home after a date, they sneak up on her and use threats and violence just like stranger rapists. Thus, even though victims and rapists are acquainted, there can be no doubt that these acts are rapes. Consent is not at issue. The elements that have historically made date and acquaintance rape controversial are eliminated. The only thing that has changed in these episodes is that the victim and rapist are known to each other.

Simple Rape: Conventional Date Rape Scenarios

A number of later episodes depict date rape in ways that are more recognizably realistic. Rather than portraying an extremely violent, weapon-yielding maniac as the "date" or acquaintance, these episodes portray apparently decent, normal men with whom female victims have chosen to associate socially. Beyond this, the episodes do not share a set pattern, but they do tend to avoid legal issues and questions in favor of moralistic discussion of ethical and acceptable behavior of men in relation to women. The specific details of their treatment of masculinity are discussed in the following chapter. Here I focus on the ways the date and acquaintance rapes themselves are depicted, focusing on the ways these new stories are clearly open to much more interpretation than the basic plot attacks, and on the progression of date/acquaintance rape representation through 1990. By leaving issues unresolved or failing to depict the incident in question, these episodes usually leave the question of how to understand date and acquaintance rape open for viewer interpretation.

Date and acquaintance rapes became more common as genre modifications more easily incorporated complex interpersonal interaction than the crime- and action-based genres of standard detective and police dramas. One of the first detective episodes to feature a realistic date rape is the *Spenser: For Hire* episode "Rage" (1986), in which the opening scene depicts a girl jumping out of a parked car, closely followed by her "date," who blocks her path. The girl is clearly in disarray and starts to cry. The attack itself is not shown, leaving the question of what happened in the car open to the speculation of viewers and of characters within the show. The rest of the episode unravels clues about the character and feelings of the girl involved, and sympathy turns in her direction.

21 Jump Street, produced by Fox, aired six rape-related episodes between 1987 and 1990, including two date rape episodes. In general the *21 Jump Street* treatments are complex, sensitive, and more progressive than those on most other programs, featuring articulate victims, structural analysis of rape, and complex webs of relationships that give the show a realistic edge. The show's rape episodes examine difficult issues such as racist attitudes and attitudes about rape, fraternity gang rape, date rape, and false accusation. The program centers on a group of young undercover agents sent to investigate crimes in high schools and colleges. The multiracial cast includes a black male police captain, an Asian male detective, a black female detective, and three white male detectives. Johnny Depp stars, but he shares the central role with other members of the "team" in many episodes. The program grants more legitimacy to feminist or victim-centered views than any other program represented here. The detectives (with one exception) are unusually progressive, and the police captain sometimes voices feminist views on rape. Despite its progressiveness, however, the program maintains the late 1980s characteristic of ambiguity with relation to rape, leaving some explanations and interpretations open to the viewer's opinions.

The *21 Jump Street* episode "Stand by Your Man" (1989) features date rape with an important dimension of ambiguity. There is no doubt that the incident is date rape because the accuser is a regular character, an undercover detective, and a flashback of the rape is shown. But the episode makes it seem that the rapist was genuinely mistaken in his views about rape and sex, rather than doing something he knew to be wrong or criminal. In this episode, detective Judy Hoffs is raped by a suspect while posing as a student and "seeing" him socially in order to gather information on his activities. One of the few date rape episodes that includes the legal ramifications of the crime, this episode ends with the attacker being dismissed from medical school. However, Hoffs is convinced that the man did not know that what he did was wrong or illegal, and the two of them have a conciliatory conversation near the end of the episode. Thus, even though the episode features visual verification of the attack, strict moral judgment is withheld. Victim and rapist are said simply to have different understandings of what happened, and they are effectively reconciled at the end of the episode. Although the victim is black and the rapist white, the episode does not provide discussion of the relationship between rape and race.

Three additional programs in the group analyzed aired date rape portrayals in the late 1980s. One of these, *Miami Vice*'s "Blood and Roses" (1988), is discussed in detail as a focus episode below. This and other date and acquaintance rape stories often feature the victim blaming herself or taking most of the responsibility for what happened, and they tend to lack any discussion of negative outcomes for those who commit date rape (with the notable exception of *21 Jump Street*'s "Stand by Your Man"). The narratives are thus limited to an exposition of what constitutes right and wrong behavior for men, in effect accepting a modified feminist definition of date rape but not finding any useful function for that definition. Most of these episodes promote feelings of support for the victims, especially through the reaction of protagonist males, but they fail to portray date rape as a serious crime because the attack itself is usually not shown and the stories seldom end with trials and/or convictions. Prime time date rape has a negative effect on its victims, but not nearly so severe as the effect of "real" rape. *Cagney and Lacey* ("Date Rape," 1983) reverses some, but not all, of the general patterns in date rape portrayals. Rather than having the victims feel guilt and self-blame, it features strong victims who will not accept the partial blame placed on them by others. Like other episodes, however, it does not show the attack, and it verifies the victim's word (and the moral evil of the rapist) by including a second witness who accuses the same man. The story suggests, however, that it would be virtually impossible to sustain a legal case on charges of date rape without the second witness.

L.A. Law's "Sparky Brackman, R.I.P.?" (1987) depicts the trial of a man for date rape. The episode includes a great deal of ambiguity, as the victim is adamant about the fact that she was raped even though she willingly accompanied the rapist to his home. After insisting that the case not be settled out of court, the victim wins at trial, but is awarded only one dollar. Like other *L.A. Law* episodes discussed in Chapter 5, this one ends on an unsatisfying note for the victim, and it seems that legal remedies may not be effective after all. The dialogue that leads up to and analyzes the mixed verdict is also ambiguous, and, as Projanski notes, ultimately suggests that the victim should take some responsibility for the rape.[16]

A date rape episode was aired on *Different World* during the 1989 season. The title, "No Means No," clearly echoes feminist ideas about date rape, but the episode is fairly balanced between male and female views. It portrays men as confused about what constitutes rape, as do the *Miami Vice* episode "Blood and Roses" and *21 Jump Street*'s "Stand by Your Man." Much of the dialogue is between male characters, with a regular character representing the "correct" view that "no means no" even if a woman seems to be giving mixed signals with her body. The person who commits the date rape acknowledges that he thinks it is fine to go ahead in such a situation, but the episode clearly ends with the "no means no" character proving that he is right. His confused friend ends up admitting he doesn't understand women, and his victim files charges against him even though other characters point out that a date rape charge is hard to prove. Other variations on date/acquaintance rape that appear occasionally include gang rape and false accusation, discussed below.

False Accusation Plots

The idea that rape claims are more likely to be fabricated than claims of other crimes has been perpetuated in legal and popular culture for hundreds of years, traceable at least to Sir Matthew Hale's famous pronouncement that rape "is an accusation easily to be made and hard to be proved, and harder to be defended by the party accused, tho never so innocent" (Hale [1650] 1847, 635). Hale's original concern was that if a couple were caught "*in coitu*" the woman might choose a claim of rape as the only way to save her character (628). His statement regarding the likelihood of false accusation was cited routinely in legal literature on rape through the 1960s, and the assumptions it voices have been a central point of contention for rape reformers. Over time, the fear of false accusation was extended to include a number of other situations in which women supposedly might fabricate rape claims, such as shame due to pregnancy or consent to sex, hatred for a partner, mental illness and delusion, or even an inability of the victim to be certain whether consent had been given (see Cuklanz 1996b, 22–24).

The fear of false accusation has certainly been linked historically with the idea that rape is a horrendous crime that could ruin a man's reputation forever. It fit with, and helped to justify, legal protections for the accused during rape trials, which in turn fostered the low conviction rates feminist reformers observed in the early 1970s. Not only were victims' sexual histories considered relevant evidence at trial, but special jury instructions stating the likelihood of false accusation were also included. In addition, to further reduce the likelihood of false accusation, in many jurisdictions corroborative evidence or witness verification was required to obtain conviction. Accusations of rape were considered with suspicion in part because they represented such a serious questioning of the honor of the accused, and the distinction between good and bad men was considered easy to make, as reflected in Henry de Bracton's thirteenth-century instructions that a rape victim should report the attack to "men of good repute" (Sanday 1996, 57). Penalties for rape conviction were thus traditionally severe. Conviction for rape in the United States could carry the death penalty, until this was struck down under feminist pressure in 1972 (Coker vs. Georgia, 75-5444), with the idea that juries might be more likely to convict if they did not fear that the death penalty would be given for a noncapital offense. A graduated code of sexual offenses took its place over time as reformed rape statutes replaced traditional law.

In part because ideas about rape have been passed down from a social and political environment very different from today's (where the stigma of premarital sex was severe for women and the violent sexual attack of women was considered such a breach of masculine norms that it could be punished by death), the mythology of the false accuser is so firmly entrenched in legal writings and history as well as popular culture that it is unlikely it will ever disappear. Because of the history of rape and trial practice, whenever false accusation is at issue, the key questions involved are the circumstances of the incident, the identity and character of the accuser, and the identity and character of the accused.

A notable variation of the prime time rape narrative from 1976 to 1990 was the false accusation plot.[17] The eight false accusation plots over a fifteen-year history do not warrant a claim that this version of the story was central to prime time's vision of rape, but they do deserve attention as a group that followed a somewhat predictable narrative line and thus provided an alternative to the basic plot formula. Also all are acquaintance rape stories. The eight false accusation plots include variations as well, with three deliberate fabrications of a claim, two mistaken identifications of the wrong man by a legitimate rape victim, one unintentional accusation, and two "twist" narratives where the claim seems false but ends up being true. In one of these latter two, the victim first makes a false identification of her abuser out of fear, so the episode combines false and truthful accusations in one story. These episodes offer insights into prime time's construction of hegemonic masculinity and its handling of issues of power in relation to rape. False accusation episodes follow the "limited variability" rule. The formula features young victims, accused rapists who have authority or power over their accusers, a focus on the masculinity of the accused, and serious discussion of rape and false accusation. Protective or domineering fathers often play an active role, and most of the stories demonstrate a predictable pattern of circumstances in which victims lie. If the accusation is truly false, or is a false identification, the accused is often the protagonist detective. Yet none of the episodes include all these characteristic elements, and each element is missing in at least one episode. Two episodes follow the formula of the teenage accuser and older accused, with the revelation late in the episode that, while the accusation seems false, it is actually legitimate.

Like basic plot stories, episodes that follow this story line clearly take masculinity as their central problematic, and in most cases they focus on the ways the protagonist detective maintains his caring, responsible, and professional demeanor in the face of a serious attack on his character and his masculinity. Because the accused is the protagonist, viewers know from the start that the accusation must be false. When the falsely accused is not a detective, he is usually still the program's central protagonist (for example, Mr. Kotter in *Welcome Back, Kotter*). All but one of the false accusation plots feature accusers who are eighteen years old or younger, and several revolve around high school life and involve accusations of teachers in positions of authority over their accusers. Although these plots deal with the issue of abuse of power through threat and sexual assault and provide a good deal of dialogue about the power dynamics of rape, they do so in the context of obviously false claims. And although date and acquaintance rape often involve abuses of power such as the threat of losing one's job, the date/acquaintance rape episodes discussed in the previous chapter do not deal with this issue. Nearly all the prime time rape narratives dealing with abuses of power by bosses or other authority figures do so in the context of false (or seemingly false) accusation. The complex issue of actual abuse of power is almost never treated outside this context in episodes through 1990.

Because four of the eight false accusation plots feature claims against familiar and upstanding characters who are the central focus of their programs, these plots share certain elements. First, the assumption from the beginning of the episode is that the accusation must be false, and in most of these episodes viewers are visually privileged to view the incident in question and thus know for certain that no attack occurred. Any discussion of the doubts surrounding rape accusations will thus be undertaken from the presumption that in this particular example the victim is lying. The two "founded" claims of rape (*21 Jump Street, The Bronx Zoo*), where the victim appears to be lying but is actually telling the truth about her attacker, feature rapists who are not regulars on the shows. The *21 Jump Street* victim first identifies a protagonist cop, however, providing a stark comparison between the reactions of an innocent man and a guilty one (identified by the victim later in the episode). Most of these episodes focus not on the question of *whether* accusers lie (obviously they do), but rather on what causes women to lie, or under what circumstances women become liars. Almost all the victims who make false accusations are underage, and most explanations are related to parental pressure (usually from the father) to show innocence and come up with a rapist to explain a pregnancy or relationship, a young girl's need for attention or a sense of power, and the confusion and hysteria that follow a violent sexual assault (in the case of mistaken identification). These stories are clearly drawn from the traditional mythology of rape, explaining rather than questioning the occurrence of false accusation and showing how easily false claims can create problems for good men. Two episodes involve racial issues as a further test of the protagonist's character, primarily to demonstrate the innocence of the non-Caucasian accused and to denounce traditional or outdated stereotypes. Protagonist males falsely accused of rape react violently, defending themselves in the most vehement terms and even risking their careers to prove their innocence.

Early false accusation plots, less complex and less interesting than the later ones, tend to focus on one-dimensional relationships and stereotypes in an effort to make a simple point about the error of stereotypical thinking. They often take place on non-detective shows (*Welcome Back, Kotter, Gibbsville*, and *Dallas* had false accusation plots in the late 1970s). The earliest false accusation plot in the group, and one that clearly follows this formulation, is *Gibbsville*'s "The Price of Everything" (1976), which features a rich white high school student's accusation of an African-American teacher. The accusation takes the form of an anonymous letter sent to the school paper asking how long a certain teacher will be allowed to "menace" the students. Although the letter does not name accused or accuser, it quickly becomes clear who is being discussed. The teacher in question notes that he will say nothing in his own defense because he is innocent, and that if he was from a different area of the city the publisher "would have thrown away that letter." It turns out that a student's mother tried to frame the teacher because her daughter was failing his course, and she was upset at the added shame of flunking a course taught by "someone from the patches." She thought that the frame-up would work because the teacher's class and race would make him a believable rapist in spite of his record and position. The episode is similar to other false accusation plots in that it features a high school student as the alleged victim and a high school teacher as the accused. But, it is unique in dealing with race and rape, and it includes significant dialogue on the fact that race was thought to be something that would make the accused appear guilty. The accused is cleared when the woman who wrote the letter confesses her attempted frame-up.

Like the *Gibbsville* episode, *Welcome Back, Kotter*'s false accusation episode (1978) features the alleged rape of a teenager by a teacher. The treatment of rape in this episode is one-dimensional and simplistic, failing to delve into substantial, difficult, or complex issues related to rape, power, and false accusation. This is the only false accusation narrative to take place on a situation comedy. The episode opens with a threat of false accusation from a girl who passes out in Kotter's class. She has given a sworn statement after the "passing out" incident that she remembers Mr. Kotter holding her before she passed out and "being on top" of her when she regained consciousness. Although this sounds like an accusation of rape, it is actually just poor phrasing; when her classmates tell her she has gotten Mr. Kotter in trouble she says she did not even mean to accuse him of attacking her. The episode includes several jokes revolving around sex, rape, and appropriate behavior. In one, Kotter comments that the accusation cannot be true because no one would attack a girl in a classroom because it would be smarter to go outside behind the gym. A high school classmate of the unwitting accuser (Barbarino) says that "fooling around" with young girls is no big deal—he does it regularly. Because the accusation is unintentional and the misunderstanding is cleared up immediately, the episode deals more with light humor and character relationships (the principal immediately believes the girl and speaks against Kotter) than with rape and false accusation. It is not critical of rape, and its discussion centers more on the ease with which an innocent man can be thought guilty of rape.

Big Hawaii's "The Trouble with Tina" (1977) depicts a fifteen-year-old motherless girl who falsely accuses protagonist Mitch to get his attention and to support her father's assumption that any relationship between his daughter and Mitch must have been forced. The opening scene visually establishes that nothing resembling a rape, or even sexual contact, occurred: Tina appears unexpectedly in Mitch's house to seduce him, wearing only one of his shirts, and is kicked out immediately by the shocked Mitch. The episode is very much about masculinity as demonstrated by Mitch in the face of the accusation. It is the earliest episode in the group to treat the issue of false accusation seriously in light of the character and masculinity of the accused. Mitch is clearly innocent, and demonstrates this in his gentle and understanding treatment of the young accuser. He is the only character to realize that her accusation must be caused by some trouble or trauma at home, and he makes several attempts to understand her motivation and help her despite his difficult legal predicament (and the fact that further "contact" with the accuser hurts his legal position). The possibility of a plea bargain is discussed, but Mitch refuses to play along with this "admission of guilt" in the face of warnings that a jury could find him guilty and ruin the rest of his life.

After a preliminary hearing and the information that the DA has a witness who saw Tina leaving Mitch's apartment wearing only his shirt, Mitch searches out Tina and confronts her, demanding why she is doing this to him. When he asks if her father is behind it, she begins to cry and runs off. During the actual trial, Mitch rejects the idea of cross-examining Tina even though she testifies that he ripped off her dress and forced her. Eventually she admits that her father bullied her into making up this story when he shouted and slapped her after her return from Mitch's apartment. The episode ends with a scene in which Mitch saves Tina at the top of a cliff. She cries in his arms and admits that her father was abusive, sometimes giving her gifts and sometimes getting angry and hitting her. Her father asks for "another chance" and comforts her, and the episode ends on this note of resolution. By modeling proper masculinity for the father, through his own behavior and through his reaction to and treatment of the "victim," the detective is able to alter the behavior of the father and mend a family situation beset with problems. Without compromising any of the traditional characteristics of masculinity, Mitch is able to demonstrate understanding and caring for a confused young girl and her equally confused father.

In the Heat of the Night's "Accused" (1989), like the Gibbsville episode, deals with race and false accusation. Bubba, a main character and (Caucasian) police detective, is falsely accused of rape by an African American woman, and her story is later supported by a Caucasian woman who claims that Bubba also raped her three weeks earlier. Eventually it turns out that both women were raped by the same man, and that Bubba was accused based on circumstantial factors and mistaken identity. Here the racial elements are essentially the reverse of those in the Gibbsville episode a decade earlier. Not only are the racial identities of the accuser and accused reversed, but whereas the Gibbsville episode uses the racial identities of the characters to illustrate the problems created by stereotypical thinking, the *Heat* episode uses race to make the point that social attitudes toward race and rape have shifted, such that the rape of black victims by a white perpetrator is now the "hot-button" issue. While it was thought easy to make a false accusation of a black attacker against a white victim in the 1976 episode, the 1989 episode is based on the opposite premise: that it is relatively easy to make a false accusation alleging a white attacker of black victims. In both, race is depicted as the reason why false accusations are successful.

This episode deals extensively and complexly with rape in a social and political context, but without diverging much from the traditional formulas. The episode touches on the issues of rape, race, and power, but most of the screen time is taken up with Bubba's search for the rapist and his encounters with various obstacles in doing so. Several scenes highlight the intersection of race and rape. In one scene a group of black men, who want to protect the victim from the white-dominated power structure, physically fight Bubba with a baseball bat. A morality of race is played out between Bubba and his black colleague Virgil Tibbs, who vows solidarity with him and swears to the accuser that Bubba could not have attacked her. The dialogue emphasizes the male bonding of the "good" protagonist detectives regardless of race, in contrast to the behavior of others. The (Caucasian) DA, for example, goes on a political crusade to convict Bubba in order to demonstrate the town's fairness and lack of racism. Fortunately for Bubba, and typical for prime time rape plots, the real rapist returns to the scene of his second attack and goes after the same woman again, allowing for his capture. The episode has little dialogue about false accusation, but it does include an explanation for why the earlier victim did not report her attack. The real rapist, a (Caucasian) auto parts store owner, is her boss, and she didn't want to lose her job because she had no skills and was single with a young daughter to support.

The episode is ambiguous in its portrayal of the victim's attitude toward Bubba. She begins by reacting to him with extreme fear, and he adds legitimacy to this fear by following her and demanding to speak with her. However, she is easily persuaded to help him in an ultimately unsuccessful effort to get a different (and black) man to confess. In the final scene the victim leaves the bar alone and is attacked again, and Tibbs and Bubba step in to save her. While Tibbs grabs the assailant, the victim clings to Bubba and apologizes for accusing him. The victim's role is difficult to interpret, but the emphasis on the detective's masculinity is clear. In spite of being falsely accused, Bubba is able to understand the victim's fear and mistaken identification, and he makes an alliance with her to catch the real rapist. His ability to see the accuser as something other than an enemy is typical of the protagonist reactions in this group of episodes. His volatility and use of violence is typical of detective reactions to rape in prime time episodes generally.

An unusual *Hill Street Blues* episode ("Invasion of the Third World Mutant Body Snatchers," 1982) features the false identification of an innocent man who happens to be walking home in the wrong area at the wrong time of night. The woman who identifies him as her attacker seems certain at first, but as he insists that he would rather go to jail than admit to a rape he did not commit, her resolve wavers. She eventually admits that she decided he had to be guilty since he was the only one nearby at the time. The victim is only eighteen years old and claims that her father "browbeat" her into fingering someone for the rape. The episode includes dialogue about the clear possibility of conviction of the innocent accused in such a case, including the observation that the pre-trial system puts the accused in a less favorable position than that of the worst criminals. His defense attorney tells him that if he pleads guilty to a reduced charge of assault or sexual abuse he might be sentenced only to probation or minimal jail time, but that if he insists on his innocence and goes to trial he could be sentenced to "10 years or more." As long as his alibi witness cannot be located (throughout most of the episode) he is in trouble. The accused man follows the formulas for innocence and honorable masculinity, and is willing to go to jail and ruin his life in order to maintain his claim of innocence rather than admit to something as shameful as rape. The stigma of a sexual assault "rap" is so negative that he will not even consider it, no matter what the costs of refusing to do so.

The *Dallas* episode "Lessons" (1978) features the accusation of a high school teacher by Ewing granddaughter Lucy, who has been left in the custody of the Ewings. After refusing to go to school and demonstrating unhealthy predatory sexual behavior, Lucy rebels against the idea of attending school by staging a false rape accusation against the teacher who has most actively tried to help her. It is clear from the beginning that her claim is a fabrication, because the camera shows through an open door that the teacher is sitting at his desk facing away from her when she rips off her own jacket and runs out screaming. Although no one close to the event believes the accusation, it is dealt with "seriously" and there is discussion of how the teacher could lose his job, be sent to jail, "or worse." Although her actual father is not part of the show, a surrogate father, uncle Bobby Ewing, appears on the scene. The episode ends with a "happy family" shot of Bobby, his wife, and Lucy agreeing to work together as a family in the future. Thus the episode features a number of familiar elements of the typical false accusation plot including an underage accuser and an accusation that is obviously false but is used to gain attention from adults. Like the *Welcome Back, Kotter*, *Big Hawaii*, and *Hill Street* episodes, it emphasizes the ease of false accusation and the severe threat to the reputation of the accused.

In addition to these traditional stories lending credence to the idea that young women falsify rape claims for a variety of reasons and that an innocent man can be in serious trouble if falsely identified as a rapist, two of the false accusation plots complicate such traditional views on false accusation and offer counter-explanations (other than the problemed teenager) or question whether false accusation actually occurs. An episode about teacher-student rape featuring an accusation that appears false but is probably true was aired on *21 Jump Street* ("Higher Education," 1987). The episode retains a good deal of ambiguity in its characterization of the rape, with the student claiming nonconsent but seeming uncertain, and the teacher claiming consent but coming across as a thoroughly hateful character. Strangely, this episode is framed as date rape and not as statutory rape. The questionable morality of having a relationship with a young student is raised by the father character, but the illegality of the situation and the very real criminal nature of the teacher's role regardless of consent is never raised. This adds further ambiguity, because the girl's age enhances the immoral dimension of the teacher's role as well as the possibility that she entered the relationship willingly but was misled about the teacher's feelings and intentions. It appears that the issue of consent is only raised because the girl is pregnant and this fact has ended whatever relationship they had. In this story, the pregnant student first names an (Asian) undercover police officer as the baby's father and her father insists that she is telling the truth. Race is not discussed at all: the student simply names the Asian cop because they went on one brief computer-arranged date and she knows his name. Eventually it becomes clear that the accusation is false, and that the student merely chose the cop to avoid fingering the real father of her baby, a teacher with whom she may have had consensual sex. The episode contrasts the denial and callousness of the real father with the honorable behavior of the falsely accused undercover cop, who risks his career and reputation to go to the girl's house and discuss the situation with her. Like the falsely accused in *Big Hawaii* and *In the Heat of the Night*, the cop cannot stay away from his accuser and is compelled to contact her and discuss the situation. He and his colleagues understand date rape very well and the police captain labels the crime as date rape, noting that "they knew each other, they were in a social setting together after the alleged incident occurred. It's not unheard of in date rape, particularly if the girl is naive and misjudges the relationship." He concludes that rape is hard to prove in such cases. Another detective confronts the teacher with the accusation of date rape, with malice and contempt in his voice.

Meanwhile, the real culprit tries to avoid all contact with the accuser and treats her cruelly when she contacts him. Early in the episode the teacher and student have a lengthy conversation in which he says that it's her "own fault" she is pregnant since she knows about birth control. Thus the dialogue depicts the accused teacher-rapist as having no remorse and no feeling of responsibility toward his child or his student-victim and suggests that their sexual relationship was consensual. In the final scene, when he is confronted by an angry, baseball-bat-wielding father, he refuses to call the relationship rape until his life is clearly in danger. Throughout the story it is unclear whether their sexual encounter was consensual or forced, even after the girl confides to Hoffs (a female undercover cop) that she was forced and asked him to stop. Hoffs tells her that it was rape if she wanted him to stop and he would not, but the girl seems uncertain about the truth of what she tells Hoffs. The officers discuss date rape and the difficulty of proving it in court, noting that it will be especially difficult in this case since the victim began with a false accusation of someone else. Since there is really no court case, the episode ends with an extra-legal solution. The girl's father threatens the teacher with a baseball bat while the undercover cop who had earlier been accused yells at him until he confesses to rape.

A second episode contradicting traditional views on false accusation by depicting a story that seems false but is actually true was aired on *The Bronx Zoo*, in an episode entitled "Behind Closed Doors" (1987). Here a student accuses one of her teachers of repeatedly taking her off campus and raping her and of repeatedly locking her in his classroom and abusing her there. In the final minutes of the episode, it is revealed that the high school student victim's very serious original accusation is warranted. Before that, the episode includes substantial dialogue on the subject of veracity, as two detectives discuss whether the victim's initial claims should be believed. The female officer believes the claims, asking why a high school student would invent a story of this magnitude and detail. The male officer is skeptical, focusing on the teacher's record and career that could be ruined if the rumor of rape is spread through the community. There is lengthy discussion of how rape accusations are the primary fear of male teachers, and how a teacher at another school had his career ruined by just such an accusation. Throughout the episode, the female detective believes the girl, but her conviction is shaken when the accuser wants to drop the investigation rather than allow her father to be informed of the situation. The episode's treatment of these points is complex, showing the victim being teased at school for her story and featuring interviews with other students, some of whom suggest that the teacher was a problem and some of whom support and defend him. Since the truthfulness of the accusation is not revealed until the final moments of the episode, a lament about the difficulty of discerning truth is also included, from the perspective of having wrongfully believed a false accusation and placing a "black mark" on an innocent man's career. Finally, the victim reveals her reasons for taking back the true story, explaining that she had thought she could make her problems disappear by naming a father, but that when this didn't work she realized she would have to go back to the true story.

As the only plot dealing substantially with the question of false accusation while going against traditional ideas about rape and lying, this episode focuses on delineating negative masculinity. The accused denies the charges and talks to other male characters about how the accusation will ruin his career, emphasizing the fact that he has a perfectly clean record after many years of teaching. He is willing to conceal his criminal behavior by lying deliberately and vociferously, and he shows no care for the student he has been sexually abusing. The character of victim's father, like most fathers in these episodes, has little depth and is limited to an attitude of protective bullying of his daughter. When she comes forward with her story, he immediately accuses her of playing along. Even the male police officer in this episode fails to give credit to the victim's initial story, instead buying into traditional ideas about lying victims. Thus the episode is a complex and unusual treatment of rape for prime time, and is part of a late 1980s shift toward complex and sensitive treatments of date and acquaintance rape.

In general, prime time's false accusation plots suggest several conclusions. First, men who are falsely accused and are truly innocent react in two ways. They try to contact the accuser and talk to her, possibly even taking a sympathetic and nurturing role toward her and trying to understand the problem that caused her to make up a rape story. Sensitive and honorable men do not become defensive or self-absorbed, but actively seek contact with their accusers to try to understand their problems and motivations. Falsely accused detectives are even willing to go against their training and the orders of their superiors to confront accusers and track down the real culprits in order to clear their own names. Second, they insist on their innocence and are willing to go to jail and ruin their reputations and careers in order to avoid admitting to a sexual assault they did not commit. Men who are accused truthfully and who have actually committed rape behave much differently, showing their bad character by reacting with denial, evasion, and blaming the victim. They reject the accuser and try to avoid talking to her, and they try to shore up their own credibility by talking about their fine record, career accomplishments, and so forth. Accusers who are lying are usually young (underage) girls who are often under pressure from their fathers to support their own innocence by presenting a story that places blame on someone else. Overall, these stories support the central myths of false accusation. A false charge of rape is "easily made" and "difficult to disprove" even when the man is obviously innocent.

The following section examines two focus episodes for this chapter, with emphasis on the portrayals of the crime of rape within the narratives. The episodes were chosen to illustrate the basic parameters of the two dominant types of rape portrayal discussed so far in this chapter, the basic plot stranger rape type and the date/acquaintance type. Since the small number of false accusation plots have all been covered in some detail, no false accusation plots are featured in this focus episode section. The pattern of focusing on one early episode that employs the basic plot formula and one later episode that breaks away from this mold will be followed in Chapters 2–4. The focus episodes in each chapter will provide a clearer view of some of the details of representation that cannot be included in the generalized discussion, and will also offer analytical discussions of some of the more typical, interesting and significant episodes in the collection.

Focus Episodes: *Baretta,* "Shoes" (1976) and *Miami Vice,* "Blood and Roses" (1988)

This section closely analyzes two episodes in detail in order to illustrate through example the similarities and differences between the original basic plot formula and the later date rape portrayals. While the emphasis on masculinity remains in both types, the key differences are in the shift from clarity to ambiguity regarding the actual rape and in the change from a simple and easily "read" plot to one that is complex and open to interpretation. The *Baretta* "Shoes" episode is a typical example of the basic formula plot, with all Caucasian characters. The story opens with several intercut images of Baretta and his colleagues staked out on the street. The viewer is privileged to observe a man gaining entry to a young woman's apartment by showing a police badge and telling her that the building is being evacuated because there is a rapist nearby. The door of the apartment closes after the man enters, and the attack is not shown. Baretta hears an anguished scream and rushes to the scene to find the woman dead. The signs of rape (bruises, cuts, and torn clothing) are clearly marked on her body, and Baretta recovers the leather strap used to tie her wrists. The scene moves quickly to a Christian community center where the next victim, Sister Olive, is working to help the homeless. A deaf-mute shoeshine boy, nicknamed "Shoes," hangs around and actively follows events around him, showing keen powers of observation. When the rapist attempts to gain entrance into Olive's room using the same "police protection" ruse, Olive refuses, saying there is no need for such things in "the house of the Lord." But her lack of fear proves misguided: the rapist breaks into the room and attacks her. The first part of the attack is shown, with the victim struggling to escape, shouting for him to stop, and trying to kick him. Finally Shoes, alerted by the victim's stomping her foot on the floor during the attack, comes to her rescue. Shoes saves Olive's life but does not prevent rape. The rest of the episode focuses on Baretta's efforts to locate Olive and figure out what happened to her, after she flees from the hospital emergency room and goes into hiding, presumably out of shame after she finds herself unable to answer intake questions in the hospital emergency room.

Baretta goes to great lengths to locate Olive before the rapist does, searching the room of a suspect, racing about in his car, arguing with his police captain that the search is worthwhile, and questioning various potential witnesses. Eventually he gets Shoes to reveal where Olive is hiding. Meanwhile, the rapist has decided to come back and kill Olive since she can identify him as the serial rapist murderer the police have been trying to find. The episode culminates in an exciting rooftop struggle between Baretta, Olive, and the rapist, with Shoes providing the final tackle that disables the rapist. The story ends with Baretta's successful shooting of the rapist, which causes the criminal to leap off the rooftop to a noisy death. Baretta also rescues Olive by pulling her back onto the rooftop from which she has been dangling by her fingertips over the street below. The closing scene is a happy family framing of Baretta and Olive talking, and the final shot has Baretta, Olive, and Shoes embracing and smiling.

This episode fits almost all the parameters of the basic rape plot formula. It features stranger rape, helpless victims, and all white characters. The seriality of the crimes offers Baretta the opportunity to capture the offender. The rapist is caught because Baretta takes a personal interest in Olive and because the attacker returns to the same victim, not because of any clues or legitimately collected evidence related to rape. Most of the episode's action focuses on Baretta, since the victim is introduced into the story just before the rape and disappears just after it. The attack is shown in enough detail to leave no doubt that consent is not a issue and that the incident qualifies as "real" rape. The rapist is neatly killed at the end of the story, and the victim says absolutely nothing about her experience of rape or her future needs for counseling, safety, or even conversation. There is no mention of rape counseling, post-rape evidence gathering, rape trauma, or crisis intervention. The victim has no female friends, but a semi-personal relationship between her and Baretta is developed through the events in the episode, making him the central figure on whom she relies to cope with the rape ordeal. Coping consists of coming out of hiding and living to see the death of the attacker.

The Shoes character serves as an alternative model of masculinity against with whom Baretta can interact and be compared. Of course Shoes is too marginal to provide the hegemonic masculine model, and he poses no real threat to Baretta's superiority (Baretta even functions as a sort of father figure to him). Baretta must interpret his silences and figure out how to make use of him to help solve the case. Only because of Baretta's volatile, at times insensitive, and idiosyncratic style is he able to solve the case and save Olive. Although Shoes helps and is depicted as an honorable person, his version of masculinity is not the central feature of the show and he serves primarily as a foil for Baretta. Shoes helps, but Baretta is the one who makes things happen. There is not much open to interpretation: the rape is a surprise, a nonconsensual attack between strangers, and the detective is responsible for handling the post-rape case in a way that saves the victim and eliminates the evil rapist.

The 1988 *Miami Vice* episode "Blood and Roses" illustrates some of the key shifts toward date rape and toward ambiguity in rape representation in contrast to the simplistically formulaic *Baretta* episode described above. *Miami Vice* has been called "undoubtedly the most ambiguous series of all time" (Buxton 1990, 158), and its rape episodes open up questions of morality, blame, personal responsibility, and meaning that were not examined in earlier police programs. The episode depicts Cuban police officer Gina on an undercover operation to gather evidence against mob boss Mosca. The assignment is dangerous, and protagonist detective Sonny Crockett (Don Johnson) is particularly nervous about it because a friend of his was killed by Mosca. In order to get close enough to the gangster to gather information, Gina agrees to date him. On their second "date," Mosca seduces her after an evening of dinner and several drinks. Although she resists and says "no" twice, he over-powers and rapes her. The scene shows that Gina clearly says no and makes some attempt at resistance, although a camera angle from behind the couch shows her hands resting above her head rather than pushing to get Mosca off her. It is unclear whether this posi-tion merely mimics prime time's usual portrayals of rape, where vic-tims often use little resistance and appear hopelessly overpowered, or whether it is included to suggest that Gina herself is unsure of whether she "wants it" or not. The rape is made more ambiguous in the following scene, in which Gina discusses the evening with her female colleague and admits "I know he's bad news. But, it was something about him, and I can't explain it." Like other prime time victims of date and acquaintance rape, she seems to take respon-sibility for the incident. When she says she made a mistake in letting things "go this far" and is horrified at what has happened, it is unclear whether she means the sexual intimacy with Mosca in the "line of duty" or her lustful feelings for him.

In order to continue the undercover operation, and after an apol-ogy in which Mosca says "I'm not gonna defend myself what I did, because it was a lousy thing to do . . . I'm sorry," Gina agrees to another date. It is unclear whether she actually forgives him or is simply pretending to. However, by this time the gangster has discov-ered her identity and plans to kill her. Sonny is alerted to her peri-lous situation and drives off to rescue her. He and partner Rico Tubbs arrive just in time to surprise Mosca while he is telling Gina that he knows who she is. Although Gina spoils the rescue operation by standing close to Mosca and being grabbed and used as a hos-tage, she escapes again and the episode culminates in a dramatic chase scene in which Gina shoots the gangster herself. Thus, while she has let her identity be found out and therefore required the help of her male colleagues to carry off the capture of Mosca, and has further bungled the operation by allowing herself to be taken hostage by him (possibly because she underestimated the danger due to her feelings for him) she is the person who in the end stops him and brings the job to a successful completion, thereby also resolving any conflict between her feelings for Mosca and her duty as a cop.

The episode differs considerably from the basic plot formula, yet certain key elements remain intact. It is different in that the rape is not a violent stranger attack but rather a "seduction" that takes place after a consensual date but goes over the line of consent. Although the moral opposition between male detective Sonny Crockett (who repeatedly shows his concern for Gina and eventually rescues her) and the rapist (a mob leader who practices torture and murder as well as date rape) is clear, *Miami Vice* is generally more open to interpretation than some of the earlier detective shows such as *Baretta* and *Rockford Files*. Here there is some ambiguity about the extent to which the incident can be considered rape, and the rape is not the central action around which the plot revolves. It is used to add excitement, sexual titillation, and danger to the story, which in this and other ways calls attention to how female police officers are different from males. In one scene Sonny arrives at Gina's house as she prepares for the second date with Mosca. Placing his arms protectively and lovingly around her waist as they both gaze into the mirror, he assures her that he is not being so protective because he doubts her professionalism and skill as a cop, but his belief that Mosca is "psychotic, cold-blooded, [and] sadistic" appears to make him unable to let her handle it on her own. The victim is not anonymous but a colleague of the protagonist. At various stages in the narrative, her own uncertainty about her feelings and commitments appears to affect her judgment and actions, but these are only suggestions of the narrative, not clear implications.

"Blood and Roses" maintains some of the traditional elements of prime time rape representation as well. Although it is a somewhat ambiguous date rape, the rapist is a thoroughly evil mob boss whose very presence carries with it the implicit threat of death. It might be understandable that Gina does not fight him off during the rape scene simply because of his character and history. It would be safer to go along with him than make him angry, particularly in her vulnerable position as an undercover cop. The rape scene is thus quite open to interpretation, and it is played for some sleazy connotations as well. After the first date but before the second, Sonny remarks that "if Mosca makes her, she's history." The remark could mean either (or both) that if he has sex with her she will lose her ability to work effectively on the case, or that if he figures out her identity as a cop he will kill her. The episode does not dwell on the rape and does not offer any suggestions of counseling or support groups for the victim. Only one scene features Gina discussing the rape with another person. The ambiguities of this complexly contrived rape situation are presented with very little commentary on the part of the characters to provide direction in interpreting the action. Gina is tough but vulnerable, effective but incompetent, shooting the rapist gangster in the end but only after she has allowed him to first take advantage of her and then escape. As police officer and victim, she still needs Sonny to rescue her, but not to help her deal with the trauma of her rape, if there was a rape.

Conclusion

The crime of rape on prime time television changed drastically between 1976 and 1990, evolving from the basic plot formula of violent stranger rape and victim helplessness toward more realistic representations of date and acquaintance rape. Throughout these years, very little visual representation of rape is included in these episodes, although later attacks are more likely to be shown onscreen. For the most part, the crime of rape in the basic plot episodes is represented through formulaic cues such as a gloved hand covering a woman's mouth, visible marks on the victim's body, or frantic screaming offscreen. Dialogue also adds to viewer understanding of rape, as characters describe the physical and mental state of the victim and compare what they have seen to their previous professional experience with rape victims. Rape in the earlier episodes is an almost ritualistic invoking of formula elements such as the masked face of the attacker and the isolated venue of the attack. In later episodes there is much more variation, particularly in the late 1980s, when date rapes become commonplace on prime time. More varied than the earlier ones, these later depictions are also more open to interpretation and "reading." In contrast to the formulaic and often-repeated rehearsing of terror and violence in the basic plot episodes, these later depictions sometimes leave the question of consent open to viewer understanding, leaving ambiguities in the dialogue and visual representations that can be filled in by specific viewpoints and experiences.

Throughout these changes, the focus on masculinity remains central in prime time episodic representations of rape. The next chapter shows how, no matter whether the rape depicted was a clearcut stranger rape between a violent attacker and an unsuspecting victim, or an ambiguous encounter between a woman and her date, prime time's concern was to show how masculinity could be defined and demonstrated in relation to rape. Detectives in the early years were sensitive enough to take care of victims and effective enough to capture or kill their attackers; by the late 1980s they had acquired even better skills and were able to provide advice to a wide range of victims, demonstrate enlightened views toward rape according to developments in rape reform, and show knowledge of rape treatment and counseling options for victims. Detectives led the way for other males, often teaching them how to handle issues related to rape or themselves struggling to do their best in the face of rape-related difficulties. Meanwhile, whereas basic plot rapists were repellent and marginal characters easily identifiable as criminals, the problematic nature of their late 1980s counterparts extended primarily to outmoded attitudes toward women, sex, and consent. Their unenlightened and insensitive attitudes and beliefs were the cause of rape in many late 1980s plots. Only on extremely rare occasions did prime time suggest that rape was caused by something other than individual problematic males whose failure to live up to the hegemonic ideal demonstrated by protagonists ended up leading to criminal activity and causing problems for other men as well as for female victims.

Chapter 3
Hegemonic Masculinity and Prime Time Rape

Chapter 2 traced the basic evolution of portrayals of the crime of rape on prime time episodic programs. This chapter further develops the book's central argument by examining the treatments of masculinity in these episodes, focusing primarily on constructions of rapist and detective character and on detective-rapist interactions. It examines what the rape plots do with masculinity in the context of the evolving genre — how these rape narratives treat, define, and contextualize masculinity, usually in predictable, patterned ways, but sometimes with surprising and complex results. Although the individual elements that constitute prime time's authorized brand of honorable masculinity are visibly altered between 1976 and 1990, the variables of this change remain predictable and relatively fixed. As in the earliest episodes, rape stories through 1990 continue to use the subject matter of rape in order to spotlight the performance of hegemonic masculinity. As models of this ideal, detectives and male police officers serve as clear moral contrasts to rapists, also demonstrating their superior understanding and compassion by helping peripheral male characters in the roles of relatives and boyfriends of victims to learn about rape, its effects on female victims, and the appropriate ways to handle traumatized rape victims. These male relatives of victims serve as foils or contrasts for the detective's model response to rape and rape victims.[18] Protagonist detectives, and sometimes peripheral male characters, are contrasted clearly and explicitly with the rapist through dialogue, behavior, attitude, and interpersonal connections. In the years approaching 1990, the typical protagonist detective becomes

ever more concerned with and characterized by his feelings, compassion, and relationships.

With only rare exceptions, emphasis on masculinity is maintained just as clearly in the minority of rape episodes aired on non-
detective programs. Even non-detective programs treat the subject
of rape in ways that highlight masculine attitudes, postures, behaviors, values, and feelings. Women's reactions, though not entirely eliminated, are peripheral in such episodes. Male characters
are more numerous and more central than females, and the narrative action centers on these male protagonists. Rather than pushing
these male characters to the sidelines, the subject of rape seems to
be used to throw them into high relief, often contrasting a protagonist's enlightened and sensitive approach to rape with the confused
and outmoded attempts of others including rapists. This chapter
includes detailed analysis of four episodes, two in the following
section as a sort of introduction to the subject of masculinity in
prime time episodic rape narratives. The two episodes analyzed in
that section illustrate how far prime time episodes could go in emphasizing masculinity in a wide range of ways. Thus these episodes
also illustrate many of the methods or formula elements used to
bring masculinity to the center of the story, marginalizing rape
victims and other women in the process.

The two episodes discussed at the end of the chapter follow the
book's regular pattern of illustrating differences in representation
between an early basic plot episode and a later, somewhat altered
version.

Masculinity as Central Theme: Illustrative Episodes

On the extreme end of the continuum of rape episodes relating to
masculinity are plots that revolve almost exclusively around this
theme and have very little to say about rape-related issues and questions. Even though such stories may not fit the basic plot formula
discussed here, the reactions that are caused still involve questions
about the nature of masculinity at the expense of the rape story.
Two episodes, one from the 1970s and one from the late 1980s,
illustrate this masculinity-centered extreme, though only one took
place on a detective-centered drama. The *Dallas* episode "Winds of
Vengeance" (1978) is an excellent example of a story illustrating
ineffective masculinity in relation to rape, as illustrated by the char-

acter of J. R. Ewing. His actions are contrasted to those of his more honorable brother Bobby. In this episode, no actual rape occurs. However, the threat of rape is held throughout the episode, and various familiar narratives about rape are reproduced, all with the subject of masculinity at the center. The episode opens with J. R. Ewing and his hired man together in a motel in Waco, Texas, in the early morning. The men are in separate rooms preparing to go home. They exchange sleazy looks over the still-sleeping women, but it is clear that any sexual activity the night before was consensual. As he prepares to leave, J. R. drops his wallet, and (unknown to him) one of his business cards falls out. The card is picked up in the next scene by the extremely jealous husband of J. R.'s overnight companion Wanda, who vows to go straight to the Ewing home and exact vengeance on the whole family by raping whatever women he finds there. His brother-in-law goes along, remarking that they need to see "how the Ewings like it when their women are treated the way they treated ours."

The "pre-rape" scene that follows is played to maximize both dramatic tension and the evil characters of the two men from Waco. After making the Ewing family guess why they have come, they reveal that one of them is married to a woman named Wanda. While Bobby Ewing models hegemonic masculinity by acting on his concern for the women's safety (eventually saving them), J. R.'s masculinity is questioned. Since J. R. is the one who slept with Wanda and "left his calling card" by her bed, they declare that his wife Sue Ellen will become the first victim. The bad guys taunt her after finding a photo of her as "Miss Texas," and force her to go get a bathing suit and her "Miss Texas" banner and perform her part from the "talent" contest. In this scene J. R. is a captive of the criminals, just like his wife and the other Ewing women, and he is forced to watch helplessly as his wife is humiliated. As Sue Ellen begins to comprehend what is happening (she will be humiliated and raped because J. R. was unfaithful to her), he tries weakly and unsuccessfully to jump one of the gunmen.

While J. R. is completely ineffective, Pamela Ewing, Bobby's wife and also a potential rape victim in the scene, turns the tables by playing one of the gunmen against the other. Reminding the leader that his sidekick told her how Wanda likes to sleep around, she demands to know whether he actually intends to carry out his rape revenge plan even though he knows that his wife was having a consensual affair with J. R. This challenge immediately deflates his ego, and he visibly shrinks and stops tormenting his victim, admitting that it's true that his wife probably consented to the night with J. R. With this predator out of the way, however, the sidekick announces that he still wants his "justice," and he selects the teenage Lucy to be his victim, since she is a "real" Ewing. Just as he drags Lucy out of the room, Bobby Ewing appears and knocks him out.

The final scene further underscores J. R.'s emasculation. Unable simply to go to his wife and comfort her, he very hesitantly approaches her and tries to place a coat around her shoulders as if to help cover her humiliation from the incident. She rejects his gesture and throws off the coat, standing up in her bathing suit and "Miss Texas" banner and striding out of the room. J. R. has been refused any credible masculine role in relation to his wife. He has not saved her from rape and in fact has created the conditions under which she has become victimized. He has sat mutely by and watched her be humiliated in front of her whole family, and he has even proven unable to help her express her emotions and recover from her experience. The episode ends on a shot of J. R. standing by himself in the Ewing living room, the only character who has not acted honorably, rejected by his own wife after her victimization. In contrast, younger brother Bobby has correctly guessed that something is wrong at home, left work and rushed home during a tornado, and arrived on the scene just in time to save his wife and niece.

Apart from its obvious attention to masculinity in the characters of J. R. and Bobby, the "Winds of Vengeance" episode also examines the subject in relation to the two criminal characters who travel from Waco to the Ewing home in pursuit of a clearly warped idea of justice. These two characters spew horribly outdated ideas about women, possession, and rape, referring to "our women" and "their women," and "getting what they came for." They are depicted as bordering on the criminally insane. The leader, played by a young Brian Dennehy, is repeatedly featured in extreme close-up, highlighting his crazed expression. Both characters are thoroughly offensive in word and deed. Not only do they deliberately humiliate women, they do it in order to get back at what men have done, and they do it in offensive, insulting, and sexist terms. Some of their language is no doubt characteristic of *Dallas* as a whole, but these characters are nonetheless particularly offensive, even in *Dallas* terms.

A second episode centering almost exclusively on masculinity is *The Equalizer*'s "Shades of Darkness," which aired in 1986. The story has many of the defining elements of the basic plot, including a rapist who is a stranger to his victims and who is the personification of abnormality and evil, commission of serial crimes, and the use of an enormous knife during the attacks. In some ways it could be considered a prototypical prime time rape narrative, since it centers on three key male characters, using them to define and delimit good and bad versions of masculinity. The three characters are the protagonist private detective McCall, a violent murderer-rapist, and the hapless but well-meaning man who tries unsuccessfully to save one victim and unwittingly exposes his sister to attack. The story opens with an attack scene, which takes place in a dark and empty parking garage and is designed for maximum terror. As the episode begins, both victim and rapist are anonymous characters rather than program regulars. The rapist emerges from behind a pillar as the victim approaches her car from the elevator. He tells her that he has been watching and following her and that he knows personal details about her life. When she starts to run, he tells her that this is good because it will be "more exciting." He grabs her, threatens her with a knife, and asserts that he will do whatever he wants to her. She begs him not to hurt her, but when a young National Guard officer happens on the scene, the would-be rapist fatally stabs his victim and runs away. The victim stumbles into the arms of the witness, who holds her for the few remaining moments of her life.

"Shades of Darkness" takes a turn when a second witness drives up and mistakenly thinks the National Guard officer is the killer, since he is holding the dead woman and is covered with blood. His guilt is further suggested when, after being told to stay still, he runs off in pursuit of the real killer, whom no one else has actually seen. The real criminal is skilled in making a getaway, while the innocent man stands out in the open waving his bloody hands until the police arrive. The next scene opens with the innocent man's sister worried that he has been arrested and will be falsely convicted. She hires the Equalizer, McCall, to find the murderer, since the police do not believe he exists. There is virtually no discussion of the merits of the case in a legal sense. The assumption is simply made that ruin by a false conviction for a rape/murder he did not commit is a likely fate for the brother without the intervention of McCall.

McCall is allied with the accused's sister (who also becomes a target of rape by the insane criminal and is saved by McCall), a priest (a friend of his), and the falsely accused National Guard officer. McCall discovers that the rapist was a deserter who ran away from his war post after causing the deaths of ten of his buddies. He is also an escaped convict who was jailed for a previous rape. Only if the rapist also enjoyed torturing children could the moral opposition of the episode be any clearer. Rape here is a sign linked to others that indicate a man's complete moral and mental breakdown, and by the end of the episode the rapist can no longer even maintain a facade of normalcy. From the moment that McCall is hired, and with the victim silently dead, the episode centers on masculinity and the parameters of good and bad men. The sister exists primarily as the vehicle that brings the men together, and as the object of their protective actions. Because the priest and McCall were old war buddies, and because the rapist is mentally unstable, there is quite a bit of dialogue related to warriors, service to the country, and the effects of war trauma on men's psyches. At numerous points in the dialogue, the rapist is called a coward or insists that he is not a coward. McCall uses the taunt "coward" to lure the criminal into a state of incautious rage, bringing him out of hiding where he can be tracked and captured.

In addition to dialogue about how the criminal is a coward and McCall and the National Guard officer are not, the episode includes other behaviors and actions on the part of all the male characters that clarify what constitutes real masculinity. Beyond the absence of cowardice, true masculinity as modeled by McCall involves the protection of innocent persons and the selfless performance of chivalric duty. He takes the case because the sister begs him to, even though the brother has already told him they cannot pay for his help. At the end of the episode McCall simply tells the man all he can do to repay the debt is to get on with his life. The middle section of the plot centers on McCall's painstaking efforts to keep the brother and sister safe, which he accomplishes by hiding them in his priest friend's church and ordering them not to go out for any reason. However, the brother is uncomfortable with his role as a helpless partner of his sister, and refuses to stay in hiding while McCall chases the murderer and solves the case. Although the sister does not object to waiting patiently for others to solve her problems, the brother says that he simply cannot sit still and allow this to happen. Eventually McCall agrees to let his priest friend take both brother and sister along if they follow in a separate car and stay away from the action. McCall takes all the risks, breaking into the criminal's apartment, booby-trapping it to enrage him, and later facing the heavily armed man alone in an abandoned warehouse. The final face-off in the warehouse, between the two men with real military backgrounds (McCall's military history is a mythic part of the program's general story line), with the much more innocent and ineffectual National Guard officer on the sidelines, highlights an additional dimension of masculinity. Experience in war, it seems, can have disastrous effects on some men while producing model citizens of others. The rapist's dementia is attributed at least in large part to his weakness (he was a deserter who couldn't take the pressure) combined with the horrors of war. Rape is once again related not to gender socialization and norms, but rather to a volatile mixture of harsh masculinizing experience (war) with a weak male character.

These two episodes, one from 1978 and one from 1986, show the extremes to which prime time was able to go in presenting a story revolving around rape and dealing almost exclusively with issues related to masculinity. In both episodes, no actual rape occurs, but the crime remains at the center of the other plot developments and dialogue. Women characters have very few lines and the discussion is among men and related to how they should act and what sort of character they have. Rapists are thoroughly despicable characters in thought, action, and speech. Protagonist males interact with other men and with women, demonstrating their superior sensitivity, versatility, and effectiveness. Honorable masculinity in these two episodes is the opposite of cowardice and involves the protection of women, the potential victims of rape, even when prime time rape plots do not take place on detective/cop dramas, as the discussion of the *Dallas* episode illustrates. Many of the elements that make up these two episodes are repeated over and over in prime time's rape-centered offerings through the 1976–1990 period.

Masculinity in the Basic Plot: The Rapist

Rapist characterization in the basic plot episodes without question contributes to the traditional conception of rape as a brutal stranger attack. Especially in episodes through the early 1980s, rapists are depicted as marginal beings far removed from the masculine ideal demonstrated by the protagonist detective. Rape is certainly not, according to these episodes, the result of a general social conception of masculinity that can be harmful or dangerous to women. It is almost never connected to structural elements of American life such as socialization, patriarchy, pervasive depictions of violence against women, or oppositionally defined gender roles. Rather, it is the result of sick, perverted, and even psychopathic individuals. Rapists in these episodes are rarely normal men or characters who have any regular connection to the show or to respectable characters, and on the rare occasions that they are respectable in some way they are almost always depicted as quite abnormal or extremely evil in other ways. For example, the rapist in one early episode turns out to be a corporate vice president (*Dog and Cat*, "Live Bait," 1977). However, this perpetrator is otherwise marked as among the most disturbed of the prime time rapists of this era. The script offers a psychological diagnosis of him, noting that he has a domineering mother and seeks strong women on whom to exact revenge. He is said to have a subconscious desire to be captured, leading him to commit serial rapes of escalating violence, and he enjoys listening to tapes of his attacks. Later rapists are more likely to be normal men in appearance, dialogue, and behavior, especially in cases of date/acquaintance rape. But even some of the very latest episodes examined here depict rapists as visibly abnormal. Rapists through the early 1980s serve as poor examples of masculinity, possessing none of the admirable traits exhibited by the detectives.

Even if they are not obviously psychologically damaged, rapists in the earlier episodes are depicted as extreme in their violence. Basic plot rapists are uniformly depicted as menacing or terrifying strangers who unexpectedly attack and beat their victims. Through their crimes, methods, and personal characteristics such as habits, language, and attitude these rapists are all clearly placed beyond the margins of the normal, and many are visibly abnormal. In *Strike Force* ("The Predator," 1981), the attacker holds a switchblade to his victim's throat and wears a stocking mask that distorts his face. He tapes his victim's eyes and shows pleasure in the "anticipation" of his crime. Similarly, *MacGruder and Loud*'s "The Violation" (1984) features an attacker who wears gloves and a ski mask and threatens his victims with a hunting knife. In *TJ Hooker*'s "The Confessor"

(1984), one serial rapist wears a frightening hood with a military appearance. The crime scene in *Tales of the Gold Monkey* ("Sultan of Swat," 1982) reveals that the victim died of strangulation by a phone cord. One episode (*Barnaby Jones*, "Deadly Sanctuary," 1978), features a rapist whose evil can be seen in his eyes; another describes the rapist as the kind of man who has low self-esteem, who blames his shortcomings and problems on other people, and who could have been a Nazi in a different era. The rapist is remembered by one victim because of his taunting and scary voice (*Quincy*, "Let Me Light the Way," 1977). The rapist in a *Rockford Files* episode ("Return of the Black Shadow," 1978) is violent and bordering on insane, and is the leader of a raucous biker gang who all wear rattlesnake emblems on their clothing. After raping a woman he has kidnapped he knocks her off his bike with his hand. A very similar plot on *Walking Tall* (pilot, 1981) features a biker gang whose leader is responsible for the rape of a young victim. After she has been assaulted, left in the woods, and found by local detectives, he remarks that she "belongs" to him. "Anatomy of Fear," a *Barnaby Jones* episode (1977), includes a survivor who has been raped and robbed a second time by the same man because she told the police about the first attack. She says the rapist returned with friends to exact revenge because she reported the first rape to the police.

Racism and sexism characterize rapists and add to their abnormality, especially in contrast with the enlightened views of protagonist detectives. Sexist and outmoded attitudes about women, sexuality, and rape consistently appear as markers of the extreme evil of rapists, often in contrast to much more progressive or enlightened attitudes of detectives. In *Matt Houston* (Episode 26, 1983), the perpetrator victimizes a teenage factory worker described as having the innocence and vulnerability of youth, though his male companion expresses shock that he is even approaching such a young girl. The rapist is so inhumane that he nearly kills a young diabetic boy who may have witnessed the rape. The episode includes elements of exploitation and racism because the victim is Mexican and the attacker is a colleague of the factory owner who illegally employs her. The young witness is also Mexican, and the rapist attempts to get rid of him by having him sent away with a group of illegal immigrants who are being deported. The episode features no dialogue on the part of the victim, who is killed by the end of the opening scene. In this episode, as in others, the racism of the perpetrator is used as one dimension of his evil. Confused attitudes about women and sex are also expressed by rapists. The rapist in "Anatomy of Fear" (*Barnaby Jones*, 1977) tells Betty (a victim) that he thinks his rapes didn't have to turn out so badly, since all he wanted was for the victim to pay attention to him. He concludes by telling her, while her hands are tied behind her and he strokes her face, that he desires her and that after he is finished she will desire him in the same way. Similarly, the perpetrator in "Deadly Sanctuary" (*Barnaby Jones*, 1978) asserts that his victim was looking for a man when she came to his bar, implying that she has gotten what she wanted through his attack.

In a slight variation, *TJ Hooker*'s "Big Foot" (1982) features a serial rapist who is a radio DJ who says on the air that the rapes may be caused by the fact that women are looking too alluring and dressing too provocatively. *Lou Grant*'s "Rape" (1980) features a truly demented Caucasian attacker who continually asks for encouragement and praise from his black victim, asking her whether she liked it and whether she wants him to do it again. In *McClain's Law* ("Time of Peril," 1981), the rapist instructs his victim to make it easier on herself by not struggling, and threatens to "cut" her with the switchblade he is holding. He has a frightening appearance achieved through black gloves and a trash bag worn over his head with holes cut out for his eyes. In *TJ Hooker*'s "The Confessor" (1984), the attacker instructs his victim to "keep quiet" so she won't get hurt. The attacker in *The Mississippi* ("Murder at Mount Parnassus," 1983) tells his victim to "behave," and the rapist in "The Predator" (1981), a *Strike Force* episode, verbally humiliates and threatens his victims, telling them that they should be compliant and do everything he tells them to do. The rapist in *Hawaii Five-O* ("Requiem for a Saddle Bronc Rider," 1977) brags that he raped a young bride on her wedding night as a way of doing the husband's duty for him.

The apparent need of these men to continue committing brutal crimes adds to their ethos of extreme evil. Two 1981 *Strike Force* episodes feature multiple victims, one with five attacks and the other with sixteen. In *Starsky and Hutch*'s "Rape" (1976) the detectives locate the rapists by looking through mug shots. They note that both are already wanted for rape and assault and that both have long criminal records and are to be considered dangerous. These perpetrators have raped a mentally challenged girl in an out-of-service city bus, and one returns to her house later to kill her. A *Serpico* episode ("A Secret Place, 1976) underlines extreme disgust similarly, with a victim remembering that the two rapists were so drunk that one of them got sick (1976), while a *Hill Street Blues* episode features a serial attacker who uses mace on his victims and has a female accomplice who helps him identify women to rape ("Dressed to Kill," 1981). Numerous rapes are committed by more than one attacker, playing up the violence of the attack and the helplessness of the victim. In *Serpico*'s "A Secret Place" (1976), the victim fights off one attacker but is pinned down by a second who asks what else she can do for him. In the *Strike Force* episode "Lonely Ladies" (1981) the attackers show "hate and malice" in their expressions and laugh as they approach the terrified victim. The *Hill Street Blues* episode "The World According to Freedom" (1982) begins after the rape has been completed, but detectives survey the scene and conclude that the damage is so severe that it had to have been a gang of men who tortured and raped several victims in a bar bathroom.

The visibility of rapists, the ability of others to recognize them at least as abnormal if not as rapists per se, is sometimes also underscored by dialogue from other characters. In one episode, a character describes the perpetrator as a maniac (*Barnaby Jones*, "Deadly Sanctuary," 1978). Another episode notes that the rapist is the same one who earlier committed rape and got away. The detective refers to the rapist as "slime" and bemoans a system that forces him to cut a deal with such a man (*Baretta*, "Somebody Killed Cock Robin," 1977). In another episode, a character observes that the rapist beats up his girlfriend too. These criminals are depicted as identifiably evil or decidedly crazy. Their immorality, including their attitudes and actions toward women, are clearly contrasted with the thoughts and actions of the protagonist detectives, who swear repeatedly to protect, defend, and avenge the female victims. Outmoded ideas about women and rape are linked with evil and brutality. These episodes through the early 1980s include almost no explanation of rape that reach beyond the depraved individual, such as gender socialization, mass media imagery, or power imbalances between men and women.[19] The self-justifying adherence of criminals to offensively sexist ideas regarding rape and sex suggests another way in which they are simply out of touch with the mainstream of society.

Rapists in Later Episodes

Rapists in late 1980s episodes are more likely to be acquaintances of their victims, but this later period also features some of the most brutal stranger rapes of the 1976–90 group. Thus those rapists who are not acquaintances or dates of their victims follow the basic plot model and even exaggerate some of its characteristics, as in the *Miami Vice* episode "Honor Among Thieves" (1988). This episode depicts an exaggerated basic plot story in which the deranged serial rapist injects his victims with cocaine before raping and killing them, and leaves a doll next to each victim. The victims are all teenagers, the most recent of whom is a fifteen-year-old. The episode includes a lengthy argument about whether the attacker knew what he was doing, after he confesses that he couldn't stop himself and that "it was like being in a bad dream you can't get out of." The rapist not only is a big-league drug dealer but is also clearly crazy. He talks to himself using high-pitched doll voices in conversation with his usual speaking voice. When other drug dealers discover that he is the notorious "doll" rapist/murderer, they capture him and put him on trial, making righteous speeches about how they think someone who does this kind of thing is beneath contempt. The episode is open to interpretation as to the relative moral condemnation it offers for drug dealing in relation to child rape/murder. In the final scene the crazed rapist, after confessing and explaining his uncontrollable compulsion, jumps to his death. He lands on one of the other drug kingpins, and both men are killed. When an officer arriving on the scene asks detective Sonny Crockett which one is the murderer, he tells him "take your pick," suggesting that rapists and drug dealers are on the same level. Although some elements are open to interpretation or alternative readings, the plot exaggerates the violence and psychotic nature of the rapist and fails to provide any role for the victim. No matter how it is read, the story is one about men, their interactions with each other, and their relative moral and social positions. Both drug dealer and rapist are dead in the final frame, leaving the detective with the last word of moral condemnation.

Many of the late 1980s rapists are "normal" characters who are acquainted with or are dating their victims. Because the accused in these stories is usually someone with friendly relationships with other characters, rapists in these date/acquaintance narratives are seldom portrayed as thoroughly evil. Like the basic plot attackers, these men are often portrayed as people with traditional ideas about women and sex. However, although they sometimes shock other characters in their expression of these ideas, they are for the most part unrecognizable as rapists. They usually do not talk to themselves, wear strange masks and clothing, carry weapons, or threaten their victims with physical injury and death. Nonetheless, moral clarity is usually maintained by contrasting the character of the detective with that of the rapist. The "bridge" episodes, in which acquaintance rape is depicted as nearly the same as stranger rape, are unusual in their portrayal of seemingly normal men who perform horrible acts of violence. One of the more menacing of these acquaintance rapists was featured on the *Crime Story* episode "King in a Cage" (1987). The episode opens with a conversation between the rapist and his victim, who pleads with him to leave her alone. He does not leave, and is clearly aware of the fact that he is her fiancé's boss, using that fact to justify his actions to himself. He openly tells her that she belongs to him. Like the basic plot attackers, he uses offensive language, asking his victim what she is "good at," as he continues to touch her against her will. A nurse tells detectives arriving at the hospital after the rape that the rape survivor is in shock and that the man who abused her must be severely mentally ill.

A *21 Jump Street* episode ("Blackout," 1990) deals with gang rape by a group of seemingly normal (and mostly white) males who commit deliberate and horrific violence. The episode is somewhat atypical in that it deals with gang rape, but typical in that the story follows the pattern of portraying rape as violent stranger attack. In this (somewhat altered but easily recognized) copy of the Central Park jogger case, a group of out-of-control teenage boys knock over trash cans and chase a lone female jogger through a park at night. Rape is not fully depicted, but they pin down the victim, rip her clothes, and smash her face with a rock (the scene ends as she blacks out from the blow). Most of the episode focuses on the group psychology and behavior of these boys, as they again lose control and take over their high school after a flood and power outage traps everyone there for hours. The episode ends as a female officer is about to be raped by the gang but is saved through the intervention of a female peer of the gang members, who reminds them that they would never act like this on their own. Although the plot is fairly unbelievable (in the depiction of the way the gang of normal teen-agers becomes a murderous pack out for the blood of teachers and anyone in their way, and in the way in which a short monologue brings them back to their senses), it characterizes rapists as average males who act violently when in a group. The episode includes some discussion of group behavior, but does not clearly link its analysis to rape per se. Thus it mirrors much of the media coverage of the Central Park case, which handled the brutal attack and rape primarily as a phenomenon of group behavior and generalized inner-city violence rather than as a rape (see Benedict 1992).

While *21 Jump Street* includes unusual portrayals of rapists as somewhat normal men, *L.A. Law* differs in tending to eliminate or marginalize the rapist (see Projanski 1995). Collectively, the *L.A. Law* episodes[20] provide a glimpse of how rape stories could be different from those usually offered on prime time through 1990. Because the program centers on legal proceedings, the stories tend to omit graphic actions such as rape and focus instead on unusual, exciting, or even bizarre fact patterns that make interesting legal dilemmas. Thus rapists often are not part of the episode's narrative at all, and the stories focus more on victims than do the detective programs of the earlier period.[21] Since *L.A. Law* is not a detective/crime drama, detectives are usually omitted from its rape stories. And, as one of the series depicting several rape episodes from the late 1980s, it also provided plots that are ambiguous and open to alternative readings. Only one *L.A. Law* episode ("Romancing the Drone," 1988) includes extended discussion of issues related to rapists. The episode deals with the pro bono representation of a rapist by the firm and an argument over the ethics of taking on this work and being committed to doing it. From the "reformed" perspective, the case is clearly a legitimate rape that should result in conviction of the thoroughly unsavory rapist character. The rapist is clearly guilty, shows no remorse, asserts that the victim enjoyed it, and even antagonizes his attorney by ordering him to obtain acquittal.

In this story, it is the ethics of the attorney that are open to question. The attorney knows that his client is guilty, but is willing not only to take on the case but also to use text from the victim's personal diary to try to win it. The rape is described as humiliating and as lasting for several hours, not as something that resembles consensual sex, but the attacker claims that he read the diary (con-

taining an explicit fantasy of having sex with him) without the author's permission or knowledge and took it as a form of consent for
what he did. In his closing argument, the attorney (Kuzak) sums up
the facts suggesting lack of coercion: "no weapon was used, no
screams were heard and no signs of physical struggle were de-
tected." He also employs familiar rape myths in concluding that the
victim is not necessarily lying because she may have regretted her
"invitation" after the fact and altered her memory to fit her feelings. The rapist is convicted and the defense attorney is repeatedly
criticized for his role, with one of his colleagues accusing him of
making sure that the victim would "think long and hard about
enduring a trial the next time she's raped." Using traditional myths
when he knows they are false is a breach of ethics and a breach of
model masculinity as it is defined on prime time. Though the rapist
is predictably offensive, the character of the attorney, which should
normally be held in contrast with that of the rapist, is instead compared to him and judged negatively.

Rapists in these prime time episodes changed a great deal from
the 1970s basic plot characterizations to the late 1980s date and
acquaintance rapists. The earlier versions are depicted in starkly
negative terms and are usually visibly abnormal. Basic plot rapists
are extremely violent, can be recognized as psychologically damaged, and spew out sexist and offensive beliefs about women and
sexuality. Later rapists are more likely to seem normal to other
characters, although occasional psychotic and marginal characters
still appear in the later years. The several *L.A. Law* episodes tend to
marginalize the rapist and focus attention on the masculine characters of the attorneys who are central characters in the show. Thus
the moral positioning of masculinity in relation to rape becomes a
bit more ambiguous, but masculine behavior stays at the center of
the drama.

Masculinity in the Basic Plot: Detective

In contrast to these depraved, psychotic, and sexist rapists, the male
detectives who discover and capture them embody the traditional
masculine qualities of competence, volatility (wildness), and freedom observed by Fiske as well as the qualities of compassion, morality, and caring for women noted by Hanke to be elements of altered
hegemonic masculinity that respond to feminist critiques of tradi-

tional conceptions. Through their work on rape cases, these detectives express their manhood in ways that emphasize and even call attention to positive, traditionally feminine qualities. Through their interactions with other characters, both men and women, protagonist detectives show that they have a superior understanding of women and their feelings about rape, and even that they are willing to learn if their understanding occasionally falls short of expectations. The rape story in these detective fiction episodes works to adjust hegemonic masculinity in such a way that critiques of male socialization and cultural norms of masculinity are defused because they seem to be no longer valid. Furthermore, when feminist dialogue appears in these episodes it is most often spoken by male detectives: hegemonic masculinity incorporates and encompasses the feminist critique, and the episodes usually simultaneously eliminate feminist and even female supporting characters. The male detective on the case is usually the primary moral and psychological support for the victim, who seldom has female friends or family to comfort her. It is the detective who questions the victim about her experience, who encourages her to press charges, remember details that could lead to the rapist's capture, or return to the crime scene, and who generally helps her to learn to trust and enjoy life in the aftermath of her attack. Masculinity solves, atones for, and soothes victims after rape. These elements are sometimes adjusted in the later episodes to account for female colleagues of the central male character, but most episodes continue to focus on the attitudes and reactions of protagonist males through 1990.

Detectives frequently play a nurturing role in relation to rape survivors. Sometimes, they discover the victims after they are raped and, finding them hysterical, incoherent, or in shock, cradle them and try to soothe them. This role of detective as primary caretaker of the victim is taken to its most extreme form in a *Baretta* episode where the victim latches onto Baretta after he finds her beaten, raped, and abandoned in a closet. Baretta holds and comforts the whimpering victim, trying to calm her down ("Why Me?" 1978). On regaining her senses in the hospital, the victim refuses to talk with anyone except Baretta, and she talks with him several times about how she doesn't think she can survive. These episodes portray a world in which connections among women are rare and in which the proper response to rape involves male caretaking of helpless victims as well as male concern with "justice" for what has been done to them. In *Baretta*'s "The Marker" (1978) a father comforts his daughter, cradling her in his arms and asserting that she should not feel ashamed or dirty. Starsky and Hutch ("Rape" 1976) provide comfort for the victim by bringing a stuffed toy to her hospital room and holding her to help her calm down. The *Quincy* episode "Shadow of Death" (1982) employs a twist on the basic plot structure involving the detective who protects, defends, and cares for the victim. Here Quincy befriends the murder/rape victim's grieving friend, who is also suffering from post-traumatic stress symptoms after serving as a nurse in Vietnam. Quincy assures this surviving friend that he will stick with her until she gets help for her mental problems, which are resulting in bouts of blackouts and depression. Through several rounds of denial and rejection, Quincy insists that she seek counseling, and he finally triumphs. This action eventually leads to the capture of the rapist. As in *Baretta* episode "Shoes" analyzed earlier, only the detective's perseverance and caring nature lead to the ultimate solution of the case, which his superiors want him to drop throughout the story.

As programs other than detective/police dramas increasingly include serious treatments of rape, non-detective male characters, usually white professionals such as doctors and attorneys, take the lead in dealing with rape and its victims in prime time. In a *Lou Grant* episode entitled "Rape" (1980) the victim, Lou's colleague Sharon, goes to work right after the rape and tells her colleague Rossi about the attack. Rossi provides the primary support system for Sharon in the days following the attack, following the pattern established in earlier basic plot episodes with male detectives. Sharon talks with her mother on the telephone and eventually puts her job on hold to return home for a while, but she apparently has no female friends or colleagues in whom to confide, and within the episode's narrative Rossi provides comfort, care, and advice. He thinks she should call the police, and does it for her when she asks him to. She even stays at his house. He assures her that she did the right thing in surviving, and compliments her for being talented, good-looking, and smart. He puts his arm around her and she cries. He advises her to go home and recuperate for a while and that her job will be available when she returns.

In addition to providing comfort, detectives and other protagonist males are effective and successful in performing their primary functions of solving the crime and capturing the rapist(s). The majority of rapists in the earlier episodes are dead at the end of the story, most at the hands of protagonist detectives. Thus in most episodes there is no need for a trial, and the difficult issues of gathering evidence, questioning the victim, and working toward a conviction are omitted from the story. Only a handful of episodes through the mid-1980s include any legal proceedings such as a hearing or trial. In most cases where the criminal is not killed during the episode, the story simply ends with his capture and makes no mention of the future legal process.

Not only are detectives the primary support for victims and the means through which rapists are brought to justice in these programs, but they also provide nearly all the verbal condemnations of the rapists and their actions and are even occasionally somewhat pro-feminist (see also Moorti 1995, chap. 6). Verbal condemnations serve to underscore the stark contrast between the evil criminal (violent, sexist, depraved) and the heroic protagonist (caring, concerned, self-righteously angry, personally offended). In the *Hill Street Blues* episode "Presidential Fever" (1981) a police officer refers to rapists with a string of derogatory, dehumanizing terms. In another episode of the same program, entitled "Dressed to Kill" (1981), a group of about twenty officers stare in disbelief at the woman accomplice who selected victims for a rapist in a public park. In yet another *Hill Street* episode, (Captain) Furillo expounds that he doesn't want this kind of "sickness" in his jurisdiction, and pounds the table, exclaiming that someone will pay for what they did ("The World According to Freedom," 1982). In *Strike Force* the police refer to whoever is committing the rapes as a "sex creep" in one episode ("The Predator," 1981) and call kidnap-rapists "three monsters" in another ("Lonely Ladies," 1981). Later in "Lonely Ladies," male detectives discuss how rape is getting more and more gruesome with time, noting that now there is always more than one attacker, aggravating torture, and even murder. In *Tales of the Gold Monkey* ("Sultan of Swat," 1982), the detectives vow to kill the villains. Male protagonists lament that other police detectives question a victim's credibility when she has clearly been raped by three undesirables ("Somebody Killed Cock Robin," 1978), and Baretta yells a threat to kill a rapist he refers to as scum. Hooker laments the injustice of rapists walking free to attack more women (*TJ Hooker*, "Big Foot," 1982) and expresses hope that he will be "nailed."

Hegemonic masculinity involves a violent temper directed at

criminals but not at women. As noted above, Starsky, while visiting a victim in the hospital after the rape, physically comforts her with parental familiarity. After wondering who could have attacked a mentally challenged girl in such a way, he expresses his own lack of comprehension but promises to find answers ("Rape," 1976). While looking at pictures of murdered teenage victims (in *Miami Vice*, "Honor Among Thieves," 1988), Crockett's face barely disguises his feelings of disgust. In a slight variation, JZ, a female detective on *Dog and Cat* (1977), asserts that when the victim returns to town her attacker will be safely convicted and in jail. Baretta asserts that he will protect a survivor by making sure the perpetrator is put behind bars ("Why Me?" 1977). Detectives in these programs are righteously angry and vow to themselves, to victims, and to rapists that rapists will be discovered and caught. If necessary, they use violence in their attempts to fulfill their promises. In the *Simon and Simon* episode "Outrage" (1987), the mother of the detective pair is raped in her home. One of the brothers hears the attack over the phone, having called just at the moment when the rapist appeared on the scene. He sheds a tear and then expresses rage and beats the wall with his fists, exclaiming his resolve to catch and murder the attacker. As the two detective sons arrive at the hospital, seeing their mother's bruised and swollen face for the first time, they are clearly holding back their emotions. One of them has severe difficulty dealing with what has happened. He wants to know if there is anything she can say to help them identify and capture the attacker. They do their best to take care of their mother after the attack, even inviting her to stay with them rather than going back to her house where the attack occurred. Later they talk with her about her plan to sell the house. They continue to vow revenge, threaten severe violence if the suspect is not arrested immediately, and carry out their threat.

Detectives often become so outraged by rape that they are unable to control themselves and must use violence, even at times when such actions jeopardize a legal case. This is true of Virgil Tibbs, a detective on *In the Heat of the Night* ("Rape," 1989), when his wife Althea is the victim of rape. He even tracks down the accused at home in order to beat him up. In another episode, Tibbs's colleague Bubba behaves in the same way after he is identified as the rapist by a rape survivor ("Accused," 1989). Quincy, after noting that juries will convict rapists if they are shown solid evidence, confronts the suspected rapist, asserting that he will bust the suspect on both assault and murder charges. After this tirade, he is unable to contain himself and lunges at the suspect ("Let Me Light the Way," 1977). The physical attacks of rapists by detectives may be seen as expressions of moral outrage against violations of the hegemonic masculine model. In addition, the use of violence by these characters firmly fixes the use of force as an acceptable means of obtaining just ends in extreme cases. Later representatives of hegemonic masculinity use physical force just as their more traditional predecessors would have done, but they add a dimension of sensitivity and nurturance in certain situations that augments the traditional masculine profile.

Detectives in the Later Episodes

Although early episodes in the group under examination here are straightforward and formulaic, matching inhuman criminals against heroic detectives, the later years include trends of development in favor of complexity, realism, and openness to interpretation. As 1990 approaches, nonformulaic plots and nonstereotyped characters are more common. But hegemonic masculinity remains as the central problematic, as mostly male detectives work out their relationships to other types of men and to women in general. Ensemble casts on detective programs such as *21 Jump Street* and *Hill Street Blues*, as well as on some non-detective programs like *Lou Grant* and *L.A. Law*, increasingly lead male protagonist characters to interact regularly with women and simultaneously to develop more versatile and complex personalities. Although detectives are no longer quite as predictable as in the past, they are still competent, outspoken, and volatile if provoked. Berman (1987) notes that prime time detectives of the 1960s and 1970s tend to view others as hostile and are somewhat overly emotional. They have "no ambiguities" because they are not concerned about image, love life, or relationships to others. Male detectives in the 1980s are portrayed with more intimacy and complexity, more concerned with their feelings and with what others think about them, and more likely to have multiple complex relationships with colleagues and friends. In the later years, protagonist males are increasingly likely to be friends, colleagues, or intimates of rape victims, and through the 1980s their relationships become increasingly central. But the protagonist detective still serves as a model of masculinity, often teaching other men the right way to feel and behave. The later prime time detectives actually listen to women characters and sometimes learn from them. Detective characters become more and more sensitive in their interpersonal relationships, sometimes proving perceptive enough to step aside and let someone else take over the role of primary caretaker of the victim.

The transition from more traditionally heroic detectives to people with a complex set of interrelationships with colleagues, relatives, and friends can be seen from the early 1980s episodes. Almost all the male detectives of the late '80s have female partners, and detectives tend to spend much more time discussing issues, feelings, and opinions. In short, these detectives spend much more time thinking and talking than did their 1970s counterparts. In addition, the 1980s episodes on detective/cop programs include more dialogue between female characters, expanding roles for female detectives, and more detailed and frequent use of feminist ideas about rape and rape reform. Rape narratives on programs without detective characters are even more complex, thorough, and variable in their treatments of rape, veering far from the basic plot narrative established years ago in the detective genre. However, detective and police programs still account for the vast majority of rape stories during this period. Through 1990, the primary solution to rape is still the reformed masculine figure who understands victims and their feelings, solves crimes, and captures rapists. The rare episodes that best explore a structural explanation for rape are *21 Jump Street*'s "Hell Week" (1988), which depicts a fraternity gang rape (discussed in Chapter 5), and *Facts of Life*'s "Double Standard" (1980), a situation comedy episode that depicts date rape as a problem caused by common male attitudes about women's "availability."

Male-Female Detective Relations

In contrast to the programming of the late 1970s, the shows of the '80s reveal some flaws in the ability of male detectives to handle every aspect of rape. They are often corrected or contradicted by their female counterparts, indicating that women have a better understanding of rape than men, no matter how sensitive and professional an individual man might be. In "Rage," a 1986 episode of *Spenser: For Hire*, Susan explains date rape to Spenser and takes the victim's side from the beginning, whereas Spenser believes she could have made up or changed her story because she was afraid to tell her parents the truth. Susan says she knows this girl wouldn't do that and defines date rape for Spenser. The episode, like several others in the late 1980s, contrasts women's and men's understandings of rape, while still allowing male detectives to show compassion and sensitivity. Spenser eventually finds the kidnapped victim and reconciles her and her blaming father. In *Shannon* ("A Secret Rage," 1981), the title character is complimented by his black woman partner for his handling of the victim's hospital interview. He also stays out of the way when the victim breaks down in her daughter's arms, and he sides with his partner in a dispute over how to handle the case. (They think the victim should be used as a key witness because she saw the guy's face, even though she has a previous record for prostitution and stealing.) Shannon shows his sensitivity and understanding by letting the female characters interact, and his sensitive treatment of the victim is legitimized by a female partner. However, in this episode as in many others, the male detective performs the hospital interview of the victim, although there is also a female detective on the case. Even in the 1980s it is rare that women characters perform the key role of comforting and questioning the victim immediately after the rape.

Male-female pairings and mixed-gender groups are common on 1980s prime time, and protagonist males usually get along well with their female partners, demonstrating an understanding of rape and its effects on victims and others. In *McClain's Law*, "Time of Peril" (1981), McClain and his colleagues (including one female) work together as a team to capture the rapist in the act. In *TJ Hooker*'s "Death on the Line" (1984), a lengthy conversation features a male detective explaining to a female officer how men can sometimes overreact when their girlfriends are raped, noting that when a man's girlfriend is raped he can feel many negative emotions including anger and frustration, and that a man whose girlfriend has been raped also experiences confusion because he may feel that his intimacy with his partner has also been violated. Hooker concludes that some men are simply unable to deal with the rape of a partner. He says this reaction is wrong, but empathizes with men who experience it. Thus, while he understands the usual male response to the sexual victimization of girlfriends, this male officer has clearly been able to move beyond this response. The emphasis here is definitely on the ways rape affects men, as if perhaps male viewers can be convinced of the seriousness of rape by imagining how it might affect them if someone close to them were victimized. *MacGruder and Loud*'s "Violation" (1984) features a husband-wife police partnership. Here the husband models the appropriate male response. After the wife is attacked and narrowly escapes being raped, the two discuss the incident. He asks her to talk to him about it and she refuses, concluding that it happened to "*me*, not us" and that it is her problem and not his. The wife's reaction, staunchly insisting that rape is something affecting primarily herself rather than her husband, is more common in the later episodes. The husband patiently accepts her need for distance and time to heal. The story line still makes room for the reactions and feelings of the husband, but here the police officer wife is strong, demanding to deal with the trauma in her own way, and the protagonist husband knows how to handle the situation and give her the space she needs.

TJ Hooker's "Big Foot" (1982), a classic basic plot in relation to the theme of masculinity, features Hooker watching the victim being loaded into an ambulance. He discusses rape and rape convictions with other detectives. They note that all the rapists are out on bail, and that rapists are no longer convicted, but are found mentally ill instead. They lament the fact that we as a society spend so much money trying to cure the criminals, forgetting about the victims. Although the male detectives have most of these lines, a female officer talks to the victim in the hospital scene, explaining that the detectives will do everything they can to catch the criminal and that she is available any time to talk with the victim. This female officer tells her colleagues she's covered the "pro-social checklist" with the victim, mentioning psycho-trauma and post-event depression. She warns the male detectives to "go easy" since the attack was so horrible. There is mention of "new rules" on handling the victim in this type of case, but not what those rules are. One male cop has unreformed, insensitive ideas about how to handle the case (grill the victim and get her to ID the rapist as soon as possible); Hooker is the more sensitive one, offering the victim a friendly smile and conversation. The insensitive cop leaves, saying that waiting for the victim to "open up" is a waste of his time. Hooker starts to talk with the victim, encouraging her to see the positive — that she is still alive and has a full life ahead of her. He offers to contact her mother and tell her what happened. Later he inveighs against a system that

often lets criminals go free on the theory that they need understanding rather than punishment. Thus the title character shows
sympathy and sensitivity toward the victim, respect for his female
colleague, and anger against the rapist. In addition, he even has
some knowledge of social change and indicates support for it. Later
in the episode he tells the victim about referral services in the city
that can help her find other people who have been through the
same experience and who can talk to her about it. He also explains
to her that in a trial they cannot ask her sexual history. He gives her
a crisis line number and encourages her to call it. When she says she
knows he's right and will try to do better, he encourages and compliments her.

In *TJ Hooker*'s "The Confessor" (1984), Hooker knows the victim,
an Episcopal priest. Stacy, a female cop, comforts the victim right
after the rape, encouraging her to talk about it, but later Hooker is
asked to help deal with the victim because he is a friend of hers. He
is at ease in dealing with both his female colleague and the highly
educated professional victim. After the rapist has been captured,
the episode ends with an exchange of professional favors as Hooker
asks the victim for help dealing with a troubled colleague. The *21
Jump Street* episodes "Fun with Animals" (1988) and "Stand by Your
Man" (1989) both feature a group of three male detectives demonstrating their sensitivity toward rape survivors, one of whom is their
colleague. They offer protection, comfort, empathy, and conversation to victims and are genuinely interested in their well-being.
These episodes are discussed later in detail.

Thus male detectives in the early 1980s show their human side
in the ease and complexity with which they are able to work alongside women and help victims get professional post-rape help. The
women characters sometimes take over the role of caring for the victim and giving her advice about treatment and trials. Beginning in
the 1980s, men and women work together as detectives. The men
retain their traditional masculine characteristics of strength and
volatility, but show increasing sensitivity to women and rape. These
plots show how rape affects men and how men should ideally respond to rape victims. In these programs, protagonist males are
generally much more reformed in their views toward rape than are
other men. The contrast between protagonist and other males is
especially stark in some episodes depicting male family members of
victims.

Males as Family Members and Intimates of Victims

The use of family members and intimates in prime time rape episodes provides another view of how these episodes constructed hegemonic masculinity. Male family members (and boyfriends) are included much more frequently than female relatives, and the roles of these male characters usually follow predictable patterns. Fathers typically fail to understand the "real" dynamics of rape and begin by accusing their daughters of immoral or provocative behavior, but finish the episode (through the help of the detective) by coming to understand that their beloved daughter is a victim deserving of care and love rather than a wayward child in need of correction. Husbands and boyfriends typically fail to understand the rape's impact on their loved one and usually are unable to handle the trauma, perceived emasculation, and uncertainty brought about by their partner's victimization. Victims themselves almost never convey the message about their own feelings and needs to their male relatives and intimates unless the intimate is a detective protagonist. Detectives typically help fathers and husbands understand the traumatic and complex nature of the effects of rape, presenting them with the victim's perspective and instructing the confused relative on the appropriate way to act toward her. In doing so, they demonstrate the superiority of their own brand of masculinity, in effect training the other males in the right way to react toward rape and rape victims.

Several episodes feature the victim's husband in post-rape scenes. None of these prime time husbands are as skilled as their detective counterparts in dealing with the trauma of rape, and detectives share their insights with husbands and boyfriends who are not coping well. In one episode (*Strike Force*, "The Predator," 1981) a team of one male and one female police officer talk with the husband and try to set him straight about rape. He has referred to his wife as "being with" the perpetrator, and they ask him if he thinks she wanted to be viciously attacked. They note that rapists enjoy proving how macho they are in this sick way, and they recommend that he conceal whatever negative feelings he has about his wife at the moment, and instead comfort her by holding her and telling her he loves her. The husband proves unable to deal with his wife's rape and leaves her. A male detective comments sadly that rape is a crime that has wide-ranging negative effects. In another husband-reaction story (*St. Elsewhere,* "Drama Center," 1984) the victim discusses her experience with her spouse in the hospital. He begins to cry and she comforts him, but does not tell him what she is feeling and how he can help her. He tells her it would be best to just forget the whole thing and not talk about it anymore. Later in the episode the husband presents his wife with vacation tickets and laments how he feels he failed her. She again comforts him, this time by comparing his feeling of helplessness to her feeling when watching him go off to war. Instead of explaining her feelings and describing her rape experience to her husband, she talks to a male detective, who comforts her by telling her that there is no correct way to act when physically attacked, and that survival means she did the "right" thing under the circumstances.

In *TJ Hooker*'s "Love Story" (1984), one of the victims is Hooker's "love interest," so he gets personally involved. He comforts her and says he will always love her, wrapping his arms around her after the rape. In spite of her difficulties after the attack, he stays with her and continues to assure her that he will be there for her. This is in notable contrast to boyfriends and husbands of victims who are not protagonist detectives. In "Death on the Line" (1984), another episode of the same program, the victim has a boyfriend (Dan) who arrives during the hospital scene. She describes the attack in a disjointed way. Dan is unable to find the words to ask her if she was raped, but finally chokes it out. She lies, telling him that luckily she was not raped, and that he should not worry. She has decided to deny that she was raped in order to avoid having to deal with Dan's inability to cope, and she refuses to testify or take any part in legal proceedings. The detectives beg her, saying that they need her help. They worry that, although they know she needs time to heal, the rapist may have a chance to attack someone else. Later Hooker discusses the case with the attending physician, who explains the mental and emotional stages rape victims experience. The detective assures the physician that he wishes to keep the victim's pain to a minimum while still trying to gather vital information about the rapist. He continues to try to convince her to help him, and also talks with her about allowing her boyfriend time to deal with his own shock and anger. Finally she breaks down and cries, and he holds her, still encouraging her to face the truth and cooperate with the investigation. Finally, she agrees to give him the results of her medical tests. He agrees to talk with Dan, and in that discussion mentions the Rape Center as well as various feelings that are common for both victims and their male partners in cases of rape. He tells Dan that Dan, too, is a victim.

Detective McCall deals with an even more troublesome husband in *The Equalizer*'s "Nightscape" (1986), which follows the story of a woman who is raped by three men in a subway station. The protagonist detective is hired by the victim not to capture the rapists but to locate her angry husband before he kills them. The husband has reacted badly, leaving his wife to find and kill her attackers instead of staying home to comfort her. The detective not only locates the husband, but also discovers that the husband has been having an affair and that his guilt at not meeting the wife after her evening class on the night of the rape is causing him to become enraged and seek revenge on the attackers. The detective captures the rapists, finds the husband, and enables a reconciliation between husband and wife after having a serious discussion with each of them. Thus, once again, a sensitivity that extends to a good understanding of human emotions and psychology helps the detective bring a happy resolution to the case. McCall bridges the communication gap between husband and wife, fading into the background as they get back together.

Fathers appear in these rape episodes at least as frequently as husbands, and have similar difficulty in dealing with rape. Fathers are almost never enlightened at the beginning of the episode, and, as in the false-accusation episodes discussed earlier, tend either to take old-fashioned, even punitive attitudes toward their victim daughters or to become enraged and seek revenge for rape. However, by the end of many episodes featuring a victim's father, he is able to come to an understanding of his daughter's trauma. A father in *Spenser: For Hire* ("Rage," 1986) starts out quite unsympathetic toward his victim daughter. The episode includes dialogue between the victim's parents in which the father takes a traditional view of rape, blaming his daughter for the attack because of the way she dresses and for developing a general reputation for being sexually available. He also says it's her fault because she let the guy get started, even if she later changed her mind and said no. From this point, the father's feelings and thoughts are spoken in several scenes, while the mother looks on with an anguished expression. The father clearly cares for his daughter, empathizing with her difficulty dealing with their recent move to Boston. Later, after the daughter is more severely victimized and Spenser's colleague Susan tells him to be more sensitive and supportive of his daughter, the father apologizes and says his views were mistaken. He says he is ashamed of himself rather than of his daughter and admits he cannot "read people." He holds her and his wife and says they can now go home together. The episode is unusual in that Susan, not Spenser, delivers the corrective speech to the father.

Fathers represent a form of traditional masculinity in contrast to male detectives' superior knowledge and advanced comprehension of rape and its consequences for victims. In the *Tales of the Gold Monkey* episode "Sultan of Swat" (1982), the victim's father vows revenge on the apparent (but not actual) rapist, and twice tries to strangle him. A detective colleague of Starsky and Hutch ("Strange Justice," 1978) is the father of a rape victim. He ruins his life by threatening the rapist and eventually kidnapping and killing him. As illustrated in the previous chapter, fathers play other troublesome roles in relation to rape, serving as excuses or motivations for daughters to make false claims. Afraid of what their fathers will say or do to them or their boyfriends, these victims are driven to cry rape.

Fathers can also be problematic in their ineffectual efforts to help detectives get their daughters out of trouble, unable to control their feelings of rage against the rapist enough to take any effective action. Of course, this behavior is contrasted to that of the usually calm and efficient detective, who is able to save the victim as well as calm down the out-of-control father. In one such episode, *Hawaii Five-O*'s "Elegy in a Rain Forest" (1977), an escaped convicted rapist kidnaps a young college student on a field trip with her classmates. As detectives set up their search operation, the father appears and demands to be taken along with the search party. After refusing him firmly and repeatedly, the lead detective realizes he will not stay behind, and allows him to go along. The father is predictably problematic when the convict and kidnapped daughter are found. He brings a gun out of his coat and rushes forward, serving as a perfect target for the armed escapee. The episode closes with his apology to the detectives and their competent capturing of the convict and rescue of the daughter. They are able to perform effectively and complete the job even though the father makes the case more difficult.

Fathers, husbands, brothers, and boyfriends of victims illustrate the various impacts rape can have on a man's life. These family members and intimates often have great difficulty dealing with what has happened to their loved ones, reacting emotionally or out of traditional beliefs. Detectives must teach these men the right way to act toward victims, and to solve their rape cases they must also at times overcome the added burden of troublesome family members. Usually, male family members can overcome their shortsightedness and learn to behave in a way that is helpful to victims, thanks to the detective's understanding of rape, human nature, and women's feelings. In some cases it is a female detective who provides the needed insight, but in most instances definitions of masculinity are competing for legitimacy, and the male detective's less traditional and more enlightened version proves more correct.

The two episodes discussed in detail in the next section once again illustrate the contrast between early and late representations of rape on prime time. The episodes are chosen as typical examples that balance at least a bit of rape-related discourse with the dominant theme of masculinity. Both adhere closely to the focus on masculinity discussed in this chapter, even though only one is from a detective program. Both episodes include males as intimates of the rape victim. The first, *Little House on the Prairie*'s "Sylvia" (1980), portrays an elderly father with little understanding of how to raise a daughter and certainly no sophistication in dealing with her rape. The second, *In the Heat of the Night*'s "Rape" (1989), depicts a tormented detective-husband whose wife has been brutally attacked in their own home. Through the use of multiple male characters and male family members of the victim, these episodes elaborate on hegemonic masculinity using the subject of rape to highlight different masculine positions. The protagonist male models the appropriate hegemonic masculine behavior, showing physical strength, volatility, and effectiveness as well as caring and sensitivity in challenging and complex situations. Both episodes illustrate how variations can be brought into the basic plot formula without significantly altering it.

Focus Episodes: *Little House on the Prairie,* "Sylvia" (1980) and *In the Heat of the Night,* "Rape" (1989)

The analyses included here focus on the typical and formulaic ways in which more standard rape plots turn story elements toward an emphasis on the masculinity of the central character in contrast to that of the rapist. Understanding of rape is confined primarily to central males, and female friends (or other female characters) are virtually absent from the narratives. The selection of one detective and one non-detective episode illustrates the similarities across prime time genres when the subject matter is rape.

The *Little House on the Prairie* episode "Sylvia" (1980) provides a clear example of how a non-detective program can handle rape in ways very similar to the basic plot developed in the cop/detective genre. This story was aired in two one-hour parts. The "Sylvia" plot follows the basic plot in that the rape is a surprise attack; the attacker, a stranger, wears a frightening clown mask to disguise himself; the attacker returns for a second attempt on the same victim and is killed during this attempt by the male protector of the victim; the victim has few spoken lines related to her feelings and reactions related to the rape, and the people who help her recover from and deal with her experience are all men. She has no female friends and is motherless, living alone with her elderly father. The "Sylvia" story can be read as a template for the various possible masculine positions in relation to rape, with the position of the show's central character Charles Ingalls clearly represented as the correct and exemplary position.

Although "Sylvia" deals with the rape of a child of thirteen, it is included in the discussion here because the discourse it employs is related to rape rather than to child abuse or statutory rape. The episode opens with Sylvia and her father alone at home; the father is lecturing her about her "wanton" ways and telling her that if the boys who are often found peeping through her bedroom window are seen there again, he will punish her to try to make her behave properly. Even though Sylvia says she has done nothing to entice the boys, her father insists that they would not "act that way" if she were not doing something. Thus the story opens with a father's expression of the traditional belief that women provoke male behavior and are to blame. During this opening scene it is made clear that Sylvia has no mother, and the implication is that her father (who appears to be in his late fifties) may not know how to "handle" a difficult situation. In the next scene, Sylvia is being taunted by a group of rowdy boys because of her breast size. She appears to be shy and unable to do anything to stop them. Finally, as one of the boys begins to grab her, Albert Ingalls (the son of Charles Ingalls) intervenes and tells them to leave her alone. This heroic gesture marks the start of a romance between Sylvia and the Ingalls boy, filmed in romantic and idealistic modes, with soft focus, filtered lens, and soft border techniques used on scenes of the young couple together near water, at sunset, and so on. The romance appears to last a couple of weeks, and is only possible because Sylvia has been lying to her father. When the lie is discovered, she is forbidden to see the Ingalls boy again and is told to come directly home from school every day to do chores. This further places in question the father's parenting technique (he is too harsh and allows his daughter no freedom even to develop friendships or have a good time), and also introduces the idea that Sylvia is a "liar" and is disobedient, which will later be used by her unenlightened father to question her story of being attacked.

The attack scene follows the termination of Sylvia's brief romance with Ingalls. As she walks home through the woods, a man wearing a clown mask jumps from behind a tree and chases her, knocks her down, and rapes her. After the attack she makes her way home in a battered and disheveled state. Her father shows sympathy and caring for her, but is ineffective and unable to provide real understanding of her feelings and experiences. He both blames her for the attack and wants to go out and kill the attacker. Sylvia keeps the incident a secret from everyone until she becomes increasingly ill and collapses in class. When it is discovered that she is pregnant, officials from school and the doctor's office suspect Albert Ingalls, who was recently Sylvia's "boyfriend." (It is clear to viewers that the romance between the young couple was sweet and innocent, extending to a fully clothed kiss but nothing more.) The boy refutes their accusations, asserts that he would "never do that," and storms out, hurt and offended at the suggestion and at the idea that Sylvia could be pregnant, and believing she has lied to him. His father, however, tells him not to judge people too quickly and not to "write off" Sylvia without talking to her. Charles Ingalls thus models proper masculine behavior in dealing with women, relationships, and emotions. Charles's calm and straightforward responses are contrasted to those of his son, who tries falteringly to "be a man." The episode features one scene in which Sylvia's father goes to the Ingalls house to accuse Albert of getting his daughter pregnant. Again Charles Ingalls is a model, defending his son, explaining the father's errors of fact, and helping him understand that his parenting has not been the best. Ultimately, Charles must wrestle in the pouring rain with the older man, proving his physical as well as moral superiority as a masculine figure.

Albert remains devastated by the news of Sylvia's pregnancy until she tells him of the rape, but at that moment he decides they should get married and run away together, and that he can take care of Sylvia and the baby. Charles's admonitions are ignored, and Albert plots secretly to run off with Sylvia. As he gathers the supplies needed for the journey, she waits alone in an abandoned building, where the man with the mask appears for a second time. This time she attempts to escape and injures the assailant, but he again traps her, and she is saved just in time by her young boyfriend, who attacks the assailant and slows him down just long enough for more help to arrive. The additional help is Charles Ingalls and Sylvia's father, who shoots the rapist dead.

"Sylvia" is a story about various men and their positions and reactions to rape. Her father represents the old-fashioned or traditional approach, blaming her for enticing boys and punishing her after she has been victimized, all while genuinely caring for her and trying to do what is best. He is sincere but simply wrong. As the boyfriend who loves Sylvia, the young Albert Ingalls rashly tries to defend and care for her without regard for his own well-being and their future. He is honorable but immature, first refusing to see Sylvia and then deciding to marry her. The actions of Charles Ingalls are at every stage presented as properly masculine, although he has little direct interaction with Sylvia. He gives advice to her father and to Albert and solves the problems of misunderstanding and confusion raised in the story. Charles Ingalls's brand of masculinity is caring but level-headed and strong. He tells his son not to "write off" Sylvia without getting all the facts, but he also advises him not to take on her problems as his own. He advises Sylvia's father that his attitude of suspicion and blame have caused pain to his daughter and almost made her a runaway. Although the old man's poor parenting skills have almost cost Ingalls his own son, Charles calmly provides him advice and comfort to resolve the plot. Notably, only one scene grants significant spoken lines to a female character. In this scene, Albert's mother Caroline explains to him that getting married is a very serious decision and that he is not old enough to take such a step. The story is one of various men and their ways of dealing with rape from several relational positions representing various versions of masculinity. As a 1980 episode, "Sylvia" is typical of early representations in its lack of focus on the victim and its representation of rape as a violent stranger attack, as well as in its portrayal of the show's protagonist as the enlightened protector of the victim.

In the *In the Heat of the Night* episode "Rape" (1989), a clear variation on the basic plot formula, regular character Althea is raped by a colleague of hers from the high school. The story follows all the standard elements of a basic plot: it is extremely violent in depicting the rape, the attacker has a knife and disguises his face, and the primary support system for the badly damaged victim is male police officers. The attack is particularly graphic and violent, dwelling on the attacker's deliberate effort to drag a scarf through spilled groceries (broken eggs, milk, mustard) before using it to gag the victim. Two subtle differences mark this episode as distinct from the basic plot formula. First, even though the attack is carried out in complete surprise and is extremely violent and graphic, the rapist is an acquaintance of the victim. Second, the police detective who comforts the victim is her husband rather than a stranger she meets in the aftermath of the attack. These adaptations are well suited to the preservation of the basic plot emphasis on masculine feelings about, and reactions to rape, while at the same time providing openings for pro-feminist dialogue, increased victim involvement in the post-rape section of the episode, and overt references to the definition and meaning of rape.

"Rape" is an excellent illustration of how some key elements of a formula can be altered without harming the central ideological function of the story. The basic plot elements of this episode are unmistakable, even exaggerated. Althea, returning home from grocery shopping, is suddenly and violently grabbed and forced into the house as she is fumbling with the door. The attacker shoves her to the floor, and groceries fly all over in a general scene of chaos and destruction. The assailant locks the door from the inside and holds her by the hair, pushing her to the ground with his free hand. Yelling continuously, he instructs her to lie down, stop making noise, and stop struggling. Later it is revealed that the attacker is a music teacher at Althea's school, angry with her for her leadership style and decisions that affected him adversely.

The post-rape scene is also typical of basic plot episodes. Bubba (a colleague of her husband) finds her trying to clean up the mess and wearing a filthy slip and blouse. Althea appears unable to show any emotion, although she does later give intake information to an emergency room clerk. When her husband Virgil enters the scene, she is finally able to release her bottled emotions, clinging to him and crying. The rest of the episode focuses on Althea's post-rape trauma, with some dialogue on rape kits, trauma symptoms, and Althea's efforts to "cleanse" herself and regain psychological control. Meanwhile, Virgil struggles just as valiantly to deal with the rape, and much of the remaining narrative is focused on his feelings and problems in understanding and trying to help his wife.

After Althea is attacked she experiences severe trauma manifested by a fear of going back to work, fear of entering the kitchen (where she was raped) and extreme withdrawal from other people including Virgil. He repeatedly tries to talk to her, with little success, as she continually rebuffs him and even yells at him, saying it is her problem and not his. One scene has Althea and Virgil discussing the rape. She asks him why he is so angry, and he responds that he is upset because of what happened. Althea gets the last word by blurting out that she is the one truly suffering since she has been physically harmed, subjected to medical tests and worries about disease, and then told that she has no legal case. She concludes with a line openly hostile to him, asking "Where do YOU get off being mad?" At the end of the episode, Althea is still struggling and Virgil has not worked out a way to deal with her trauma. When she later suggests couples counseling, he readily agrees.

While the episode is progressive in that it grants a number of intense lines to Althea (even one in which she accuses men, including her husband, of stacking the deck against her so that she does not have a valid court case), it is Virgil's perspective that dominates throughout. His conversations with his boss and colleagues are shown onscreen, and in one scene he expresses both a desire to get through to his wife and make everything better for her and a desire to beat up the rapist. In a later scene he drives to the rapist's house and carries through with his threat of violence. In the final scene he kneels by the bed while Althea rests and discusses her plans for her future. The episode ends as the camera zooms out, looking down on the scene of Althea turned away from Virgil, who silently watches her.

Virgil is offered as the ideal male with respect to rape, and the parameters of his masculinity fit those of hegemonic masculinity.

Virgil is kind, loving, tender, and obsessed with the pain of his wife's trauma, but he also vows revenge and prefers violence as a means of "settling the score" even when others tell him this is not the best means of gaining justice. Unlike non-detective husbands of rape victim wives, he is able to empathize with her and is patient with her post-rape process of coming to terms with what has happened. He understands that rape is traumatic and he tries a variety of means to communicate with his wife. Although continually rebuffed in his efforts, he stays by her, both mentally and physically, as symbolized by the spatial layout of the final scene. He is willing to put in the time and effort that will be necessary to help Althea heal. However, he still goes to the attacker's house and jeopardizes the legal case by beating him up and threatening him. Acting on impulse and unable to control his feelings of anger and frustration, he resorts to violence. Virgil's perspective is the dominant point of view through which the rape experience is perceived and understood. The episode shows how, in seriously affecting the victim, rape can also cause great and lasting difficulty for the man close to her.

By articulating both the victim's perspective and the husband's feelings, the episode does remain open to interpretation. Althea has enough strongly spoken lines that the episode could be read as one that focuses primarily on her feelings and efforts to deal with what has happened to her. She has some scenes alone, including one in which she drives to school but turns back, unable to enter the building. When the attacker comes back to her house, she smashes him on the head and runs out of the house, locking herself in her car and leaning on the horn until the police come to make the arrest. In many ways the episode is about her actions and feelings. However, Virgil has more lines and more scenes, and it is his perspective that is articulated in scenes with other characters, including other police officers and the rapist. The episode certainly represents substantial change from the basic plot, yet many of the original elements remain intact, including the central focus on masculinity.

Conclusion

As the extended examples illustrate, the basic plot formula represents a plausible representation of rape throughout the period under examination here, especially effective in keeping masculinity at the center of the story. Detective programs do evidence some changes between 1976 and 1990, and the rape plot shifts accordingly. While detectives retain their basic character, they gradually become even more sensitive and adept at handling complex situations. As victims become stronger and more outspoken, detectives prove able to give them space to handle their own problems when necessary. As the detective genres on prime time gradually allow for closer working relationships between women and men, the sensitive male demonstrating hegemonic masculinity becomes more attuned to the needs and feelings of his female counterpart. In the late 1970s and early 1980s, detectives like Baretta are only required to hunt down the criminal and either capture or kill him, offering some consideration for the victim along the way. As episodes like *In the Heat of the Night*'s "Rape" and the *Miami Vice* episode "Blood and Roses" (1988) illustrate, male detectives in the late 1980s are much more involved with women, not just saving them or avenging them when victimized, but also talking to them about personal issues, going out of their way to try to understand them, and expressing concern for their well-being. They also often show their reformed sensibility (in contrast to less enlightened peripheral male characters who enter the story as relatives and intimates of victims), in some cases offering helpful advice that brings a family or couple back together.

Rapists during these years begin as almost exclusively violent, psychotic, and sexist criminals who attack and brutalize their victims. By 1990 rapists are much more often acquaintances of their victims and somewhat normal-seeming men who, often through a poor understanding of women, sex, and consent, commit rape in a manner less brutal than the crimes committed by their earlier counterparts. The crime of rape continues to be characterized as something caused by rapist character: marginal people with poor comprehension of the rules and norms of social conduct, or with outright antisocial attitudes, are the unfortunate cause of rape. Socialization, media portrayals, pornography, economic inequality, and other social causes do not enter these stories as explanations of rape. Rapist character continues to be contrasted to that of the detective throughout the period under examination here, and frequently a third character serves as a foil against whom the detective can also be measured. Protagonist males consistently demonstrate ideal masculine behavior and enlightened understanding of rape reform and the needs of victims.

Over this fifteen-year period, prime time detectives learn quite a lot about rape, rape reform, and how to deal effectively with rape victims. During the same period, victim reactions to rape also become more complex, and victims generally become less passive and more outspoken, while rape crisis lines, counseling, and victim rape trauma gain more attention. These shifts in victim characterization and the representation of rape reform ideas are the subject of the Chapter 4.

Chapter 4
Representations of Victims and Rape Reform Ideas

The earliest prime time rape episodes under examination here depict victims in a routine formulaic way, suggesting that they deserve sympathy rather than blame. A consistent theme throughout the years is the idea that rape is a serious crime that unquestionably has harmful effects on its victims, a point that is often brought out verbally by male detectives. But, in prime time versions of rape even the victim's character and dialogue are structured to enhance a general focus on masculinity as the central plot theme. Thus during the period from 1976 through the early-1980s, when rapes consist almost exclusively of stranger attacks characterized by extreme violence, and when the protagonist detective helps the victim heal, victims are depicted as vulnerable and helpless, usually as inactive pawns to be discussed, nurtured, and pitied. In most early episodes, victims go into immediate post-rape shock and become unable to speak or to help detectives gather evidence of the attack. In almost all the episodes depicting violent stranger rape, victims play only a small role and are usually confined to hysterical reactions, shocked silence, and reliance on detectives for support and encouragement to help solve the case or testify at trial. A few early victims are strong, vengeful, or articulate about their experiences, and the later episodes provide a more expanded role for their victim characters. Late 1980s victims speak more about their feelings, learn more about rape trauma (usually from helpful police detectives), are more likely to take steps toward post-rape healing, and are willing or even eager to come forward and testify at trial. This increasing effectivity of victims in some ways reduces the centrality of the male detective compared to the earlier episodes. As male detectives become less central, victims gain more lines and more assertive characters, until eventually many victim characters carry feminist ideas into these rape-centered episodes.

The reactions of prime time victims, though formulaic, did have some relation to feminist research on the subject. The first major study of rape victims was undertaken in 1973 by a research team consisting of a psychiatric nurse and a sociologist (Burgess and Holmstrom 1974a). They studied 109 victims representing a wide range of ages and found that there were clear similarities in responses to rape across the group. They believed that the pattern "seemed to qualify as a clinical entity" (Burgess 1995, 240) and labeled it "rape trauma syndrome." The syndrome observed entailed a psychiatric crisis characterized by an extreme fear of being killed. In this first phase, called "acute," the victim's life could be disrupted by such severe feelings of vulnerability. The second phase, which might last much longer, involved a process of regaining a feeling of control, perhaps by returning to familiar patterns. Primary symptoms of rape trauma syndrome include "re-experiencing the trauma," nightmares, and "a numbing of responsiveness to or involvement with the environment" (Burgess 1995, 241). Secondary symptoms can involve guilt and self-blame, fear of crowded places, fear of being alone, avoidance of activities that are reminders of the attack, distrust of friends and strangers, and personality shifts (Warshaw 1988, 69–70).

Burgess and Holmstrom's work was groundbreaking in establishing the legitimacy of rape claims, and some jurisdictions allowed evidence of rape trauma syndrome to show that rape did occur. Their first article on the subject (in the *American Journal of Psychiatry*) appeared in 1974, as did their book *Rape: Victims of Crisis*. Their book on rape trauma syndrome was published in 1978. Thus the earliest episodes examined here, aired in 1976–77, were emerging at the same time as their findings. For the most part, these early episodes did reflect some of the primary symptoms of rape trauma syndrome such as a state of shock or numbness and a fear of doing almost anything. However, they did so in stories that paid very little attention to the victim. For example, in the 1976 *Baretta* episode "Shoes," discussed at length in Chapter 2, the victim has an extreme fear reaction and disappears for the rest of the episode. The early victim reactions match with rape trauma syndrome, but the stories do not follow the victims through post-rape processes of anger, self-blame, or recovery efforts. Rather, they put the victim aside in a state of extreme shock or fear and follow the detective's efforts to solve the case. Victims have few lines, seldom speak about their feelings and fears, and almost never seek any help beyond that of the detective. Although rape crisis centers began operation in many U.S. cities before 1975, this element of the anti-rape effort received only rare and passing mention in prime time episodes until much later.

By the late 1980s regular mention is made of crisis and counseling supports for victims, and a few episodes even depict feminist characters or actual counseling sessions. The later episodes are also more likely to follow their victims through a traumatic post-rape process of changing emotions and eventually some healing. The later episodes also include more professional women as victims, and they are portrayed as very different victims from others (who, as one-time characters on the show, might be college students, former prostitutes, bar patrons, and so forth). Professional women are more articulate, more active on their own behalf, more likely to resist or fight off the attacker, more likely to press charges without much coaxing from male characters, and more likely to reject or rebuff offers of help from protagonist detectives. This alternative response is discussed in the section on "macho" and cop victims.

The Basic Plot Victim

Many first appearances of victims in the earlier episodes occur after the attack has taken place. The scanty information available on the actual identities of victims during this period indicates that they are almost all single,[22] that they have very few (if any) women friends, that they are not in close contact with their families, and that most have careers or jobs outside the home. The majority of victims are not regular program characters and remain fairly anonymous throughout the episode, functioning primarily as ciphers through which the trauma of rape can be indicated and over which the detective can demonstrate his caring, commitment to justice, and effectiveness in his work. Notably, *Dog and Cat*'s "Live Bait" (1977) indicates that all the victims are well-known leaders in their fields (a judge, college president, and tennis star), but even this level of identification of victims is unusual. Some stories provide an explanation for why the victim has no female friends, as in a *Baretta* story ("Why Me?" 1977) in which the victim tells Baretta that she is shy and awkward and does not make friends easily. More commonly, the victim is simply presented as friendless and single without explanation.

The typical response of survivors of rape in the basic plot world is to go into deep emotional trauma similar to the "numbness" reaction described by Holmstrom and Burgess. Most victims end up in the hospital after they are attacked, and it is in the hospital scene where the physical and mental condition of the victim are revealed, providing further evidence of the evil and brutality of the attacker. As discussed in Chapter 2, victims' post-rape physical condition is almost always depicted as clearly indicating a savage attack that could not be mistaken for consent or acceptable sexual relations. Victims frequently experience severe injuries such as bruising, knife wounds, swollen faces, and concussion. In addition victims are shown to experience severe psychological and emotional strain to the point that they cannot function normally, and often the protagonist detective has to coax the victim to provide simple descriptive details to help locate or identify the attacker. In the *Starsky and Hutch* episode "Strange Justice" (1978), the victim is depicted in the post-rape hospital scene as totally without verbal or nonverbal expression and not able to cope with normal activities and interactions. The victim in *Shannon*'s "A Secret Rage" (1981) has lacerations on her abdomen and a bruised face and neck, and is described as being in shock. In *Rockford Files*, the victim of gang rape by a motorcycle gang is totally unresponsive and is put in "psychological intensive care" ("Return of the Black Shadow," 1978).

An episode of *McClain's Law* ("A Time of Peril," 1981) depicts a victim who suffers from a trancelike detachment from reality and spends most of her time staring off into the distance, unable to converse or help detectives with their work. A second victim attacked much later in the episode escapes before the rape takes place, but is on the verge of hysteria. This second victim, who is a reporter, vows to gain revenge on her attacker, but the episode ends without showing any actions in this direction. The link between her professional status and her attitude toward her own victimization (she wants to do something about it and not be totally passive) is typical of the connection often made in these episodes between professional women and pragmatic, less emotional reactions to rape, as discussed below.

Numerous early episodes follow the pattern of depicting the victim in extreme physical and emotional trauma in the post-rape scene. In *Hotel*'s pilot episode (1983), the victim is found wrapped in a sheet on the floor, cringing away from anyone who tries to go near her. When asked what's wrong, she denies that anything has happened and rushes out of the room. Observers remark that she resembles an injured animal in the way she is shaking, staring into space, and generally showing symptoms of being in shock. The victim, who is a prostitute, refuses to press charges, noting that the police would have a good laugh if she tried to make a rape claim. She refuses offers of help and sympathy, saying that she does not want to be a charity case and that people are really only concerned with their own interests and not with her well-being. She sticks to her refusal to press charges in spite of heavy pressure from several male characters, and she states that she will be ripped apart if she tries to go through with a trial. A *TJ Hooker* ("Death on the Line," 1984) episode depicts its victims as young, gorgeous blondes wearing bikini bathing suits and focuses on one in a series of brutal attacks. In the post-rape scene, a female doctor describes the survivor's current state, noting that physically there is little damage, but that since she is a vulnerable and sensitive person she does not want to admit she has been raped. Hooker is practically forced to beg her to help the police by remembering some detail of the rapist's appearance, because this attacker has committed several rapes in the same area and will no doubt soon strike again. But, his efforts prove fruitless and he laments her inability to speak in a later scene, where he asks the doctor when the victim will realize how important his job is and help him out. The doctor responds by describing the victim as experiencing a typical series of emotions from shock to disbelief to guilt to depression.

Some episodes emphasize the ways in which the victim qualifies as a "legitimate" rape victim who has not done anything to bring about her own attack. *TJ Hooker*'s "Big Foot" (1982) depicts a jogger who attacks several women joggers at the track. Typically, the emotionally devastated victim is shown in the post-rape hospital scene, simply staring up at the ceiling with a stiff gaze. Even when detectives begin to question her, she does not move or change expression. When she finally speaks, after being coaxed by Hooker, she cries and tells him that she is twenty-six and was a virgin, saving herself for her future husband. Hooker tries to convince her to press charges and agree to testify if there is a trial. Later, as detectives go back over the series of crimes committed by the same attacker, they note that all his victims have been in their twenties, and that all lived alone. A victim in *Shannon*'s "A Secret Rage" (1981) is the mother of an adult daughter, and her daughter remarks that she is old-fashioned and has probably not slept with anyone except her husband, remaining abstinent after his death. The daughter wonders how it will be possible to make her mother understand that rape is a violent crime rather than a sexual act caused by attraction and lack of control over desire. The victim does speak, but her daughter and the detectives who are with her see evidence of psychological fragility, and the daughter remarks that she would be happier if her mother would show some emotion by screaming or crying. A female detective informs her that her mother is in shock and that she should call the rape hotline for information and advice. Eventually the mother breaks down and cries, but we never see her coming to an understanding of the crime or working to express and deal with her feelings about what has happened to her.

In the *Baretta* episode "Why Me?" Baretta convinces a severely traumatized rape survivor to make an official statement. However, the victim is further traumatized by looking at mug books, and exclaims that she cannot bear to look at any more of them. She becomes dependent on Baretta and follows him around, prompting him to theorize that she is like a baby duck that has imprinted on him after coming out of her "shell" of post-rape trauma. Although the victim initially agrees to give a statement, she ultimately provides no help at all to the detective except the identification of the captured rapist at the very end of the episode. Instead of helping, she becomes a burden, clinging to Baretta and talking about her sad life. If the *Baretta* example seems extreme, a *Starsky and Hutch* episode ("Strange Justice," 1978) goes even farther, providing a young and mentally handicapped girl as the ultimate helpless victim. Like her counterparts in other rape episodes, this victim asserts that she does not want to see or talk to anyone, adding that she would rather die than face everyone after the attack. Barnaby Jones helps a woman who is scared to the point of desperation ("Anatomy of Fear," 1977), and detectives in another episode confront a victim who asserts that she could not go through the two necessary trials (two rapists) but prefers simply to put the whole thing behind her. She initially asserts that she cannot and will not face the rapists, but is finally persuaded by detectives to do her part. When victims are not depicted as so frightened that they cannot talk to detectives and describe their attackers, they may be physically unable to help solve the crime because they have been knocked unconscious or were not able to see the rapist, as in the *Charlie's Angels* episode "Terror on Ward One" (1977), in which a nurse victim struggles with her attacker but does not see his face.

The *St. Elsewhere* episode "Drama Center" (1984) depicts a 55-year-old victim who is attacked while trying to start her car. She is inside the car with the door locked, but the attacker smashes her window with a metal pipe to attack her, and she reacts with severe emotional trauma. This victim is stoic and specifically not hysterical; that is, she is able to describe exactly what happened and answer questions about the rapist's identity. Later in the episode, after the questioning, she has nightmares in which she screams and beats her arm against the bed railings, breaking her cast. Near the end of the episode she describes her experience and the feeling that she should have done something more to prevent the rape or kill the attacker. This *St. Elsewhere* example is thus a transitional one; it includes the older "hysterical victim" scenario with some modifications of an initial reaction of stoicism followed eventually by the ability to discuss the incident and express feelings. The victim shows some of the same signs of severe trauma as victims in earlier basic plot episodes, but she overcomes the severe trauma and acts effectively on her own behalf.

By the final years under examination here, victims of "real rape" still show signs of severe trauma, but also work to overcome the effects of rape to make changes in their own lives. Date rape episodes are more complex and more likely to include feminist dialogue. Instead of closing people out, victims may demand help and get information from detectives. In general, then, victims shift noticeably from near-catatonic helplessness and refusal to take action against their attackers, to self-blame and guilt, and eventually to acceptance of help, expressions of anger, and active attempts to achieve emotional healing.

Victim Dialogue and Feminist Ideas

Discussions of victims and victim dialogue are often the vehicles through which rape law reform material is included in rape episodes, particularly in the early 1980s. In the earlier episodes, when talk about victims brings reform ideas into an episode, such lines are usually spoken by male detectives although victims and peripheral female characters discuss the issue more often in the later episodes. Detectives worry that antiquated rape laws and trial practices will prevent conviction in cases where detectives have worked hard to identify and capture a rapist, and they offer suggestions about rape crisis counseling and rape trauma. An excellent illustration of detective use of reform ideas is in the "A Secret Rage" (1981) episode of *Shannon*, in which the victim is attacked while sleeping in her own home. She expresses a desire to seek justice even if it means going through with a trial, but when detectives investigate her background they find that she once worked as a prostitute and has a record of conviction for possession of stolen goods. The detectives discuss how these facts will affect the case, with one noting that the victim's sexual history is now barred from evidence at trial, but also noting that a convicted felon is not the ideal key witness in such a case. One detective critiques the victim's "style," meaning that she is too forceful and determined in her desire to have the rapist found and convicted. The one female officer, who is African American, sides with the victim and reminds her male colleagues of the specifics of the attack. In the end, the rapist is shot, so no trial is needed and the treatment of law reform and victim character extends to discussion only.

In the earliest episodes, male detectives inform victims of recent changes in rape procedures and complain to their colleagues about limitations in legal procedures. An early example is the *Barnaby Jones* episode "Anatomy of Fear" (1977), in which Jones informs the victim that police have new ways of handling rape cases, and that they provide "female officers to help." The episode demonstrates this new procedure in having Jones's colleague Betty comfort the victim while Jones does the talking. Baretta frequently bemoans the ways victim credibility is questioned, because it makes conviction in legitimate cases very difficult. An entire episode of *Quincy* is devoted to Quincy's crusade to teach hospital emergency room personnel how to preserve evidence to enhance the probability of conviction ("Let Me Light the Way," 1977). The earliest expressions of ideas related to rape reform cannot for the most part be classified as articulations of feminist ideas. Rather, they report on material changes in trial practice, laws, police procedures, or hospital routines for gathering and preserving evidence. Detectives in these episodes are usually approving of changes in rape laws and help options for victims, often lamenting the fact that some elements, such as trial procedures, have not changed enough to help them obtain justice from their crime solving efforts. But, the ideas expressed are not identified as feminist, and when the rare feminist characters are included, detectives tend to disagree overtly with them.

In *Quincy*'s "Let Me Light the Way" (1977), the pre-1980 episode with the most thorough discussion of feminist ideas about what causes rape and how best to deal with it, Adrienne Barbeau is featured as Carol, a feminist rape crisis center director. Although she is Quincy's friend and he invites her to provide her expert opinion on one of his cases, they disagree in an opening scene. While Quincy thinks that better evidence collection can lead to a better conviction rate for rape cases, Carol is less optimistic, and she states that the real cause of the escalating problem of rape is an aggregate of social ideas, beliefs, principles, and morals. The dialogue includes a doctor's defeatist attitude that juries never convict no matter how conclusive the evidence may be, even if it extends to a film of the attack. Thus, although teaching about rape law reform is clearly not central to these programs, some of them do include discussion related to cultural changes regarding rape.

A number of women-authored episodes from the early 1980s include lengthy discussion of rape reform issues with references to crisis centers, counseling, hotlines, and special police and hospital rape units to help victims. In the *Vegas* episode "No Way to Treat a Victim" (1981), author Anne Collins includes a young female officer who meets the victim in the hospital, and a discussion of a rape crisis center and a special victim rights committee that is part of the District Attorney's office. The woman refuses to contact them, however, asserting that everyone she has talked with so far just wants to blame her for what happened. She has even lost her job because of her boss's fear of adverse publicity. A female friend tries to persuade the victim to change her mind about the crisis center, telling her that victims have recognized rights and that there are ways they can help her feel better after her experience. The friend talks to a counselor because the victim refuses to, and the counselor describes the previous era when victims would just leave town to avoid the shame of townspeople knowing what had happened. She also explains that withdrawing is not an uncommon response, but that it is very unhealthy and possibly even dangerous, and she warns the friend that based on past experience with other victims, suicide is a possibility. In a later scene, she further discusses the fact that rape is not an act of sex and that victims are not guilty of "arousing" their attackers. The episode also includes lengthy dialogue on how difficult it is for the victim to relive her experiences by talking about them with other people, and how this leads many to keep their feelings and thoughts to themselves.

Although it features little suggestion of rape law reform, *Lou Grant*'s "Rape" (1980) is similar to the *Vegas* episode in that it includes an expanded speaking role for the victim, who tells her colleague how she feels and how the attack has affected her thinking. She describes her upbringing on matters of sex and sexuality, explaining that it should be something private and given by choice. Because of the rape, she is having trouble feeling secure, self-reliant, and able to make free choices. Both this victim and the *Vegas* victim experience and articulate insecurity and anger and talk to other people about their feelings. Similar feelings are expressed by the victim (Natalie) in *Facts of Life*'s "Fear Strikes Back" (1981). After she is attacked Natalie withdraws from her life and her friends, convinced that she will always be vulnerable and unable to defend herself.

An early example of an active and outspoken rape victim is in a woman-authored episode of *Facts of Life* ("Double Standard," 1980), in which one of the four girls invites a male friend to a party, where he attempts date rape. The would-be victim, Jo, speculates that the wealthy and over-confident "date" assumed she would be a willing participant because she is from the poor side of town. The episode closes with a conversation between the rich friend (Blair) and Jo, in which the two come to the realization that they actually have something in common: both are targets of unwanted advances because people assume they will not mind. In Jo's case, the assumption is because she is low-class and "easy"; in Blair's case, it is because she is rich and bored. Another outspoken victim is featured in *St. Elsewhere* episode "The Attack" (1984), in which nurse Daniels is emphatic, insisting that the women in the hospital are not reacting hysterically, that they want to see some action on the part of hospital and city officials, not just lectures on what steps women should take to avoid being attacked. During the 1980s, victims become more conscious of what has happened to them, more articulate in expressing their feelings and reactions, and more likely to express solidarity with other victims and with other potential victims of rape.

Rape crisis lines, rape law reform, the treatment of victims during rape trials, and rape counseling services are all increasingly mentioned through the 1980s, with victims becoming stronger and more articulate and supporting female characters occasionally playing a role. However, male detectives retain their centrality in these later episodes as well. In the *Vegas* episode featuring a crisis counselor with numerous spoken lines, the male detective repeatedly urges the victim to seek counseling and accompanies her to the first counseling session. In addition, the episode includes a scene in which the detectives discuss the difficulty of obtaining a conviction in the case because the victim is a former prostitute. The rapist is shot dead at the end of the episode, thus eliminating the need to actually depict such a trial and accomplishing the detectives' work with resounding success. *TJ Hooker*'s "Big Foot" (1984) mentions the conduct of rape trials and the ways rape law reform has affected them. After giving the victim the phone number of a rape crisis center, he explains that defense attorneys can no longer ask offensive questions such as whether she enjoyed having sex with her attacker. Hooker concludes that the legal change is for the good. In *Simon and Simon* ("Outrage," 1987), one of the detectives informs his brother that if their mother's attacker is the same man she was dating earlier in the evening, she would only be one of many women to be assaulted by someone they trusted. A female character informs both detectives about post-rape effects on victims, noting that their mother is out of touch with reality and caught up in blaming herself for what happened to her. She also informs the brothers that they should seek counseling to help deal with the trauma of what happened to their mother, and that she will obviously need counseling as well. In another episode, a male detective urges a victim to contact the rape crisis center that is part of the district attorney's citizen advisory committee on victim's rights.

In addition to including a number of lines referring to rape victims and rape reforms, victims in later episodes speak more often, have more lines, are able and willing to testify and to help detectives solve the case, and are less often dead or comatose by the end of the program. In general, victims are depicted as more complex and stronger characters than during the 1970s. The *St. Elsewhere* episode

"Drama Center" (1984) includes an exchange in which the rape survivor says that the rapist did not have the right to touch her, and that she decided not to fight him because she was afraid he would kill her. She laments her choice of simple survival over putting up a fight, questioning why she did not try to kill her attacker. In another program, the victim asserts that she is afraid all the time, but that she has found the strength to attend a counseling group for rape victims (*MacGruder and Loud*, "The Violation," 1984).

Minority Victims

During the late 1970s, nearly all characters involved in rapes in these rape-centered episodes were white. In the early 1980s, a number of episodes specified that their victims were women of color while their perpetrators often were specified as Caucasian. The opposite pattern, with a nonwhite rapist and white victim, was not used in any episode for which the characters' race is known, except in the false accusation episodes discussed earlier. In some narratives, the victim's race seems to provide an additional point of vulnerability and sympathy to her characterization. Many scripts make special note of race, as in a *Hill Street Blues* episode that depicts the victim as a young Puerto Rican girl attacked by a white teenage male ("Presidential Fever," 1981). *Lou Grant*'s "Rape" (1980) specifies a rapist who wonders whether the neighbors will become suspicious that the black victim has a white male "visitor." The *In the Heat of the Night* episode "Rape" discussed above also features a white attacker and a black victim, where the victim is a regular character and the attacker appears for only one episode. As noted earlier, white rapists frequently speak in racist and sexist ways, thus contributing to their characterization as extremely evil. Very few episodes contribute significant dialogue on the complex relationships between rape and race.

The *Miami Vice* episode "Hell Hath No Fury" (1988) goes farther than most episodes in providing some discussion of race and rape. The story depicts the release from prison of a convicted rapist who is affluent and white. His African American victim is afraid he will attack her again, and race is used in the dialogue to suggest that he may have gotten off with a lighter sentence because of his race as well as that of his victim. The rapist is not depicted as someone who prays particularly on minority women, however, nor as an especially racist person. Instead, the narrative develops ambiguity around the question of whether he is rehabilitated. The racial identities of the characters are made relevant only to the question of sentencing and parole, not to the commission of the rape itself (its circumstances are never explained). There is no clearly discernible pattern in prime time's use of race within rape-centered episodes, except that when the rapist and victim are of different races it is almost always the rapist who is white and the victim who is not. It could be said that the minority identity of the victims makes up one more element of their vulnerability and enhances the idea of their victimization, and that racism on the part of the attacker is sometimes used to underscore his extremely evil nature. When the issue of race is not avoided entirely (by casting both characters as white), it is often simply included without comment at the level of dialogue. Minority victims in these episodes do not discuss their minority status or racial issues and, like other victims, seldom have friends to help them recover.

Macho/Cop Victims

Even before *Cagney and Lacey*, a number of prime time episodes that feature female cops depict their victimization. The earliest of these center on single female characters in otherwise all-male casts, in traditional male detective/police dramas such as *Barnaby Jones* and *Matt Houston*. The pattern in these narratives includes several fairly predictable elements. First, the female cop victim is fearless and tough before, during, and after the attack. Unlike almost all non-cop victims, she fights hard to escape the attacker and sometimes succeeds. Often she knowingly accepts the role of potential victim by serving as a "decoy" in a police operation designed to tempt a serial rapist to attack again. In this variation, equipment and communication failures result in the near-completion of the rape, but in every case the woman cop is rescued by her male colleagues who arrive on the scene just in time to prevent serious injury. After an attack, whether in the line of duty or not, female cops act much differently from their non-police counterparts. Instead of collapsing in hysteria or retreating into post-traumatic shock, these victims react with anger and resolve to do something about the attack. Much like their male colleagues, they seek revenge and the capture of their attackers and work to bring about these results. Rather than becoming incapacitated by rape, they react in an almost opposite way, becoming more active and committed to their professional roles, eager to see justice done to their attackers, or simply stoic and unwilling to allow the trauma of rape to make any difference in their professional effectiveness.

Thus the female cop serves two important functions in the evolution of the rape narrative on prime time. First, she blurs the lines between victim and cop, placing one character at the nexus of experiences of both rescuing and being rescued, both vulnerability and proficiency. At the same time she calls into question the possibility of true gender equality, highlighting the differences between women and men with respect to this important prime time profession. In some cases it appears that having female cops is unwise because it eliminates the perfect strength and effectiveness of the formerly all-male force. In others, the presence of this new character type suggests new possibilities and competencies for the police, because female cops can better empathize with victims and can function in ways men cannot (such as acting as decoys to induce rapists to repeat their crimes). In most individual episodes, however, and certainly in prime time's rape programming taken as a whole, the presence of the female cop highlights gender differences and leaves open the question of the effectiveness of female cops for viewers to answer according to their own personal, political, and philosophical positions. The dialogue and actions surrounding women cops are certainly open to interpretation. Julie D'Acci asserts that women officers on prime time police dramas upset "general cultural codes of masculine activity and feminine passivity as well as conventional codes of appearance, figure, movement, and spheres of action in TV dramas" (1994, 117). Prime time's female officers have different roles and symbolic meanings from those of male officers. The presence of female officers in rape episodes provides for the inclusion of dialogue among women as well as for the presence of strong, professional women who are not afraid or hysterical. It also sometimes makes women who should be in positions of strength, self-sufficiency, and competence vulnerable and reliant on male help to do their jobs and stay alive. In cases throughout the middle 1980s, women cops represent difference more than anything. They cannot be the same as other cops simply because they are women, and rape is an effective subject in highlighting this difference. By the late 1980s women police officers are routinely included without question of their competence.

If women are different from men, then one possible way to resolve any question of their competence is to make them behave in a more masculine way. In several episodes, victims display masculine traits such as stoicism and toughness, refusing to be thought of as victims. In these episodes, male detectives do their jobs by trying to persuade the tough victims that they should show emotion or accept help. Thus detectives "choose" the "right" path toward healing for a variety of survivors, encouraging some to trust and reach out and urging others to be less stoic and more in touch with their emotions.[23] One early episode features a detective who fights off her two attackers for quite a while before being overpowered and raped (*Serpico*, "A Secret Place," 1976). The initial attack is played out identically to those in other "real rape" episodes of this period, as a shadowy figure emerges suddenly and seizes the victim from behind. The victim's partner criticizes her for refusing to call for help, saying she is just trying to be "supercop" and warning her that people who act this way usually die young. This rape victim is dispassionate even as she describes the attack to her colleagues while filing the official report, and provides a derogatory description of her attackers. She takes a pragmatic, unemotional attitude toward the rape, asserting that this sort of event is nothing unusual in New York City, and continues to function effectively as a detective helping her colleagues identify and capture the rapist. When her partner criticizes her for refusing even to appear weak, she asks whether he would prefer a reaction of hysteria. Although he continues to badger her to talk and emote about the experience, she staunchly refuses, later proving her professional competence when the pair successfully take on a gang of five hoodlums. The two become emotionally close and, when the female cop wins a commendation for her bravery, they embrace with tears in their eyes. Though open to interpretation, the episode suggests that, even though men and women are different, they can be the same in many important ways, and that being raped need not necessarily ruin one's life or damage a professional's confidence and effectiveness.

Many women police characters are attacked (especially in the early 1980s as women cops first make their appearances on many detective shows), usually because they are used as decoys to lure a repeat rapist. D'Acci notes that "posing as sexual bait and as decoys was, in fact, probably the major police duty performed" (1994, 118) by female cops on early programs such as *Charlie's Angels*. The use of female officers as decoys continued to be a common element in later programs featuring women officers as part of mostly-male casts. In spite of their police training, women officers are almost never able to fight off a single deranged rapist on their own. The female officer in *Strike Force*'s "The Predator" (1981), Rosie, is the one to think of a complicated plan for taunting the rapist to attack again, and she later serves as a decoy to capture this same rapist. She is attacked by the suspect and appears unable to fight him off alone, but is saved by the arrival of her male colleagues on the scene. In another decoy episode, "The Violation" (1984) on *Mac-Gruder and Loud*, a female officer functions as comfort and support to a frail victim, helping her get involved with a counseling group and holding her when she breaks down. At the end of the episode the officer serves as a decoy and is grabbed by the throat and dragged by the rapist. She fights back, but she is too weak, although she does throw acid on him just as her colleagues break in and save her. She takes a tough attitude toward her experience in discussing it with a male colleague, noting that narrowly escaping rape seems nearly as traumatic as actual rape. Her male colleague compares attempted rape to being under sniper fire; the female officer refuses his offer of help and insists that she is fine. A later episode of *In the Heat of the Night* ("First Deadly Sin," 1990) uses a female cop decoy in much the same way as these early examples. In another episode, a female reporter functions as an unintentional decoy and is similarly rescued by detectives on the case.

Perhaps not surprisingly, in these episodes female rape victims who are members of other highly respected professions (such as ministers or doctors) react to rape with resolve, will power, and a noted lack of emotion. There seems to be an element of class identification in these stories, with professional women reacting differently from victims who are non-professionals or whose job classification does not enter the story. Victims who resemble the typical male hero of prime time by virtue of their professional status are marked as different in their victimization, as if to suggest that rape trauma syndrome is a symptom of femininity as much as a symptom of rape. The "masculinization" of these victims through education and powerful position carries through to make them atypical victims according to the prime time formula. In a *Rafferty* episode where the victim is a doctor and the rapist is her patient, the victim refuses to reveal the attacker's identity because of doctor-patient confidentiality. She acts as a doctor rather than as a victim and is dispassionate throughout the episode, delivering a firm message near the end of the program stating her desire to be treated as a doctor and not as a woman ("Point of View," 1977). A *TJ Hooker* episode ("The Confessor," 1984; see Chapter 3) features a victim who is an Episcopal priest who insists on going about her normal life without dwelling on her attack. Unlike basic plot victims, these women are not made hysterical, helpless, and mute by their experience. The professional identity of some victims thus seems to preclude their reacting to rape in the usual prime time way. They refuse to become emotional, but instead continue in their usual lives and calmly discuss their experiences with male colleagues. In prime time, a professional woman is just as vulnerable to attack as any other. However, though she can technically become a victim, she will not assume a victim identity by passively accepting rape, going into shock, or letting others solve the case without her active participation. Male detectives seldom accept the stoic, macho reaction to rape on the part of their female colleagues, usually insisting that they talk and get in touch with their feelings about the attack. In the later episodes, the unemotional and stoic response is more frequently augmented by characterizations of victims who undergo a more complex post-rape emotional process. In most of these later stories, males are still there to help out.

Nonprofessional rape survivors who are proactive and "refuse to be a victim" are rare on prime time through the early 1980s. One unusual example is in a *Baretta* episode featuring a strong, active victim who is neither a regular character nor a police officer (her occupation is not revealed). Here ("Somebody Killed Cock Robin," 1977) the victim, who has been raped before as a teenager, becomes convinced that justice will not be served through the legal system and shoots two rapists, one in self-defense and one because he refuses to sign a confession. She criticizes the way she was treated by the legal system in the earlier rape case, where she says she was blamed for the attack and her words were twisted to sound perverted and guilty. As the episode ends Baretta warns the woman that nobody can get away with such a revenge murder, and she leaves town. All these events make this plot a rare portrayal of victim action.

Date/Acquaintance Rape Victims

Victims of date and acquaintance rape, where the specifics of the incident may be quite different from the violent stranger rape scenario, react somewhat differently to their attacks. Date and acquaintance rape stories appear mostly in the late 1980s, and victim characters in general are better developed in them than in the earlier "real rape" stories. In the later episodes, as discussed earlier, victims in general have more lines and speak more about the effects of rape trauma and even the causes of rape, and those in date and acquaintance rape episodes are granted the most lines and the most articulate expressions of their own experiences and views. Views that could be labeled feminist are much more likely to be clearly articulated in these as well as other late 1980s episodes, and some of the date/acquaintance rape episodes seem written deliberately with public education in mind.

In the *21 Jump Street* episode "Stand by Your Man" (1989), black female undercover officer Hoffs is date raped by a suspect while on a case. The episode includes an exchange in which dating is described as a "battle" where "guys try to score" and "girls try not to be scored." It also features a subplot of a man's story about how he dated a girl who kept saying no but who called him a "giant homo" when he left her alone. Hoffs's immediate reaction to rape is to take a shower and spend the night at the home of a male colleague, but after this initial phase she steadfastly refuses offers of help and even refuses to call the crisis center for support. She claims she does not want to be "with a bunch of crybabies bitching and moaning about how awful men are." Eventually, however, she does succumb to severe pressure from her (male) boss and pursue the "correct" path toward post-rape healing by attending sessions at the center. By the end of the episode she has overcome her resistance to seeking emotional support and has gone on with her life and work without serious effect. Her initial "tough cop" reaction is reminiscent of the behavior of the macho cops in earlier violent stranger rape episodes, but her eventual willingness to accept help and admit her feelings represents a key change from the earlier scenario and could be seen as constituting the final stage in victim development through 1990.

Different World's "No Means No" (1990) includes several conversations among male and female college students during which positions on date rape are articulated. The episode's conclusion is firmly that "no means no," making it one of the clearer of the available feminist statements of this period's prime time rape narratives. The victim on *L.A. Law*'s "Sparky Brackman, R.I.P?" (1987) is one of the central characters for that episode, with numerous spoken lines detailing her feelings and thoughts about how the trial process should proceed. Though open to interpretation, this episode also voices support for the feminist notion that date rape is a serious crime that warrants legal remedy.

Typical of the victims in the acquaintance rape scenario is the middle-aged woman on *Simon and Simon* ("Outrage," 1987) who blames herself for the attack and surmises that if she had agreed to sex with her date, he would not have returned to attack her. She further concludes that this means it is her own fault that she was attacked because she insisted on having her own way and desisting from sexual contact. The episode mentions guilt, shame, and how "most victims" feel and react to rape. Another story following the "real acquaintance rape" pattern of ambiguity is *In the Heat of the Night* episode "Rape" (1989), discussed in detail in Chapter 3. After being savagely attacked in her own kitchen by a colleague from the high school where she works, the victim's reactions echo those of the victims of violent stranger rape in the earlier episodes. She reacts initially with hysteria and incoherent babbling, and later describes her shame and humiliation, in part based on the fact that she must return to work and face the man who attacked her. In trying to understand the attack she echoes other victims of acquaintance rape in asking "What did I do? What did I do to make him hate me so much?"

The *Cagney and Lacey* episode "Date Rape" (1983) follows many basic plot elements, including depiction of brutal attacks that leave visible marks on the victim's body, attacks on more than one woman, *and* attack on the same woman twice. The episode ends with the capture of the rapist. It is different in its inclusion of a great deal of feminist dialogue about rape and date rape, including a number of lines spoken by the angry and frustrated victim. Unlike most of the date rape examples, however, it truly focuses on date rape, bringing out a variety of viewpoints and myths by allowing many characters to make some comment about the case. Male police officers voice opinions about whether there is a legal case and how difficult this kind of case is to prove. Cagney and Lacey defend the legitimacy of the victim's claims against the comments of their colleagues, but the victim accuses them of making subtle negative judgments about her. Thus the treatment is more complex than many others.

The *Facts of Life* episode "Double Standard" (1980) includes feminist dialogue critiquing the date rapist as a creep who is outside the norm of acceptable male behavior. The episode includes discussion of why date rape occurs, placing blame on male attitudes rather than on female behavior or dress. It also is unambiguous in its endorsement of the idea that the victim in the incident did nothing wrong. She successfully fights off her date as he attempts to force himself on her, thus taking action on her own behalf and showing that victims need not be passive and helpless.

The *L.A. Law* episode "Noah's Bark" (1990) and two subsequent episodes that deal with the rape of SiFuentes's girlfriend Allison feature a great deal of discussion of the legal process with respect to evidence and trustworthiness. The defense attorney argues that the victim's word is not sufficient evidence to hold the defendant, claiming she invited him to consensual intercourse and that she is "aggressive"; the prosecution asks why the woman would go through the pain and humiliation of an emergency room examination and a trial if she were not actually the victim of a crime. Exhibiting an attitude unusual for TV victims, Allison wavers back and forth on whether to accept a plea bargain, but eventually decides to push for a trial because she wants the attacker to know he chose the wrong victim and she wants him to have a rape conviction on his record. Although the attorneys have informed her that a conviction in this kind of a case, with just her testimony and no corroborating physical injury or other evidence of rape, is almost impossible, she decides to stand up for the truth. The episode ends with a scene in which Allison is informed that another woman has come forward to report rape by the same man, after seeing Allison's statement on the news. Thus the correctness of pressing charges, going through with a trial, and testifying at great personal cost is reaffirmed by the positive outcome of Allison's ability to help another victim. This outcome is quite different from other *L.A. Law* episodes discussed in Chapter 5, in which trials do not bring such positive results for victims.

Prime time victims in rape-centered stories are predictable stereotypes in the late 1970s episodes. Their roles do expand, but in fairly patterned ways. While the early basic plot victims react to rape with severe emotional trauma, shock, and silence, later victims are more outspoken and tend toward guilt and self-blame. Victims without friends, families, and colleagues to help them turn to detectives for support and comfort, while victims with professional identities turn primarily to their male colleagues. Professional and cop victims are tougher, less emotional, and generally more "masculine" than their nonprofessional counterparts. By the late 1980s, elements of the rape reform movement such as crisis lines, support and therapy groups, and special police units and procedures are mentioned regularly. However, feminist characters and endorsement of feminist ideas are rare. Ideas recognizable as feminist are voiced occasionally, mostly by male detectives in early episodes and mostly by victims in later years.

As in previous chapters, the close analysis of two selected episodes will illustrate in more detail the general ways early and later episodes differed in their treatment of this chapter's central themes. Here, the episodes were chosen for both their representativeness and their ability to illustrate key changes in prime time episodic programming on the subject of rape. The *Rockford Files* episode "Return of the Black Shadow" (1978) typifies the early approach to victims on prime time, emphasizing vulnerability and severe trauma and marginalizing the victim from the main action of the plot. The *Cagney and Lacey* episode "Open and Shut Case" (1983), one of the few episodes from the late 1970s and early 1980s to center on a victim, illustrates the extent to which a television episode can move away from the basic plot formula of an absent, passive, silent, or helpless victim. It places the victim at the center of the story, eliminating the rapists and focusing on victim feelings, actions, and decisions. The *Rockford Files* episode epitomizes the masculine-centered basic plot approach to rape. The *Cagney and Lacey* version represents a variation on this model, highlighting some of the tensions and formulaic limitations of the basic plot, but retaining allegiance to a masculine model of dealing with rape.

Focus Episodes: *Rockford Files,* "Return of the Black Shadow" (1978), and *Cagney and Lacey,* "Open and Shut Case" (1983)

The *Rockford Files* episode "Return of the Black Shadow" fits solidly within the basic plot formula. The opening scene shows a gang of tough motorcyclists getting ready to hit the road. The leader is even more greasy-haired and foul-mouthed than the other gang members. The scene cuts to Rockford driving his car with his friend Gail beside him, talking vaguely about the past. It becomes clear that Rockford was good friends with Gail's younger brother and that sister and brother are each other's only family. Gail is a bit fragile, and Rockford keeps assuring her that she is "all right." As the two chat amicably, a loud noise approaches from off-screen, until Rockford looks at his rear-view mirror and sees the motorcycle gang gaining ground. He refuses to pull over and let them pass, instead honking his horn at them. Later, when he stops for gas, the same group arrive at the isolated station and begin to taunt and threaten him. A fat gang member called "Animal" says that he will make Rockford's "woman" pay for his mistake of honking his horn. When Rockford tries to get back into the car, he is beaten up by several gang members, and Animal kidnaps Gail by stealing Rockford's car with her in the passenger seat.

Like most of the early rape episodes, this one does not depict the rape at all, but instead uses pre-rape terror and the condition of the post-rape victim to suggest the horror of the attack. In this case, although Rockford borrows a tow truck, rushes off after the gang of about thirty kidnappers, locates them, and fights them, he is too late to prevent rape. As the police arrive on the scene, the gang scatters, dumping a limp female form on the ground. From a distance, Rockford sees Gail's bruised face, debris-filled hair, and torn clothing. They are both taken to the hospital, where Rockford is found to have a broken rib threatening to puncture a lung, and Gail is in "PIC: psychological intensive care." Her brother arrives at the hospital and is devastated to learn of the rape and of the fact that his sister is in a "head ward." This rough character nearly cries as he discusses the events with Rockford, and sets off on a personal quest to exact revenge from the gang. He also absolves Rockford of any guilt, since Rockford risked his own well-being and was clearly outnumbered. The discussion about the rape is between men, and the meaning of the rape is defined by them. They discuss the rape over the mute victim, who stares blankly into space in a state of shock. The rape is a horrible event that requires violent revenge on the part of the outraged men. Here, because Rockford is badly injured, the victim's brother takes over the masculine role of detection and apprehension. However, Rockford is still the one to offer Gail physical affection and personal attention in the final scene.

Conveniently, Gail's brother was himself once a member of a tough motorcycle gang, so he knows their language, customs, and hierarchies. He still "wears colors" and is able to flash his tattoos whenever necessary to establish his credentials. He quickly infiltrates the gang, discovers that they are planning a raid the following morning, and alerts Rockford. When the raid takes place the gang is caught in the act. The episode ends with Rockford and his friend in Gail's hospital room. She has come out of shock and is able to speak to them. Rockford again tells her how great she is and offers to take her on a date, promising that he is sincere and not doing it out of pity. He strokes her face and gives her a kiss.

Thus, like the *Baretta* "Shoes" episode described earlier, this one focuses most of its screen time on the quest of a male protector to find the rapist. The only deviation from the basic plot here is that Rockford himself does not find the rapists. In the *Baretta* episode the focus is on Baretta's search for the lost victim, whereas here the quest is for the brother's revenge against the biker gang. In each episode, the victim's screen time is limited to under ten minutes, and in each her post-rape appearance conveys much of the message about rape. Both victims have torn clothing, disheveled hair, and facial injuries, and both are essentially unable to communicate, having been thrown into shock by their experience. Neither victim has any female friends or family. The episodes focus on male efforts and end with the death or capture of the rapist. In addition, both episodes include a second central male character who has more screen time than the victim.

The *Cagney and Lacey* episode "Open and Shut Case" (1983) is in some ways much different, and its handling of the victim is one area in which it retains little similarity to the early formula. In fact, with no central male characters (even the district attorney in this episode is female), "Open and Shut Case" may appear to be a thorough departure from the masculinist tendencies of prime time discussed so far. However, even with its nearly all-female cast and its implicit critique of some elements of the method of handling rape used in the basic plot, the episode still legitimates some central themes of the original formula.

Because of its uniqueness as a police detective drama with two female protagonists, *Cagney and Lacey* has been the focus of a number of scholarly works. Most thorough is Julie D'Acci's 1994 book *Defining Women: Television and the Case of Cagney and Lacey*. D'Acci argues that the show was "unique in television history" because it "drew from and engaged with liberal Western feminism" (1994, 142). Her book traces the ways Cagney and Lacey included "many explicit feminist lines, gags, and runners," which at times were criticized in the mainstream press as being "heavy-handed and didactic" (148), but which in the earlier seasons included linking analyses of sexism and racism in several episodes. D'Acci's analysis matches Bonnie Dow's observation that *Cagney and Lacey* could be judged by some as the most explicitly feminist show on prime time during the 1980s (1996, 103). In the first season, D'Acci documents, the show linked race, class, and gender issues together. She shows how over time the program moved away from this sort of "general" feminism and toward "women's issue feminism" primarily by moving away from any sort of structural analysis of economic and social inequalities. "Open and Shut Case," aired in 1983, is a good example of the show's early efforts to connect various issues, and provides some structural analysis of the problematic way "the system" handles rape. However, the episode still does not link the issues of rape and race in its critique or analysis.

John Fiske's 1987 work *Television Culture* also pays specific attention to *Cagney and Lacey* in its chapter on masculine gendered television narrative. Fiske argues that *Cagney and Lacey* is an "interesting mixture of masculine and feminine form" because "the 'end' of the narrative is often neglected in favor of a feminine emphasis on the process by which that end is achieved" (216). Thus the "enigma of the narrative" is no longer whether the detectives will nail the criminal, but rather how the various women characters, including the detectives, can learn to identify with each other and locate and act on "their common interests in patriarchy" (216). This significant shift in the detective genre had a direct effect on the rape narratives within the show—a variety of nonformulaic and realistic rape stories including one on male prison rape, two on date rape, and one on the retrial of the rapists described here. Another writer has noted that "the women of . . . *Cagney and Lacey* are perhaps as much in conflict with masculinity as they are with crime" (Berman 1987, 88). The rape episodes highlight the ways the socially constructed position of "woman" is at odds with that of "police detective" (or prime time police detective), but in ways that often question the ideological and social roles more than the women caught between them. The program does not focus on a single-minded effort at capture or vengeance on the part of the protagonist detectives, but rather depicts them in a variety of roles in relation to victims. However, many generic conventions are also maintained in *Cagney and Lacey*'s treatments of rape.

This episode is unconventional in many important ways, especially for a rape narrative taking place on a detective fiction program. It begins well after the rape itself has occurred, and even after the successful conviction of the attackers. Thus no rape, pre-rape, or off-screen rape is included. The "rape" story line begins when the African American victim appears at the precinct to talk with Cagney and Lacey, saying that the conviction of one of her attackers has been overturned and that she wants to refuse to testify in the new trial. She literally begs Cagney and Lacey to help her avoid testifying. Throughout the episode, the detectives struggle with their dual identities as women who sympathize with the victim's difficult position and as (television) police detectives who must uphold the law. They empathize with the victim and consider her feelings and experience of the trial to be important factors to consider. But, it is clear that the demands of the job and their official duties are at odds with their empathy and solidarity with the victim in this case. This is one way in which the episode points to possible structural problems related to women — the detectives cannot fully resolve their feelings as women with their responsibilities as cops. Mary Beth Lacey, the one coded as the more "feminine" and more "feminist" of the two (she is the one with a husband and children, is less ambitious in her career than Christine Cagney, but voices or agrees with most of the feminist positions on the show), considers advising the woman to lie on the stand or flatly refuse to testify, imploring Christine to "think how she feels." Christine, who identifies more fully with her professional role than does Mary Beth, reacts with shock and disappointment that her partner could suggest such an unethical and illegal course of action. Ultimately, the detectives agree that they must function first as detectives and only secondarily as friends to the victim, although they take the role of "friend of the victim" much farther than any of the male prime time detectives, becoming real buddies with her and spending many hours helping her cope with the new trial. They offer to sit with her while she awaits her turn to testify, and even take her out for dinner and drinks. The evening ends with teasing and giggling, signs that the three women have become close and comfortable with each other. They even call themselves the "three musketeers."

When the detective partners let the victim choose which of them will stay with her while she waits to testify, she chooses Christine, the more traditionally masculine of the two. So it is Christine who delivers the emotion-filled lines urgently asking the victim to stay and give her testimony rather than run away (the usual line presented to rape victims by prime time's male detectives). In an exchange that encapsulates a great deal about prime time's views on rape, Christine responds to the victim's question "What do you want me to do?" with the answer that her response is exactly the same whether the victim is "asking me as a detective" or if she is "asking me as a friend." Either way, she says, the victim should testify and try to send the perpetrators back to jail. Her "friend" position has shifted and is the same as her "detective" position. Having Christine stay with the victim as primary caretaker during the trial allows this line, which underscores the sameness between the role of masculinized detective and female friend, to be spoken. If Mary Beth had been chosen, according to her position throughout the episode, she would not have been able to utter these lines, but instead would have had to delineate the differences between subject positions: for her, "friend" and "detective" are in conflict here. The episode could be read either as highlighting the differences between subject positions (detective and female friend of rape victim) or as delineating how these positions are similar, depending on which elements appear most prominent to a particular viewer. In either case, the show uses its female detectives to produce some unique rape-related dialogue for prime time.

The episode is true to the basic plot formula in other ways. The victim has no friends and tells the detectives that her husband has left her because he could not deal with the idea of the rape. Thus, although she is in some ways strong and sympathetic, she is even more alone than many of the pathetic examples helped by male detectives in the earliest formula plots. The episode also maintains an optimistic outlook that working within the legal system, although frustrating, can lead to justice for rape victims. Although the detectives briefly consider the fact that her original agreement to testify against the attackers has now placed her in a terrible trap (testify again in however many cases may be re-tried, or be subpoenaed and face contempt of court charges for refusing), the story is resolved happily when the victim is made to understand that testifying is really the best choice for her and for the justice system. A story that more heavily focused on the creation of a trap that the victim cannot escape (ending perhaps with her suicide or arrest for refusing to testify) would have moved the story much farther away from the traditional narrative, but then the elements of police effectiveness, constructive female solidarity, and working within the system to achieve justice could not have been carried through to their requisite conclusion.

The episode ending also calls up scenes from earlier prime time rape stories, but in its contrast rather than its similarity to them. In what seems to be a direct response to earlier episodes, the victim ends the story by rejecting the help of both detectives after Cagney tells her to "quit being a victim," saying that if she relies on them any more she might end up losing the ability to be self-reliant. Thus, after creating a relationship of dependence very similar to those developed in earlier basic plot episodes with male detectives, this story breaks the dependence at the victim's initiative, and ends with the detectives and victim embracing and walking away from each other. The episode creates a narrative of victimization, following the victim through various stages toward eventual independent strength.

The episode is typical of rape episodes in general in its avoidance of direct dialogue about race or the relationship between race and rape, even though the show as a whole has been commended for its thoughtful treatments of the intersection of race, gender, and class. By leaving the race of the attackers unspecified and by eliminating any same-race support system for the victim, the episode omits race as a relevant factor in the victim's experience of rape and rape trial. The victim does not discuss race as a part of her feelings about what has happened to her. Likewise, Cagney and Lacey do not mention the fact that, as a black woman, she was fortunate to obtain a rape conviction in the first place. They do not suggest that race may be a factor in why the case has been overturned. The victim's race stands perhaps as a silent reminder of the racist history of rape and rape convictions in the United States, but the episode fails to provide any specific articulation of the relationship between race and rape, instead implying that the victim's identity as a woman is the only salient element of her identity with relation to rape. Her race is presented as nothing more than an incidental factor that is apparently not noticed by any other character in the episode.

The *Cagney and Lacey* episode inverts the basic plot in its emphasis on the victim and in its striking elimination of the rapists as characters. Whereas formula plots rely on the attacker to provide a moral opposite to the protagonist detective as well as a point of focus for his anger, rage, and sometimes violent outbursts in the name of "the system," here there are essentially no rapists at all. Multiple rapists are mentioned, but all that is given is the name of one of the attackers. The rapists do not speak, are not described, and are not discussed by either the victim or the detectives here. Rather, the victim is at the center of the story. She initiates the telling of the central narrative, brings Cagney and Lacey up to speed on what is happening with the case, and tells them what she would like to do. She describes feelings that are clearly articulated and that make sense given what happened to her. Finally, she describes a life that has been seriously affected by the attack: her husband has left her and she is very much alone. In every way the victim is a sympathetic character, and there is no doubt that she was raped, even though there is no rape scene and not even any verbal description of the attack. Simply by seeing and hearing the victim, we know that a rape occurred. Thus, the episode goes farther than any up to this point in suggesting that the truth about rape can be known solely through victim testimony uncorroborated by either physical or eyewitness evidence. Although the viewer does not see the devastated body of the victim, does not see or hear the attack, and has no idea who are the accused, the presumption is clearly with this victim. By simply seeing her, hearing her story, and following her anguished attempts to deal with a very difficult situation, the audience is left with no doubt. It is simply not possible that someone would go through all this to make a false claim, or that the woman could fabricate this complexity and severity of emotional response.

Conclusion

As the two focus episodes illustrate, prime time's basic formula left much room for variation among episodes on different programs, even within the same genre. During the years under examination here, masculinity remains central to most episodes, yet there is great variation in content elements such as victim characterization and discussion of issues related to the rape reform movement. Particularly in later years, feminist ideas about rape and rape reform are likely to be included even within the masculine-centered framework of prime time episodic television. Victims in the 1970s basic plot episodes are silent, passive, helpless, and even refuse to take part in the pursuit and trial of their attackers. These elements change gradually as victims are granted larger and larger speaking parts. While many rape survivors in the middle episodes express guilt and self-blame, by 1990 many have moved beyond these negative responses to experience and express anger and a desire to do something to bring "justice" to the criminal and go through the necessary steps toward returning to some enjoyment of life. Over time, then, victims become fuller characters with more complex responses to rape, less physically damaged and less incapacitated by the trauma rape has caused.

Feminist ideas increasingly enter these narratives, often through the victim character and often through the male detective trying to help her. While victims attend counseling sessions, detectives describe legal changes in the handling of rapists and victims, sometimes using this information to encourage victims to do their part in putting the attacker behind bars. While both victims and detectives improve in their reactions to rape according to the perspective of the rape reform movement, victims in later episodes still have few resources apart from detectives with which to deal with the trauma of rape. Most rape-related dialogue continues to involve the protagonist male, and very seldom is a peripheral female character, such as a victim's friend, involved. These general rules are not always followed, though, and exceptions to even the broad parameters set out so far are examined in the next chapter.

Chapter 5
Unusual and Groundbreaking Episodes

While the majority of prime time's rape-centered episodes followed predictable formulas, several were unique in their sensitive treatment of issues, their depth of analysis, or their relatively early examination of a difficult subject. This chapter examines eleven specific episodes that were either groundbreaking in handling new subjects, or unusual in their treatment of more typical subject matter. The discussion of unusual subjects will center on the groundbreaking treatments of marital rape (*Barney Miller*, "Rape," 1978); male rape (*Kaz*, "Day in Court," 1978; *Cagney and Lacey*, "Violation," 1985); and gang rape (*21 Jump Street*, "Hell Week," 1988). These episodes are the only ones in the collection that treat these three important issues in depth. The other episodes discussed in this chapter handle more standard rape cases in unusual ways. These include a *Miami Vice* episode featuring a paroled rapist whose former victim has him killed ("Hell Hath No Fury," 1988), three *L.A. Law* episodes, two of which deal with the trials of people who fail to protect women from rape, and a *21 Jump Street* episode in which a high school girl is attacked, beaten, and apparently raped in the school showers ("Fun with Animals," 1988). The *Facts of Life* episode "Fear Strikes Back" (1981) is included as an example of a very early treatment of "real rape" that reversed nearly every element of the basic plot formula. Finally, the *All in the Family* episode "Edith's 50th Birthday" (1977), which depicts the attempted stranger rape of Edith Bunker, is included as an unusually sensitive and complex treatment from the late 1970s. Discussion of each episode will emphasize how its treatment of rape was unusual or groundbreaking, standing apart from the standard rape stories available on most prime time episodic programs. Though they were unusual in many ways, most of these episodes still maintained the emphasis on masculinity characteristic of rape-centered episodes in general. It is worth note that three of these eleven episodes took place on situation comedies, and that these three episodes (from *Barney Miller*, *All in the Family*, and *Facts of Life*) represent very early (1978, 1977, and 1981 respectively) and quite thorough departures from the basic plot formula established in detective genre programs. These sensitive early portrayals, with central female characters, consideration of rape reform ideas, and no visual depictions of violence, fit the observation of Dow and others that situation comedy can often carry a more progressive or ideologically critical message because the use of comedy in some ways undercuts or softens the political dimension. The rape episodes on these programs did do a better job of presenting information relevant to the current political and social context than did most of the detective genre episodes.

Unusual Subject Matter: Marital Rape, Male Rape, and Gang Rape

Marital Rape: *Barney Miller*, "Rape" (1978)

This episode was aired in 1978, just before the Rideout marital rape case in Oregon made national headlines, and just after the first three states had made marital rape a legal offense. It is the only episode in the collection examined here to treat marital rape as a main theme. Prior to 1977, "marital rape" had been considered a contradiction in terms since women were supposed, at the time of marriage, to have forfeited their right to refuse consent. State rape statutes before the late 1970s were written to include a "marital rape exemption," meaning that rape was illegal except in cases where the victim and attacker were married to each other. The *Barney Miller* episode thus made its way into the public discourse on rape at a precisely timed moment, when the nation was considering the meanings of the terms "marriage," "rape," and "consent" in relation to each other. At the time of the highly publicized Rideout case in 1978–79, public opinion had not shifted far from this traditional notion, so that John Rideout's violent behavior was largely overlooked in news accounts that instead focused on Greta's sexual history and character (Cuklanz 1996b). The *Barney Miller* episode illustrates that television writers can and do respond directly to cultural and political context in writing for prime time entertainment programs. It focuses on marital rape and provides some information about the changing laws, but does not take a position on the issue except to say that violence is wrong in any domestic situation.

The episode opens with a woman coming into the precinct and complaining of rape. When she claims to have a picture of the rapist, the officers are skeptical, but she produces a photo of her husband and quickly converts their doubt into shock. After showing her husband's photo, she claims to know she has "rights," and proceeds to describe what could be interpreted as an unsatisfying sex life in which the husband dictates the terms of their physical relationship. When the husband arrives at the station, he strongly asserts that having sex with your own wife cannot be against the law, but Barney has already contacted the district attorney and is waiting for instructions because the law is "unclear" in the area of marital rape. When the DA says they can prosecute for marital rape there is discussion about how to proceed, with the woman and the seemingly unreasonable DA in favor of charging marital rape, and others urging her to consider a lesser charge.

The episode includes a lengthy discussion among the police officers, DA, and husband and wife of what is the "real" issue, and contrasts the traditions of "English common law" (which held that marriage was equivalent to consent) to the feelings and rights of a woman "as an individual." One character takes the traditional line, using phrases like "basic biological laws," and they all consider what might be the result if this case became a test case for the law, with some arguing that it would surely be difficult for the courts to adjudicate in marital relationships. Meanwhile, wife and husband discuss their relationship quietly, expressing their feelings and needs and coming to an understanding. The husband is confused by his wife's dissatisfaction, noting that he has bought her everything she wants including a recent gift of a garbage compactor. Although the wife has asserted that she was "assaulted" and that her "privacy" was violated, in the discussion it seems rather that she yearns for small sentimental gifts such as flowers and candy and for a sexual relationship that makes her feel worthwhile and loved. When detectives join in the conversation, they add that women deserve attention as individuals and respect as human beings. A small argument ensues about the relationship between respect and English common law. Although the "problem" described by the wife would not qualify as marital rape under any statute (the husband has failed to express care and consideration in their sex life but the wife does not assert that he has used force, threat, or other illegal means to obtain sex), thus adding credence to the notion that marital rape is a dangerous and inappropriate area for the law to intrude into, it does include some direct and clear dialogue on two opposing views of marital rape, and it goes beyond the simplistic legal understanding of rights and into the realm of human relationships and needs. As the only marital rape episode in the collection, and one of the very few prior to 1985 to discuss sex and rape together, the episode provides an unusually complex and subtle treatment that remains open to interpretation as to whose view is the best or most correct one. The wife is right that she is not being treated appropriately, but wrong that her husband's actions (as described) are illegal, even under a reformed marital rape law. But, like media treatments of the Rideout case a year later, the episode does not provide much help in clarifying what is probably the most difficult and controversial question related to marital rape, that of how disputes over consent in marital conduct can or should be resolved. It could also be seen as trivializing of very serious, unquestionably violent and coercive cases of marital rape. The episode ends with the wife apologizing to the DA for wasting his time, and the husband offering to stop on the way home and pick up some wine and records. The couple agree to go dancing together. Because the program is a situation comedy, the marital rape subject is played for humor in ways that undercut the legitimacy of the wife's marital rape claim. When she first makes her claim, the officers note that it is "weird" and compare it to another case where a priest was caught carrying a gun. Her insistence that the husband be prosecuted for rape rather than any lesser charge is absurd given the facts of the case as she has presented them. And, the over-eager DA is really the only person who thinks her claim has any legal merit, zealously pushing for prosecution and talking about all the women who will be glad he did not compromise or sell out on this case. The problem is resolved quickly without the intervention of the law, and the couple go home happily together. Although the episode is unique in its attempt to deal with marital rape at all, it diminishes the seriousness of the crime and the severity of violence experienced by many married women at the hands of their husbands.

Male Rape: *Kaz*, "A Day in Court" (1978) and *Cagney and Lacey*, "Violation" (1985)

The group of over 100 episodes analyzed here includes only two rapes of male victims, both by male attackers. The first took place in 1978 on the one-season program Kaz, which featured an attorney who had gotten his legal education while in prison. The male victim provides a distinct contrast with most female victims of rape in the early episodes. Rather than reacting with hysteria and withdrawing from contact with other people, or refusing to cooperate with the police investigating the crime, the man quickly agrees to take the stand and testify against his attacker. The victim's brother is supportive and refers to the attacker as a "monster" and the rape as an "outrageous experience," and he encourages the victim to distance himself from the idea of homosexual sex. When the victim's brother and others urge him not to testify at the trial because of how he will be treated, he shrugs it off and says that he has to testify. Although an earlier scene shows that the defense will portray him as a bisexual and the attack as a seduction on his part, he notes that no one can destroy him except himself, implying that he is not afraid of what the defense will do. He will do what is right even though his masculinity will be questioned.

Thus, while the female victims in violent stranger rape plots during this time are hysterical, broken, and silenced by their attacks and nearly always hesitate or refuse to testify, the male victim comes forward immediately and firmly, in spite of the fact that the trial experience will be grueling and humiliating for him. While male detectives have to persuade and cajole female victims into doing their duty by testifying at trial, the situation is reversed in the case of the male victim, whose male advisors tell him not to testify. Here the male victim more clearly understands his duty with respect to the legal system and performs it willingly in spite of personal costs to himself. Questions that will be raised about his character are no obstacle in his quest for justice. He does not receive advice or encouragement in fulfilling this role from his male friends and associates, but volunteers and stands firm in his resolve to be a good citizen and tell the truth of what happened to him. In contrast, female victims seem unable to comprehend the workings of the system and the harm they will do future victims and trials by refusing to give their testimony. Only through the education provided by helpful masculine figures are they able to comprehend their duty and find the strength to perform it. Thus this episode reinforces the definition of masculinity as involving pride, honor, knowledge, courage, and strength, as well as working within institutional structures to gain justice.

Cagney and Lacey's "Violation," the second of the two episodes to deal with male rape, aired seven years later in 1985. In this episode a high school boy leaves home for the senior prom, stops to steal some liquor, and is arrested. After using a fake ID to verify his identity, he is booked as an adult and ends up spending the night in jail, where he is raped. Cagney and Lacey spend the rest of the episode interviewing prison inmates to find out who was responsible for the attack. As in "Open and Shut Case" (see Chapter 4), the detectives divide their police work and attitudes into the traditionally masculine perspective and an arguably more feminine response. Cagney, the less traditionally feminine of the two, questions the attacker, threatens him, and knocks him down. Lacey, however, commits an error when, in trying to comfort and empathize with the victim's parents, she admits that the police department made a grave mistake in its handling of their son. The rape is not shown or described in detail, but dialogue notes that the attack took place repeatedly over a four-hour period. Only the condition of the post-rape victim is similar to the basic formula portrayal. The boy is said to be in severe pain, shows symptoms of shock, and has bruises and cuts covering his face. Like female basic plot victims, he declines to explain what happened, preferring instead to try to make the experience go away by maintaining his silence. Although the victim here continues to insist that nothing happened except a little "hassle," he soon begins to worry that his father will blame him and say that he could have prevented the attack. Finally, he admits that some prisoners "messed" with him and "used" him, never using the word "rape," even when the detectives ask him directly if this is what happened. By the middle of the episode, he is sitting alone in his darkened bedroom and refusing to talk to anyone including his parents. Similar to female basic plot victims, he never makes any contribution to the detectives' search to find the attacker, and his primary speaking role is confined to the initial post-rape interview scene. The boy's father defends his son and tries to obtain justice for him, but believes the rape made him a "faggot."

Although the victim does not use the word rape, Cagney and Lacey insist on labeling the attack for what it is, even when other characters use terms like "brutalization" instead. The episode includes some discussion of what constitutes rape and is critical of some versions of masculinity. In a conversation with Cagney, a male colleague brags that he used to handle a lot of rape cases and that he was very good at it, since he was sensitive and helpful to the victims. However, he laments, now women officers handle all the "sex cases." He is quickly corrected by Cagney, who notes that they should not be called sex cases, but rather "humiliation" cases. As they proceed to interview prison inmates, the detectives are treated to a variety of even more offensive opinions about rape, with one inmate stating that the boy asked for what happened to him when he accepted a gift of a package of cigarettes. This inmate refers to prison rape victims as "fruit hustlers" and clearly has no sympathy for them. In a later scene in which the prison warden explains the cause and frequency of prison rapes (men cooped up with each other and no other sexual outlet), the detectives are subjected to truly menacing ogling, taunts, and whistles from the inmates as they cross the prison yard, clearly making a connection between the position of rape victims and the gender of the detectives.

The attacker is a typical reprehensible prime time rapist: a convict who committed several crimes and got away, and finally robbed an all-night drug store, shooting a customer and a pharmacist. He tries to place blame for the rape on three "soul brothers," tells the detectives to ask the boy whether he enjoyed it, and taunts them with the fact that, since he is serving three consecutive life sentences, they cannot really do anything to hurt him. In short, he is a thoroughly evil person, like most of those who commit violent stranger rape on prime time. He shows no remorse, but tells the detectives to keep "sending" him young boys.

Thus this episode follows many of the basic plot elements even though the victim is male and the detectives are female. The rapist is violent, racist, remorseless, and has outmoded ideas about sex and consent. The victim reacts with severe symptoms and has almost no role in the episode. The detectives actively pursue the case until it is solved and try to provide comfort for the victim and his family and some insight on the nature of rape. Some of their lines reflect feminist ideas. The episode is groundbreaking only in the simple fact that it deals with male rape and prison rape, and in so doing develops some discussion on the socially constructed interrelationships of homosexuality, male rape, and masculinity. In many ways the episode, like other *Cagney and Lacey* examples, reverses the normal prime time constructions of masculinity and femininity, with the female detectives fulfilling the traditional masculine role and trying to help the victim, who is feminized not only by his victimization through rape but also by his reaction to it, which is reminiscent of the passive and self-effacing behavior of the earliest basic plot victims.

Gang Rape: *21 Jump Street,* "Hell Week" (1988)

Gang rape is the violent assault on a victim by two or more perpetrators. Often real-world gang rapes follow the standard pattern of "real rape," in which a victim is selected at random by attackers who do not know her, attacked by surprise, and subjected to force that causes physical injury. Because of the circumstances in which many gang rapes take place, the phrase "acquaintance gang rape" has been used to refer to situations in which there are multiple rapists, at least one of whom is known to the victim. This label covers most rapes taking place on college campuses, because those crimes tend to involve members of fraternities or sports teams who attack female students at the same school (O'Sullivan 1991). The phrase "date gang rape" has also been used to refer to cases in which one man arranges a date with a woman and then lures her to a location where she is gang raped by himself and others. These labels underscore the fact that, rather than representing total depravity and chaos in the streets, gang rapes very often represent the degree to which seemingly normal men in normal social settings are capable of violent sexual behavior. Many of the real world gang rape cases that made the news in the 1980s were cases of fraternity gang rape, which according to Peggy Reeves Sanday tends to follow a pattern in which a young woman who is drunk, high on drugs, or the unknowing recipient of a spiked drink is locked in a room at a fraternity house and raped sequentially by fraternity members (1996). The practice is called "pulling train," and is seen as the result of certain male attitudes toward women and sex. Men who engage in these assaults claim to believe that their victims are willing participants, that women often say "no" when they mean "yes," and that violence is sexually stimulating or necessary for women (see Koss 1988; Sanday 1996).

Gang rape received almost no attention on prime time episodic television through 1990, and this episode is the only one in the collection that deals extensively with it. A few other episodes, such as the *Rockford Files* episode "Return of the Black Shadow" (1978) and *21 Jump Street*'s "Blackout" (1990), depict gang rapes but include very little dialogue about rape. The Rockford episode includes an (off-screen) rape by a biker gang, and the *21 Jump Street* episode is a retelling of the Central Park jogger case with lots of attention to the "gang" elements and very little to rape. Besides these two, a few episodes (such as *Vegas*'s "No Way to Treat a Victim," 1981) have two attackers, but the focus is never on the crime as a gang rape per se. Rather, multiple attackers simply represent another dimension of evil for rapists and underscore the severity of the brutalization and helplessness of the victim. The *21 Jump Street* episode reflects feminist research and arguments on the topic of fraternity gang rape, providing a complex and subtle treatment of this documented problem, but nonetheless retaining a number of basic plot elements. Although the show features a group of undercover detectives of both genders and of many races, only one of the group is female.

In this episode, all five members of the team go undercover on a college campus to investigate an alleged gang rape, but the story primarily focuses on the two members assigned directly to the suspected fraternity. Thus the action focuses on male members of the team, who go through fraternity hazing, or "hell week," in order to gain the trust of the rape suspects. The victim appears only in the final scene after the case has been successfully completed and the perpetrators have been arrested. Her brother has a larger role, befriending the detectives, attempting a break-in at the fraternity to find an alleged tape of the rape, and encouraging the victim to return to school when the rapists are arrested. The focus is on masculinity, but in order to interrogate how one dominant construction of masculinity is related to rape. In making this connection between the social construction of masculinity and rape one of its main foci, the episode is truly unusual.

Through the vehicle of the "hell week" theme, the episode focuses on the exemplary masculinity of the male undercover cops, in marked contrast to the young and "cool," but also very conformist fraternity version of masculinity. Not only do the detectives endure disgusting and physically challenging experiences such as eating raw liver, drinking raw eggs, and having chili pepper rubbed on their lips, but they also twice save the lives of their fellow pledges when the hazing activities get out of control. On one occasion a cop must climb to the top of a ladder carrying a semiconscious drunk "pledge brother" on his shoulder. On another, the two cops perform CPR on a pledge who has nearly drowned. The two detectives are clearly superior to any of the pledges or fraternity brothers. They are stronger, in better shape, more knowledgeable, and more willing to speak up. Their revelation at the end of the episode that "you weren't saved by your fraternity brothers . . . you were saved by two cops" succinctly sums up their superiority and the superiority of their version of masculinity over the "male-bonding" version practiced by the fraternity members, who were so scared they were going to watch the pledge die rather than take action.

While it in some ways falls into the same patterns as the basic plot episodes, especially in its focus on masculinity, this episode is groundbreaking for several reasons. First, it examines gang rape within a college fraternity, suggesting that socially accepted male group dynamics may be at least in part at fault for the fact that brutal rapes occur. The episode features a great deal of situational evidence, but not much dialogue, in support of this point. The older fraternity brothers are depicted as not knowing "where to draw the line" in their hazing of the pledges, a clear parallel with how the rape probably took place. They think that bonding and trust among men is the key to success in life, and they routinely act as a group to harass other people, including passersby on the sidewalk in front of the fraternity house and their neighbors in the "nerd" fraternity. The fraternity brothers are described in glowing terms by the members of their sister sorority, and it is clear that they are from wealthy and well-connected families. Thus, even though they hold the sexist attitudes characteristic of many prime time rapists (when women say no they really mean yes), they cannot be described as thoroughly evil. Rather, they are depicted as examples of what a segment of society views as the masculine ideal: wealthy, well educated, good looking, well respected, and well connected.

The episode contains some subtlety on the issue of sexual relationships, and also connects sexism to other negatives such as racism. In the opening scene three undercover male cops attend various fraternity parties. At the party of the suspected fraternity, one cop comments that the women there are not only gorgeous but also "legal." His colleague (the central character, played by Johnny Depp) reminds him harshly, "hey, we're on a rape case," to silence him. In the same scene the fraternity brothers scan the room full of potential pledges, eliminating one because (from sight) he is a "Jew" and another because he is a "druggie." They invite the "chink" to pledge because they think it will benefit their image in the future. The racial slur is not repeated, but underscores the egocentric attitudes of the rapists and is reminiscent of the link between racist attitudes and rapists in earlier formula episodes.

The episode certainly leaves some room for interpretation, particularly in the characterization of the neighboring "nerd" fraternity, which is used as the butt of jokes. Far from serving as alternative models of respectable masculinity, the caricatured nerds wear glasses and talk constantly about computers. They drink nonalcoholic beverages and download software for fun. When their next-door neighbors harass them and tell them to clear the sidewalk, they back down immediately and are only saved from humiliation by the "cool" undercover agent who has joined them. Unlike any of the nerds, he does not hesitate to use violence, and he punches the harasser in the face. As in more typical detective episodes, the use of physical force is linked with acceptable hegemonic masculinity. The ridiculousness of the nerd characters may preclude understanding them as models of masculinity even though they are serious, hard-working, smart, and nonviolent. With the next best alternative spending all their time studying, talking about computers, and lamenting that their GPAs are only 3.8, the cops stand out easily as the best version of masculinity available, even if they do punch their way out of trouble. The nerds do offer an alternative, but the mocking caricaturization of them offers little challenge to the masculine superiority of the cops.

Another potential source of different readings is a pair of scenes in which the fraternity and sorority members describe each other. After the men describe the women as the type of girl they can take home to their parents' house and then "nail" on the sofa, the women praise the men as the type they don't have to be afraid to introduce to their parents, because the parents will feel confident leaving them alone with boys like this. This juxtaposition could be seen as showing how the attitudes of members of a particular social circle are unhealthy and objectifying with regard to sex and relationships, possibly connecting those attitudes with rape. It also suggests that women are complicit in some level of objectification and sexual repartee with the fraternity members. Even though the victim is not a member of this sorority, the comments might be read as showing how women's attitudes in general are no better than those held by men. On balance, though, this episode is an unusually subtle and thorough treatment of a subject seldom seen on prime time episodic television. It creates legitimacy and sympathy for the victim and provides detailed character portraits of the smug rapists, one of whom even asserts openly that when women say no to sex they really mean yes.

Groundbreaking Treatments

All in the Family, "Edith's 50th Birthday" (1977)

Norman Lear's popular and social-issue oriented situation comedy *All in the Family* aired perhaps the earliest rape-centered episode to feature a central character as the rape victim and to focus on the victim's reactions and feelings after the attack. In an episode entitled "Edith's 50th Birthday," Edith Bunker is attacked by a man who gains entry into the Bunker home by representing himself as a police officer. Edith, who is home alone at the time while the rest of the family prepare for her surprise birthday party next door, is slow to realize the man's intentions. Her character was usually portrayed as ill-at-ease with topics related to sex and sexuality, and in this episode she does not pick up on the sinister man's ogling and innuendo at first. As the man becomes more physical with her, Edith expresses shock and disbelief and resorts to a series of verbal ruses to try to save herself, eventually escaping by rescuing a burning cake from the oven and smashing it into her tormenter's face. Although it is not very violent compared to other prime time rapes, the episode is graphic and almost excruciating in its detailed portrayal of the attempted rape. Protesting and cringing, Edith is forced onto the couch and told what is going to happen to her, while the attacker threatens her with a gun. Later, the rapist unzips her dress and again pushes her down. Thus, more than most other episodes, this one dwells on the elements of helplessness and physical domination, with the unusual resolution of Edith escaping before the rape is completed. The rest of the episode focuses on the aftermath of the attack, with Edith afraid to do ordinary things and her husband Archie urging her to just forget it because it is over and nothing really happened anyway (as he sees it). Like some of the detective episodes, this one places quite a bit of emphasis on Archie's post-attack processing as well, with several intense scenes featuring his unsuccessful attempts to talk with Edith. Edith rebuffs Archie's efforts, refusing to call the police because she is afraid her attacker will return to kill her. Daughter Gloria also plays a key role here, instructing Archie on how to make Edith feel loved, appreciated, and safe. Gloria actually yells at Archie and says he is not doing the right thing, and later she provides the needed impetus to get the reluctant Edith to make an official report to the police. At another point Gloria functions as Edith's mouthpiece, explaining to Archie that she is feeling afraid, angry, and guilty. Although Edith has up to that point followed the basic plot scenario in saying she is too afraid to make the report (even though the man left some of his clothes in the house, making hers a potentially strong case), Gloria eventually convinces her that it would be more like Edith to make the report because she is usually concerned for the well-being of others. Gloria employs logic familiar from the detective programs, telling her mother that other women could be hurt by the same man if she does not go to the police and give a description. During this key interchange, the central male characters stand and watch, making this a very unusual prime time scene indeed.

While this episode includes some elements regularly seen in detective genre rape episodes, its thorough attention to the aftermath of rape for the victim and her family is totally unique among the episodes examined here. In addition, the episode makes clear a number of elements of a reformed understanding of rape. The realism of rapist-victim interaction during the attack combined with Edith's escape (thus the depiction of attempted rather than complete rape) make for a significant change in the representation of violence here. The horror of forced "intimacy" is made clear through the dialogue and physical contact between the attacker and Edith, but without the use of brutal extremes such as blood, bruises, restraints, or frightening disguises. The idea that any woman can be victimized regardless of age and sexual attractiveness is also emphasized through Edith's attempts to suggest that the man might have more fun somewhere else and her initial inability to understand what is happening. Finally, Gloria's important role in discussing issues with her father as well as providing the final persuasive push to get Edith to testify are a fairly realistic representation of how the dynamics of post-rape trauma might play out within a family. No outside professionals provide the primary support for Edith, and she is finally able to gain some strength and understanding from her longstanding relationships. The episode, although part of a situation comedy, provides one of the most complex and realistic portrayals of a rape situation on prime time during the entire fifteen-year period under examination here.

The Facts of Life, "Fear Strikes Back" (1981)

Like *Barney Miller* and *All in the Family, Facts of Life* is a situation comedy in some ways free to depict rape in ways that greatly diverge from the dictates of the detective/cop formula. As we have seen, many non-detective episodes (such as *Little House*'s "Sylvia" and *Welcome Back, Kotter*'s false accusation) fit some of the parameters of the basic plot. However, both episodes aired on *Facts of Life* deviate directly and thoroughly from the usual prime time formula. One of these episodes, "Double Standard" (1980) is not only a very early treatment of date rape, but also one that features substantial victim dialogue, supporting female characters, and feminist perspectives on rape. The second, "Fear Strikes Back," aired in 1980, and for this reason alone it would be worthy of recognition as one of the earliest rape-centered episodes that has almost no resemblance to the basic plot formula. It depicts female relationships, does not show the attack, deals only with attempted rape, does not have any central male characters, and does not end in the capture or death of the rapist. However, the episode represents an even more meaningful deviation from the usual formula in that it focuses almost exclusively on the victim's reaction to the attack and her efforts to recover from it.

Facts of Life portrays a group of four girls living away from home at a boarding school with their housemother Mrs. Garrett. Most episodes focus on these five central characters and their life at the school. "Fear Strikes Back" begins with a report by Mrs. Garrett that a school employee has been raped nearby on her way home from work. The girls first react with shock, but then make jokes to ease the tension and distance themselves from the event. One of them even asks why they can't just pretend it never happened and get on with their lives. They speculate that the perpetrator is probably "long gone" and do continue about their normal routines without much further discussion. The school officials, after considering canceling an upcoming party, decide that they will also carry on as usual. However, on the night of the party, Natalie (one of the central characters) is attacked on her way home alone. Because some passersby scare off the attacker, she is not raped, but she is quite shaken by the event. From this point forward, the story focuses on Natalie's fears and the efforts of her friends to help her through her feelings of vulnerability. Natalie states that she now knows the world is dangerous and that as a young woman "you don't stand a chance out there." She refuses to take part in normal activities and just wants to stay in her room reading books in safety. Her friends and Mrs. Garrett coax her out by reminding her that she should not let the "bad guys" win so easily.

While her friends join a self-defense class offered by the school, Natalie feels that such a class is silly since it could not have helped her on the night she was attacked. However, when she attends the first session as an observer, the instructor convinces her that she could have avoided the situation in the first place by taking a different route from the shortcut she used, by walking with someone rather than alone, or by getting a ride home. The episode ends when Natalie decides to take the self-defense class, thus rejoining her friends, resuming an active life, and taking action to recover from her fear. While Natalie and her friends express their resentment that they must think in this way, they eventually all take positive action on their own behalf. The only male character is the self-defense instructor, who appears only in the final scene. Even though this role is a minor one, it is the male instructor who finally succeeds in bringing Natalie out of her paranoid shell and convincing her that she can take action to protect herself in the future.

This episode illustrates what prime time usually did not do with its rape plots. First, "Fear Strikes Back" does not depict any violence against women. The opening scene features only a report of rape, and the victim of that attack is never shown. Natalie's attack is also not shown. The focus of the show is the meaning of rape to women in general and to Natalie in particular. There is no titillation, no opening "teaser," no evocation of the terror building up to the rape scene. Natalie discusses her feelings with her female friends, who articulate a range of the ideas women hold about rape, from wanting to ignore it to feeling overwhelmed by fear and helplessness. Until the final scene there are no central male characters to help Natalie through her difficult time, and she relies on her friends and Mrs. Garrett for support and reassurance. There is no focus on the search and capture of the rapist. The episode presents an almost thoroughly feminized (yet perhaps not feminist) perspective on rape, with almost exclusively female characters, an absent rapist rather than a dead victim, and virtually no presence of male authority and expertise. While most prime time rape stories revolve around the interactions between the rapist and detective(s), this one revolves around interactions between the victim and her female friends. This final fact alone makes "Fear Strikes Back" a very unusual prime time series treatment of rape.

21 Jump Street, "Fun with Animals" (1988)

"Fun with Animals" presents one of the most thorough treatments of rape and black-white race relations on prime time through 1990, but it does so by depicting a case of suspected rape that turns out to be something else. It follows the team of undercover detectives working in a high school on an assignment to discover who is responsible for a racially motivated attack on some students at the school. Soon after the undercover agents arrive, they befriend a group of rowdies who are racist in that they use epithets to refer to a number of national, ethnic, and cultural groups. The officers on the job have a difference of opinion about the potential of these bullies for real violence. One argues that they are just "equal opportunity snot-wads" while the other believes that this group is probably responsible for the violent incident. Soon another violent incident occurs, involving an African American girl who is left beaten and half-clothed in the girls' shower room, with the words "nigger slut" scrawled on the wall. As often happens in prime time rape episodes, observers take a glance at the crime scene and immediately conclude that a rape has taken place. Indeed, rapes such as the one in *In the Heat of the Night*'s "Rape" (see Chapter 3) make it clear that when a "real" rape occurs anyone looking at the post-attack scene would immediately know what has happened. Thus the visual view of the bruised girl lying in the shower room (and the racist attitudes of the suspects) do seem to confirm rape in the terms previously set by prime time programming.

Race is an important element of this episode, but the discussion mostly centers on the question of what is the appropriately non-racist position for the white male cops to take regarding the case. A subplot involves the two white male officers in an uneasy relationship with each other, as one suspects the other of being the actual rapist who attacked the girl in the shower. However, their black female colleague provides a solid alibi for the suspected partner, revealing that they spent the whole night together on the date in question. Thus the partner suspected of rape is not as "racist" as his partner thought but instead has enjoyed genuine intimacy with his black colleague (she says that they "talked all night," thus also clearing him of the lesser charge of having a "thing for" black women). When it is clear that the suspected guy is not the attacker, he turns the tables on his partner, accusing *him* of being the real racist, alleging "you wanted to catch a racist so bad, you couldn't see anything else. That's racism, my friend." The episode attempts to examine the meaning of the word "racist," here and later when the white male partners resolve their differences and discuss the term.

At the victim's house, the detectives are greeted by the victim's mother, who agrees to let only one of them go inside and talk with her. The one against whom a charge of "racist" is still pending does the questioning. In a scene beginning with lines reminiscent of early basic plot scenes between victim and detective, he begins gently prompting the silent victim for information, then quickly confesses to her that he has been blaming people for the attack because he thinks they are racists, but now he realizes that he does not understand what a racist is. Eventually the victim reveals that what actually happened was not rape and was not racially motivated. Rather, the girl got into an argument with a gang of three other girls after she slept with one of their boyfriends. A flashback clearly and deliberately shows the three girls, two of whom are African American, putting gum in her hair and punching her repeatedly. She explains that she decided to lie on the floor of the showers all night because she could not decide what to do and "just wanted it to go away." The case ends there, with only one more scene to follow. In this "concluding" cliché of a scene, the two male detectives discuss their jobs while watching a stripper in a sleazy bar. This episode is thus unusual in its treatment of both rape and race. In dealing with race, it acknowledges that the concept of "racism" is open to interpretation and that individuals may have widely varying definitions of it. However, the idea that looking for a racist is itself racist is debatable, and is only stated and not supported in the episode. Various elements are left open-ended, such as any explanation for why the female detective wanted to spend the night with her fairly obnoxious colleague. In a second strand of discussion about racism, the episode features the black detective captain fighting against what he sees as irresponsible community activism: a black councilwoman is threatening to file complaints against the police department if they do not solve the crimes immediately. She is among those who most loudly proclaim that the latest incident was a rape. The police captain asserts several times that there is no direct evidence that a rape has occurred. The besieged captain, who is just trying to do his job and discover the truth of what really happened, is hampered in his work by extremists using the words "racism" and "rape" for political gain. People claiming to be activists on behalf of all blacks have misguided and mistaken views, and are simply too extremist to see that there is no proof of rape. The councilwoman is wrong, as is the earnest detective who suspects his partner of wrongdoing. Only those who have not let the *idea* of racism (not to be confused with racist attitudes themselves) cloud their thinking have seen this case clearly. Even the black female colleague of the detectives on the case immediately jumps to the conclusion that the attack was a rape, attempting to silence them by shouting that the issue is not only racial, but also a violent attack on a young girl. The female cop even suggests that her male colleagues probably think the girl enjoyed the attack, as a possible reason why they have focused only on the racial element. Here prime time moves directly to the idea that racism-hunting clouds clear thinking. It still is not examining difficult issues that link race and rape such as disproportionate conviction rates, questioned legitimacy of claims by black victims, and generalized white fear of black rapists. The episode is much more a discussion of racism than of rape, which is common in mainstream media treatments of these interrelated issues (see Benedict 1992, Moorti 1995, Cuklanz 1996b).

The episode is also unique in its treatment of rape. It does not directly show the attack at all, and only gives a brief and restricted view in the flashback (just enough to see the race of the attackers). Several narrative "stretches" have been made to fit the facts together as presented. First, the victim refuses to speak about the attack, thus allowing speculation to run free. Second, the issue of a post-rape medical examination is totally omitted, whereas in episodes that depict "real" rapes this scene is nearly always shown. Apparently the victim is not examined for rape, thus making a conviction in case the "rapist" is caught a near impossibility. Although the show has a protagonist detective who is a black female, she is not even assigned to this case. In addition, the attackers, though two are black, choose to write "nigger slut" on the wall of the shower, thus adding fuel to the idea that the attack was racially motivated. Finally, the victim stays in one position in the girl's shower room all night, thus preserving the rapelike post-attack scene for the other characters and viewers. Thus, the credibility of the story is weak: The possibility of events happening in this way is marginal at best, and the story is extremely contrived at worst.

L.A. Law, "The Brothers Grim" (1987), "Hey, Lick Me Over" (1988), and "Belle of the Bald" (1988)

L.A. Law aired seventeen rape-centered episodes during its eight seasons. Nine of these were aired before 1991. Along with *Miami Vice, L.A. Law* demonstrates the late 1980s tendency toward ambiguity and multiple interpretation in prime time and in rape-centered episodes. The show is widely recognized for its frequent portrayal of rape, and Judith Mayne has observed that the series represents "the possibility of a more complex engagement with rape, defined as a problem of representation as well as a problem of sexual violence, than is usually the case on prime-time television" (1997, 90). Mayne also observes that, while *L.A. Law* draws "on feminist discourse" (91), it presents the "most obvious and insistent" fantasy of "a utopian heterosexuality" (95), and she discusses some of the narrative techniques employed to allow for articulation of a variety of perspectives as well as a clear moral statement on what constitutes right and wrong. *L.A. Law*'s rape episodes present rape very differently from most other prime time programs. They tend to omit the attack, include a profusion of victim dialogue, and focus on complex legal issues and interpersonal relationships. The stories themselves are unusual for prime time, each one unique rather than following a template or formula.

The following discussion will focus on "The Brothers Grim" (1987) and "Hey, Lick Me Over" (1988), with a detailed description of "Belle of the Bald" (1988) as well. The first two episodes are similar in many ways, since both feature the trial of someone who failed to take action to prevent rape rather than of an actual rapist. The first story centers on a police detective who simply watched while a rape took place in a bar. The second covers the case of a security company that claimed to be better than the police, but failed to intervene while a family was being robbed and the wife/mother brutally raped. All defendants are male (a male police officer in one case and male guards and company owners in the other), as are both prosecuting attorneys. The third episode also focuses on a trial that is not a rape trial per se. In it, a woman who has murdered her attacker is found not guilty by a jury.

"The Brothers Grim" is sympathetic with the position of the victim throughout the story, and after the trial scenes are completed it seems likely that she will win the case. On the stand she describes the attack. She states that police are supposed to protect the public but now she knows that "there's no such thing as the police." She describes the effects the attack has had on her life, and how she will never be "well" again. Although the police officer is not depicted as a clearly evil character, trial testimony about his past actions suggests that he cannot act decisively in critical situations and has never drawn his gun, even when his partner's life was in danger. In one way the officer is on trial for not behaving as a good prime time cop always does. He has not responded to dangerous situations by using violence and injuring or killing criminals. Although his position may be more realistic than that of prime time's typical officer, his claim that drawing a gun might have caused further harm is unconvincing. The officer, having failed to perform in an acceptably masculine way (particularly according to the version of hegemonic masculinity established in other prime time episodes), sees that his career and reputation have been ruined by the trial, which has revealed his inaction and possible cowardice in the face of danger. At the end of the trial but before the verdict has been announced, he speaks directly with the victim, asking whether she really thinks it was his fault and whether she can ever forgive him. When she says yes, it was his fault and no, she will never forgive him, he goes offscreen and kills himself. According to prime time's logic of masculinity, his humiliation is so severe that it warrants suicide. The episode ends there, without any announcement of the legal verdict. The rapist is not part of the trial and is never seen or even described. The victim, though vindicated by the evidence revealed during the trial, is violently robbed of any feeling of triumph or even justice. The ending implies that rape is so horrible that it ruins lives without any possibility of repair. The victim's effort to heal by pursuing the legal option (though not against the rapist) that has traditionally been encouraged ends in failure and cynical ambiguity. Now at least two lives are ruined instead of one.

"Brothers Grim" suggests various interpretive possibilities, particularly in its treatment of race. The victim is portrayed as Hispanic, and her attorney Victor SiFuentes, also Hispanic, is depicted as perhaps overzealous in his push to nail the possibly racist cop who, to him, represents a police force that harasses Hispanics rather than protects them. The defendant at one point speaks the attorney's name with special emphasis on its Spanish pronunciation, but in no other way is he marked as especially racist. The defendant's suicide implicates Victor for pushing too far, but does not indicate whether he was right or wrong in his claim that the cop was a racist and his actions were in part motivated by a lack of compassion for the Hispanic victim. The racial theme focuses attention on Victor, the attorney, and his moral and professional choices during the trial. While the victim has a key role, she is not the central character in the narrative. As Sara Projanski notes, the narrative of this episode centers on the masculinity of the attorney and the defendant (1995, 85).

This episode is quite similar in its cynicism to another *L.A. Law* offering ("Belle of the Bald," 1988) in which a woman is placed on trial for the murder of her rapist, the son of a diplomat, who has been released by police (in spite of his confession of guilt) on the basis of his "diplomatic immunity." Although the defense attorney tries a risky and possibly illegal strategy in claiming temporary insanity when all evidence shows that the murder was premeditated, the jury finds the woman innocent on this basis and she is acquitted. However, on the way out of the courtroom, while she is beginning to savor her freedom, the rapist's brother steps forward with a gun, says "for my brother," and kills her. The male attorney is the only one there to weep over her dead body and, like SiFuentes in

"The Brothers Grim," his legal strategy is implicated in a senseless death. Both episodes suggest that there is no way out and no satisfaction for rape victims. In the first episode the system fails twice, first in the inaction of the police officer and then in the inability of the trial to provide vindication for the victim. In the second story the system again fails at every turn, first in releasing an "immune" rapist to possibly repeatedly torment his terrified victim, and then in providing a legal verdict that ultimately does not help her at all. In their cynicism, both endings are also ambiguous. It is not clear what action, if any, the woman or her attorney should have taken, or whether any other course of action would have better.

The verdict is also ambiguous in "Hey, Lick Me Over" (1988). It finds a security company that failed to protect its clients from rape and robbery innocent of harm but guilty of breach of contract, and awards the plaintiff over two million dollars. The verdict is specifically split such that the company is found not guilty of negligence. Although the verdict vindicates the wife, who was adamant about publicizing the company's responsibility for her victimization, it also once again suggests that there is no remedy for rape. The defense attorney's closing argument emphasizes this point, stating clearly that the jury will want to convict because they will want to believe that security companies can and should prevent violent crimes like this one. He argues that this is just an illusion and that the jurors should admit to themselves that ours is a dangerous world and that there is no certain protection no matter how much money is paid. In the end, the company is guilty of promising the impossible but not for failing to deliver it. Although the victim's family is awarded a large settlement, the episode also concludes that there is no protection from rape, even in one's own home. On hearing that the verdict awards the family such a large sum of money, the wife/victim does not even smile. Once again the conclusion is quite pessimistic for victims of rape.

This cynicism is only further enhanced by a fourth episode in which a victim's personal diary is read in open court as evidence that she "wanted" to be raped. Although the jury finds the defendant guilty, the woman says she is torn apart and ruined by the events of the trial.

All the rapes that result in trials on *L.A. Law* are depicted as genuine crimes, yet few of them end in a satisfactory conclusion for the victim. Thus in general *L.A. Law* presents the problem of rape as one that has not been, and perhaps cannot be, solved from the victim's perspective. In its complex and ambiguous stories *L.A. Law* omits explanations of the cause of rape, focusing instead on factors contributing to the failure of the system to handle the crime adequately, such as racism and untrained or unskilled police and security forces. As in earlier episodes, the causes of rape are still depicted as problematic individuals, with the legal system implicated primarily for failing to deliver true justice. Elements that point to individual fault also include the need for revenge and vindication and the overzealous pursuit of legal solutions by attorneys. Even these victim-friendly, subtle, and ambiguous representations do little to examine structural causes for the problem of rape.

Some remaining focus on masculinity is retained in *L.A. Law*: the attorney for the rape victim is nearly always male and is always the focus of the episode's rape story. Furthermore, in one case that lasts for three episodes, SiFuentes's girlfriend is raped, thus once again bringing the male reaction to the rape of a loved one to center stage. However, *L.A. Law* is not just a new version of the old pattern. Although it retains the focus on masculinity, it also provides complex, subtle, and ambiguous treatments of rape that do not depict violence and that give voice to victims and other female characters. The *Miami Vice* treatment discussed below is even more ambiguous in its treatment of rape, and echoes the *L.A. Law* element of despair in locating any legal remedy.

Miami Vice, "Hell Hath No Fury" (1988)

Like *L.A. Law, Miami Vice* aired several episodes centering on the subject of rape, tending toward ambiguous representations that break out of the formula molds of other prime time programs. "Hell Hath No Fury" is similar to, but even more extreme than, many of the *L.A. Law* episodes in that it suggests a horrific world in which victims of rape can never achieve satisfaction or peace of mind. The episode deals with rape in unusually complex ways. It opens on the set of a television talk show where a convicted rapist (on parole) is one of the guests. The (white) convict is the son of a prominent and wealthy family and supposedly a model of successful rehabilitation. Guests on the talk show debate whether his recent release is fair to the black victim. The rapist claims that he is fully reformed and regrets his former actions, and requests a statement of forgiveness from the victim. Reporters track the victim at work and at home in an effort to obtain her statement, but she locks herself inside her apartment and refuses to speak to anyone except her police officer friend. The victim is still terrified of the rapist, in large part because she is receiving phone calls threatening that he will come after her again.

Although her detective friend (also a black woman) offers to stay with her as long as she wants, the desperate victim insists that no one can watch her all the time and that she can't rest while the rapist is free. The dialogue focuses on the limited range of options open to her, because the rapist has already "paid his debt to society" and presumably has a right to his freedom, if not at this moment, then some time in the foreseeable future. She tries unsuccessfully to get a restraining order against him. Finally she hires a mercenary, who successfully kills the released criminal. Up to this point, the story seems to be about whether the terrified (and terrorized) victim is justified in taking such action when there are no legal options open to her. However, the episode's ending offers a twist when, after the rapist is killed, the victim receives another threatening phone call. An imposter has apparently been making the calls, and the victim, who now has a murder on her conscience, is no safer or happier than she was before. The ending suggests that there is no way out for rape victims.

Like the *L.A. Law* episodes, this one does not stick to the traditional prime time detective drama credo that working within the system is best and that it will lead to effective outcomes for serious problems. However, unable or unwilling to condone illegal actions, it is also unable to provide any satisfactory solution. Even the friend is unable to provide a resolution to the victim's problem or to protect her, stating that in criminal matters she is a cop first and a friend second. She tells the victim that she cannot condone hiring a mercenary for any reason, and that if she ever has proof (or a confession) she will arrest her friend immediately.

The *Miami Vice* episode is unusual in that it deals with the release of a convicted rapist, thus beginning the story after conviction and failing to depict the attack. The story is mainly about the victim and her efforts to regain a peaceful life. Notably, the victim in this episode actually has a friend who is of the same race and gender as herself, and who is also holds a position of power (as a police officer). Like other *Miami Vice* episodes, this one employs feminist discourse but is open to various interpretations. One character even suggests that the rapist may have been given early parole because of his family background and race rather than because of his prison record. Although it is suggested that the black victim cannot receive justice, no further link is made between her race and the way the case is being handled. The horror of the final threatening phone call indicates that the victim has made a grave mistake, yet no other options are provided for her. Perhaps the conclusion should be that victims should take no action. On the other hand, the police have been ineffective at protecting her, and her friend's boss has tried to remove the friend from the case. If loyal friends and well-meaning police are useless, it is unclear what hope is left for the victim, and the mercenary solution, though unsuccessful in this instance, is at least an understandable choice.

Conclusion

The groundbreaking and unusual episodes chosen for discussion here either focus on unusual subject matter or treat more standard prime time rapes with unusual depth, sensitivity, or story line. In general, programs in the late 1980s become more likely to include feminist ideas, but do so in ways that are both ambiguous and cynical. Some of the most unusual and complex treatments have conclusions that offer no satisfaction for victims of rape. In addition, where these episodes break new ground they often do so in ways that undercut the potential usefulness of new elements. Thus a black woman friend of a rape victim is unable to offer anything of use to the victim, and an episode that deals at length with race focuses on the racism of the investigating detectives in a non-rape case rather than on how racism affects actual rape cases. Victims win trials only to be killed or to see themselves as the cause of another's death. Many but not all of these episodes maintain their focus on masculinity. Those that do not, such as *Facts of Life*'s "Fear Strikes Back," are the most significant and rare deviations from prime time's usual rape-centered offerings.

Together these unusual and groundbreaking episodes help to further delimit and illustrate the limitations of the familiar formulas of rape representation on prime time episodic television. The three situation comedy episodes examined in this chapter show the extent to which it was possible for prime time to break away from the traditional emphasis on masculinity, violent imagery, and ritualized juxtapositions of good and bad men. The episodes on unusual subjects such as marital rape and gang rape are useful in illustrating the general lack of attention to important aspects of real-world rape, aspects that were apparently difficult to fit into the formulaic treatments of rape favored on most detective programs through 1990. Episodes discussed in this chapter also show a move in the final years under examination toward unique and thoughtful treatments of rape on a range of important issues such as racism, legal ethics and gang violence, but they also increasingly back away from an expression of confidence in the legal and social structures that are in place to deal with rape, moving away from formula but toward cynical and depressing endings.

Chapter 6
Conclusion

This book has examined prime time rape-centered episodes, arguing that between 1976 and 1990 prime time was struggling with evolving depictions of rape, but almost always in such a way that definitions of masculinity remained at the core of rape representation. It demonstrates that most rape-centered episodes through the early-1980s were aired on detective or police dramas and that they depicted rape as a violent surprise attack involving the use of weapons and brutality. Episodes of this type were common enough to establish a "basic plot" formula for rape on prime time episodic series, and key elements of this formula were followed even on non-detective programs through the early 1980s. Later years saw the development of rape narratives on programs such as *Miami Vice* and *21 Jump Street* that evolved out of the old detective genre. In these later years, the typical representation of rape shifted from the formulaic portrayal of violent stranger rape to date/acquaintance rape, while other elements such as detective and rapist characterization shifted accordingly. Victims, who had been silent during the early years, steadily gained more prominent roles and became more articulate about their feelings, experiences, and needs. Yet through all these changes masculinity remained the focus of these prime time narratives. Detectives and other male professionals continued to be the central characters of most rape-centered episodes, working out the appropriate masculine reactions to rape in their interactions with other men and with women. Even when the attack and the rapist were removed from the story, leaving only the victim's perspective, most narratives still focused primarily on the masculinity of the detective or other male protagonist in relation to the victim. Protagonists evolved slowly from effective, volatile detectives with a soft side, to competent and concerned professionals struggling with ethical choices and complex relationships with female colleagues. Throughout this evolution, violence remained an accepted and effective means of solving problems, and protagonist detectives routinely attacked, shot, and killed rapists. Rapists shifted from being characterized as demented and abominable criminals to seeming more normal but still harboring unhealthy, sexist, racist, and dangerous ideas that led to violence against women. Their ideas, along with their abnormal and even psychotic characters, accounted for the crime of rape in nearly all episodes through the early 1980s, and individual rapists' attitudes toward women and consent were responsible for many prime time rapes through 1990.

This book demonstrates that issue- or cause-oriented studies of television are an important way to gain information about the history of this important mass medium and its relationship to real-world events and concerns, particularly in relation to social change. Many of the episodes discussed here evidenced a clear awareness of current changes in legal and social practices, incorporating references to altered police procedures, crisis hotlines, hospital procedures for collecting and preserving evidence, and post-rape trauma therapy for victims. In addition, a few episodes dealt with contemporary issues such as marital and gang rape in ways that reflected legal change, research, and publication on those topics. Although these treatments were rare and necessarily carried with them some limitations, they illustrate the ability of prime time to respond to social change in timely and meaningful ways. The dramatic shift in thematic coverage of rape between 1976 and 1990 shows that television fiction as a whole responds to, and thus participates in, social change in profound ways.

My previous book, *Rape on Trial* (1996), examines mass media treatments of famous rape trials during this same period of intense controversy and change in laws and attitudes related to rape. A comparison of the findings of the two studies suggests that prime time episodic series and mainstream news both responded to the rape reform movement in fragmented and uneven ways, seldom presenting a coherent feminist analysis of rape. On the rare occasions when complex versions of rape reform views were incorporated, they were not necessarily endorsed. However, prime time episodes were without question more consistently sympathetic to victims and their traumas and concerns, in spite of their accompanying emphasis on masculinity as a central theme. Together the two studies also demonstrate that, without question, prime time television and mainstream news select and treat subjects drawn from contemporary social change politics. Thus these central mainstream mass media discourses contribute importantly to the process of social change in important ways, supporting elements of both traditional view and opposing views. Sympathy for and legitimation of victim experiences of rape were the most common rape reform ideas to find acceptance in the mainstream mass media examined; more difficult issues such as what evidence is relevant in a rape trial were taken up much less frequently. An underlying belief in the ease of false accusation was also found in both mainstream news and prime time television.

In spite of the change observed in prime time rape episodes, this book demonstrates clear limitations to change as well. The texts examined here reveal that through 1990 most explanations for rape remained narrowly focused on problematic individuals rather than on structural elements such as socialization, pervasive violence and objectification of women in the media, widespread use of pornography, or patriarchal social structures. This finding certainly parallels the conclusions of *Rape on Trial* with respect to mainstream news discourse. Rapists through the early 1980s were depicted as deranged psychopaths well beyond the bounds of normal behavior and thinking. They were often sexist or racist, demonstrating their marginality through their ideas as well as their violent behavior. Thus the cause of rape according to these episodes is individual mental illness. The limited elements of sympathy for victims and a willingness to believe victims of brutal rape are accepted, but in most episodes masculinity emerges as the solution to, rather than the cause of, the victimization of women through rape. Victims in most cases remain mute, passive, and vulnerable, the objects of pity and aid on the part of active and successful detectives. They do little to address their own problems and have few female friends or relatives who can help them. They often blame themselves for their own rapes and rely on professionals for information about counseling and crisis intervention. There are almost no prime time episodes in which women work together to help a friend through the trauma of rape and post-rape efforts to regain a sense of confidence, security, and freedom.

Although they were seldom the central focus of these episodes, victims did undergo some change on prime time between 1976 and 1990. In some of the latest episodes examined here, victims are strong and articulate, actually seeking psychological healing and legal resolution to their problems, but often their stories still end badly. According to many of these most recent stories, even victims who obtain convictions cannot find peace. In this way, prime time stories skip from insisting that pursuing a legal case is the best solution (yet seldom depicting trials), to a phase in which trials are represented, but usually not in a such a way as to critique contemporary trial practice or provide comfort and satisfaction for victim characters. A "solution" to rape remains elusive on these programs. As prime time genres evolved to include more complex people and relationships, they also moved toward emphasis on the complexity of justice and vindication, abandoning the moral clarity of the 1970s detective shows. Thus a woman whose close female friend is a police officer is the one who unsuccessfully hires a mercenary to kill her tormentor, and a rape victim whose desperate action is vindicated at trial is killed before she can leave the courtroom. Viewing these stories it would be easy to conclude that all the efforts and successes of the rape reform movement in the areas of law, trial practice, evidence collection, and social attitudes have provided little relief for victims.

Further Change in Prime Time's Rape Depictions

The prime time episodes examined here showed significant change in their overall characterizations of rape between 1976 and 1990. However, with a few notable exceptions they did not grapple with difficult or controversial issues related to rape such as gang rape, marital rape, adjudication of consent, and the underlying causes of rape. The ways these episodes treat the combined issues of race and rape provide some of the most discouraging findings of this examination. By far the majority of the episodes omit central minority characters. Those that include non-Caucasians in central roles almost without exception include them as victims, never as rapists, thus practicing a studied avoidance of the historical myths surrounding race and rape. Minority victims in some cases bring additional sympathy to the case, as in one episode in which the victim is an illegal migrant worker considered disposable by her tormentor.

Many rapists, like the one in this story, illustrated their extreme evil by articulating racist attitudes. This linkage of racist ideas and language with rape is the most common way for these episodes to connect the questions of race and rape. At the same time, then, race functions as another way in which the (usually) white male protagonist can demonstrate his superior understanding and progressivism. The wide range of other possibilities linking race and rape, such as depicting a black victim whose claim against a white perpetrator is doubted, portraying minority crisis workers and therapists, or showing how the race of an attacker can affect trial process and sentencing, are omitted from prime time's rape story. Instead of including such elements, prime time occasionally presents a falsely accused minority male or a minority detective who defends his white colleague from false accusation. These episodes seldom go further than showing that "racism is bad," providing very little subtlety or depth in their exposition of race and rape. This area is clearly a difficult one for prime time, and it remains one where further change is to be hoped for.

False accusation stories are well represented here, but in ways that tend to lend credence to traditional myths about fabricated claims of rape and the ease with which a man's reputation can be harmed. These stories almost without exception show that false accusations are easily made and hard to disprove, following the traditional prescription passed down from British common law. Even in cases where the victim has no intention of making an accusation, men find themselves in serious trouble because of a circumstantial suggestion of guilt. In others, where young girls deliberately set out to make a false accusation, their hasty attempts to contrive a rape situation are accepted without question by other characters. In still others, mistaken identity places men with spotless reputations in grave legal trouble. Not only do these episodes show how easy it is for a man to be falsely accused of rape regardless of his previous reputation, they also provide a stock profile of the false accuser. In most cases where the false accusations are made deliberately, the accuser is a high school student, often under pressure from her father to shift blame from herself to a man. Prime time episodes seldom leave doubt about whether a given accusation is false or not. Rather, they tend to begin with the certainty of a false accusation and trace the protagonist's efforts to clear his name in this ultimate test of masculinity.

Directions for Future Research

Although research in the area of representations of rape in the mass media has been undertaken by a number of scholars in recent years, much work remains to be done. This book suggests a need for two specific projects in the near future. First, an examination of prime time representations of rape in made-for-TV movies is needed to complete the picture of how prime time has portrayed rape over the years studied here, and this group of texts will likely offer a counterpoint to the focus on masculinity found in the prime time episodes examined (see Rapping 1992, 199). The number of rape-centered made-for-TV movies aired during this period and since is truly astounding, and it is likely that these portrayals have evolved in ways no less dramatic than the episodic series. It is likely that made-for-TV movies have provided stories more focused on victims and their experiences rather than on male detectives and their responses to rape, since scholars of TV movies have shown that they are more socially oriented and that many focus on women's issues. Second, a study of prime time episodic portrayals of rape from 1991 to the present will supplement the work undertaken here. Programs such as *NYPD Blue*, *Law and Order*, and *Reasonable Doubts* have aired multiple rape episodes since 1990. An examination of these programs can chart recent directions in the portrayal of difficult issues such as the intersection of race and rape, the ability of law to handle date rape cases, and the social and structural causes of rape.

A cursory look at some of the post-1990 episodes suggests that these programs have become even more complex and ambiguous in their treatments of rape, and that extra-legal solutions have become more popular on prime time. In one plot, detectives assure the frightened victim (who does not want to testify at trial) that there may be "another way" to handle the case. They frame the rapist for drug possession and then offer him a deal whereby he confesses to his rapes but the drug charge is dropped. In another, detectives track and beat up a rapist when the legal case evaporates. These stories suggest that prime time has continued to be unable to sustain support for the idea that "the system works" when dealing with the crime of rape. Further research on episodic series representations of rape will also reveal more about the development of the detective and legal genres on prime time, including how these genres have handled gender in recent years. Possibly, rape stories will also become more popular on other genres of prime time fictional programming.

The subject of rape carries with it powerful emotional responses drawn from the physical and gendered nature of the crime, the political uses it has historically served, and the severe trauma it causes to its victims. The rape reform movement in the United States since the early 1970s has involved thousands of people working in numerous areas in every state to help survivors work through their trauma, to change laws, to produce knowledge about the crime in contemporary society, and to educate people in hospitals, police stations, and courts according to this new knowledge. Ultimately their work is designed to counteract powerful myths about sexuality, violence, and gender that have been passed down to us through centuries, and to replace old ways of thinking with new ones more in line with contemporary reality. The study of how rape is represented on television and in other mass media is an essential means of understanding the extent to which this reeducation has been successful, since television serves as an expression of mainstream ideas to a mass audience. It is hoped that future studies will continue to examine this important relationship between television and rape, which can only become more complex as the conflicting understandings of rape are reconstructed and reconciled in television's countless narratives.

Appendix 1. Program Descriptions and Episode List

Much of the factual information on dates, number of episodes, length, and networks, is from Heidi Holland, ed. (1992), *Television Programming Source Book, 1992–93* and Alex McNeil (1984), *Total Television: A Comprehensive Guide to Programming from 1948 to the Present.*

Program	Genre	Years	Min.	Network
All in the Family	sit com	71–79	25	CBS

Carroll O'Connor and Jean Stapleton starred in this Norman Lear comedy about a working class family headed by a caring father with offensive views about social groups and issues, which he debated with various other characters.

    Edith's 50th Birthday, 1977

Program	Genre	Years	Min.	Network
Baretta	detective	75–78	52	ABC

Robert Blake starred as the title character, a streetwise detective whose primary companion was his pet parrot. Baretta often went against the wishes and instincts of his police chief and police procedures.

    Shoes, 1976
    Somebody Killed Cock Robin, 1977
    Why Me? 1977
    The Marker, 1978

Program	Genre	Years	Min.	Network
Barnaby Jones	detective	73–80	52	CBS

Buddy Edson starred as a private detective whose niece and (later) nephew assisted in his investigations. His work was characterized by a thorough knowledge of criminal justice and a witty approach.

    Anatomy of Fear, 1977
    Deadly Sanctuary, 1978

Barney Miller	sit com	75–82	25	ABC

Hal Linden starred as captain in a Manhattan precinct detective division. The plots were set in the station.

Rape, 1978

Big Hawaii	drama	77	52	NBC

Cliff Potts starred as an independent young rebel whose personal life as often as his professional exploits was the focus of the program in this story of cattle ranchers in contemporary Hawaii.

The Trouble with Tina, 1977

The Bronx Zoo	drama	87	52	NBC

Ed Asner starred as principal in a Bronx high school. Episodes centered on personal and professional issues of the faculty rather than the students.

Behind Closed Doors, 1987

Cagney and Lacey	detective	82–88	52	CBS

Tyne Daly and Sharon Gless starred as undercover detectives in a New York precinct plagued by sexism. The program won a number of Emmy awards including several for Outstanding Lead Actress in a drama series and one for Outstanding Drama Series.

Open and Shut Case, 1983
Date Rape, 1983
Violation, 1985
The Rapist, part I, 1986
The Rapist part II, 1987
Do I Know You? 1987
Friendly Fire, 1988

Charlie's Angels	detective	76–81	52	ABC

Farrah Fawcett-Majors, Kate Jackson, and Jaclyn Smith starred as three beautiful young detectives who went on widely varied assignments for a boss (Charlie) who communicated with them over the phone and through his assistant Bosley.

Terror on Ward One, 1977

Crime Story	police	86–88	48	NBC

Dennis Farina, Stephen Lang, and Anthony Denison starred as members of an elite Chicago detective squad fighting underworld crime.

King in a Cage, 1987

Dallas	drama	78–91	52	CBS

Larry Hagman, Linda Gray, Barbara Bel Geddes, and Patrick Duffy starred as members of the fictitious Ewing family of Texas.

Lessons, 1978
Winds of Vengeance, 1978

Delvecchio	detective	76	52	CBS

Judd Hirsch starred as a law school graduate who failed the bar and became a top performing police detective.

The Silent Prey, 1976

Different World	sit com	87–92	25	NBC

Jasmine Guy starred in this *Cosby Show* spinoff set in a fictitious African American college.

No Means No, 1990

Dog and Cat	detective	77	52	ABC

As the title suggests, this program featured two detectives quite unlike each other. Kim Basinger and Lou Antonio starred as the mismatched partners.

Live Bait, 1977

Dynasty	drama	80–89	52	ABC

John Forsythe, Linda Evans, and others starred in this melodrama set in Denver.

The Search, 1981

Equalizer	detective	85–89	52	CBS

Edward Woodward starred as a former U.S. security agent working as a skilled private investigator helping people whose cases fell outside the parameters of the law and the judicial system. The program was set in Manhattan.

Pilot episode, 1985
Nocturne, 1986
Nightscape, 1986
Shades of Darkness, 1986
Heart of Justice, 1989

Facts of Life	sit com	79–88	25	NBC

This program followed four young girls through high school and college.

Double Standard, 1980
Fear Strikes Back, 1981

Gibbsville	drama	76	52	NBC

John Savage and Gig Young starred as small-town newspaper reporters in the late 1940s. The program was based on a the stories of John O'Hara.

   The Price of Everything, 1976
   Saturday Night, 1976

Hawaii Five-O	police	68–80	52	CBS

Jack Lord starred as the intelligent captain of a special investigative unit investigating cases on all the Hawaiian islands.

   Requiem for a Saddle Bronc Rider, 1977
   Elegy in a Rain Forest, 1977

Hill Street Blues	police	81–87	52	NBC

Daniel J. Travanti and Veronica Hamel starred as members of a unit of big-city police dealing with realistic contemporary issues and problems, mixing tragedy and humor and conveying realism.

   Presidential Fever, 1980
   Dressed to Kill, 1981
   The World According to Freedom, 1982
   Invasion of the Third World Mutant Body Snatchers, 1982
   Trial by Fury, 1982
   Moon over Uranus, 1983
   Watta Way to Go and Rookie Nookie, 1984
   Intestinal Fortitude, 1985

Hotel	drama	83–88	52	ABC

James Brolin and Connie Selecca starred in the adaptation of Arthur Hailey's novel, taking place in the St. Gregory Hotel and revolving around the activities of the hotel manager and his assistant.

   Pilot, 1983

In the Heat of the Night	police	88–92	55	NBC

Carroll O'Connor starred as police chief in this drama about a small town in Mississippi. The cast and story themes were consistently biracial.

   Accused, 1989
   Rape, 1989
   First Deadly Sin, 1990
   Quick Fix, 1990

Kaz	drama	78–79	52	CBS

Ron Liebman and Patrick O'Neal starred in this short-lived program focusing on an attorney who acquired his legal education in prison

   A Day in Court, 1978

L.A. Law	drama	86–92	48	NBC

Susan Dey, Corbin Bernsen, and Jill Eikenberry starred as attorneys working for an elite Los Angeles law firm and taking a wide variety of cases. The show has often been noted for its frequent treatment of rape. Some of its rape-centered stories were aired after 1990.

> Pilot episode, 1986
> Brothers Grim, 1987
> Sparky Brackman R.I.P.?, 1987
> Hey, Lick Me Over, 1988
> Belle of the Bald, 1988
> Romancing the Drone, 1988
> The Pay's Lousy But the Tips Are Good, 1990
> Good Human Bar, 1990
> Noah's Bark, 1990

Little House on the Prairie	western	74–82	50	NBC

Michael Landon and Melissa Gilbert starred in this family drama set in the American West and (loosely) based on a series of autobiographical books about Laura Ingalls Wilder's childhood and young adulthood in the late nineteenth century.

> Sylvia (2 parts), 1980

Lou Grant	drama	77–82	52	CBS

Edward Asner starred as city editor of a newspaper in Los Angeles in this continuation of his character from *The Mary Tyler Moore Show*.

> Rape, 1980

MacGruder and Loud	detective	85	52	ABC

John Getz and Kathryn Harrold starred as a married police team in this short-lived drama.

> The Violation, 1984

Matt Houston	detective	82–85	52	ABC

Lee Horsley starred as a part-time detective and full-time millionaire with plenty of energy for his wide range of activities.

> Episode 26, 1983

McClain's Law	police	81–82	52	NBC

James Arness starred as Jim McClain, a cop who returned to police work following a friend's murder.

> A Time of Peril, 1981

Miami Vice	detective	84–89	52	NBC

Don Johnson starred in this postmodern detective program set in Miami, Florida. The show mixed music and attitude to create a new and ambiguous version of the police detective show.

> Amen, Send Money, 1987
> Blood and Roses, 1988
> Hell Hath No Fury, 1988
> Honor Among Thieves, 1988

The Mississippi	drama	83	52	CBS

Ralph Waite starred as a big-time attorney who gave up his practice for a simpler life on the Mississippi, where he nevertheless inevitably helped defend locals with legal difficulties.

> Murder at Mt. Parnassus, 1983

Oregon Trail	western	77	52	NBC

Rod Taylor starred in this one-season story of a family's travels from Missouri to Oregon in search of free land.

> Concentric Circles, 1977

Palmerstown U.S.A.	drama	80–81	52	CBS

Jonell Allen and Beeson Carroll starred as two boys of different races in the south experiencing racial conflict with their families.

> Vendetta, 1980

The Quest	western	76	52	NBC

Brothers played by Kurt Russell and Tim Matheson searched for their sister who had been held by Indians for several years.

> Shanklin, 1976

Quincy	hospital/detective	76–83	52	NBC

Jack Klugman starred as an enthusiastic and opinionated medical examiner working in the L.A. coroner's office and functioning as a detective solving crimes. His persistent and voluble style irritated many including his irascible boss.

> Let Me Light the Way, 1977
> Shadow of Death, 1982

Rafferty	hospital	77	52	CBS

Patrick McGoohan starred as Dr. Sid Rafferty, a hospital doctor who was once an Army doctor, in this one-season program.

> Point of View, 1977

Rockford Files	detective	74–80	52	NBC

James Garner starred as a private detective working on cases formally closed by the police. His well-meaning but bumbling father helped with many cases.

Return of the Black Shadow, 1978

St. Elsewhere	hospital	82–88	52	NBC

Ed Begley, Jr. and others starred in this hospital drama centering on a group of doctors and nurses working in Boston.

Drama Center, 1984
The Attack, 1984
After Park, 1984

Serpico	detective	76	52	NBC

This one-season series was based on a film and best-selling autobiographical book by Frank Serpico, who wrote of his experiences in the New York City police department.

A Secret Place, 1976

Shannon	detective	81–82	52	CBS

Kevin Dobson starred in this story of a detective who changed cities and jobs after the death of his wife.

A Secret Rage, 1981

Simon and Simon	detective	81–89	52	CBS

Jameson Parker and Gerald McRaney starred as detective brothers working in San Diego, California.

Outrage, 1987

Spenser: For Hire	detective	85–88	52	ABC

Robert Urich starred as a Boston detective in this series based on the novels of Robert Parker.

Rage, 1986

Starsky and Hutch	detective	75–79	52	ABC

Paul Michael Glaser and David Soul starred as detective partners with different interests and habits.

Rape, 1976
Strange Justice, 1978

Strike Force	police	81–82	52	ABC

This series about an elite police unit ran two of the most gruesome and exaggerated rapes of the group, including one with a serial rapist who attacks 16 victims.

>Lonely Ladies, 1981
>The Predator, 1981

TJ Hooker	police	82–86	52	ABC

William Shatner starred in this series about an experienced police officer who teamed up with a rookie partner. Heather Locklear also starred.

>Big Foot, 1982
>The Confessor, 1984
>Love Story, 1984
>Death on the Line, 1984

Tales of the Gold Monkey	comedy/drama	82–83	52	ABC

Stephen Collins and Caitlin O'Heaney starred in this series set in 1938, in which a pilot experiences a variety of adventures while flying in the Marivella Islands.

>Sultan of Swat, 1982

Tour of Duty	Vietnam	87–90	52	ABC

Terence Knox and Stephen Caffrey starred as US soldiers in Vietnam relying on each other to survive the war.

>Nightmare, 1989

21 Jump Street	police	87–91	52	FOX

Johnny Depp and others starred in this story of a group of young detectives working undercover at various high schools, investigating drug-related crimes and other incidents.

>Two over Hard, 1987
>Higher Education, 1987
>Fun with Animals, 1988
>Hell Week, 1988
>Blackout, 1990
>Stand by Your Man, 1989

Vegas	detective	78–81	52	ABC

Robert Urich starred as private detective Dan Tanna in this program centered on the Las Vegas scene and the exploits of a private detective in this crime-ridden environment.

>No Way to Treat a Victim, 1981

Walking Tall	police	81	52	NBC

Bo Svenson starred as sheriff Buford Pusser in this show based on two movies drawn from the life of a real Tennessee lawman.

Pilot, 1981

Welcome Back, Kotter	sit com	75–79	25	ABC

John Travolta and others starred in this situation comedy about inner-city high school students and a teacher who decided to stay in town rather than seek his fortune elsewhere.

no title, 1978

Appendix 2. Timeline of Rape Reform and Related Events

1969–71   Speakouts on rape and other consciousness-raising discussions on rape-related issues.
      Establishment of early hotlines for rape victims.

1970   Publication of Kate Millett's *Sexual Politics*, articulating feminist analysis of rape.

1972   Death penalty for rape struck down by Supreme Court in *Coker v. Georgia* (75-5444).

1973   Congress establishes National Center for the Prevention and Control of Rape, with funds for state projects primarily on research and education.

1974   First reformed legal statute passed (in Michigan).
      Burgess and Holmstrom's first article on Rape Trauma Syndrome published. Publication of Burgess and Holmstrom's first Rape Trauma Syndrome article

1975   Publication of Susan Brownmiller's *Against Our Will: Men, Women, and Rape.*

1977   First reformed statutes making marital rape a crime.
      Law Enforcement Assistance Administration shifts funding toward social programs that fight crime, such as rape crisis projects.

1978–79   Rideout rape-in-marriage case gains national attention (John Rideout found not guilty).
      Publication of Holmstrom and Burgess's book on rape trauma syndrome *The Victim of Rape: Institutional Reactions.*

1979   Publication of Susan Griffin's *Rape: The Power of Consciousness* .

1982   Publication of Dianna E. H. Russell's *Rape in Marriage.*

1983–84   Big Dan's tavern case gains national attention and convictions.

1988   Publication of first book-length work on date/acquaintance rape, Robin Warshaw's *I Never Called it Rape.*
      Film *The Accused* released, based on the Big Dan rape case.

1989   Central Park Jogger case gains national attention and convictions.

Notes

Chapter 1

1. Lichter, Lichter, and Rothman 1994, 21.

2. For an excellent example of how compromises can be made in these areas, see D'Acci's discussion of *Cagney and Lacey*'s abortion episode in *Boxed In: Women and Television* (1987), as well as her book-length study, *Defining Women: Television and the Case of Cagney and Lacey* (1994).

3. For the purposes of this book, the terms "victim" and "survivor" will be used somewhat interchangeably. However, victim is more appropriate in some cases involving television representations, as when an attack is in progress or when the term is meant in a general sense.

4. David Martindale's (1991) reference volume *Television Detective Shows of the 1970s: Credits, Storylines and Episode Guides for 109 Series* provides some evidence of the completeness of the Annenberg collection. For the series *Baretta*, Martindale identifies the same rape episodes included in the Annenberg archive. The same is true for *Barnaby Jones, Quincy*, and several other programs. Martindale identifies one *Starsky and Hutch* episode involving a rape plot ("Nightmare") that is not found at Annenberg.

5. The archive also collects made-for-TV movies, of which there are dozens. Although an analysis of made-for-TV movies that treat rape would make an excellent point of comparison for the present study, this constitutes a separate set of texts and a separate project in its own right.

6. Basic information on the represented programs is also included. The collection of rape-centered prime time episodes is no doubt still incomplete because of the nature of the project.

7. Brooks and Marsh's (1995) *Complete Directory to Prime Time Network and Cable TV Series, 1946–Present* classifies programs discussed here under several related genres, including "Police Drama" (*Quincy, Hawaii Five-O, Delvecchio, Starsky and Hutch, Serpico, Baretta*), "Detective Drama" (*Charlie's Angels, Rockford Files, Barnaby Jones*), "Crime Drama" (*Dog and Cat*), "Police

Anthology" (*Police Story*), or "Law/Detective Drama" (*Kaz*). All these are variations of what I call the cop or detective genre.

8. See also Griffin 1979; Berger, Searles, and Neuman 1995; Sanday 1996.

9. See, e.g., Connell and Wilson 1974; Gager and Schurr 1976; Hilberman 1976; Horos 1974; Hursch 1977; MacKellar 1975; Medea and Thompson 1974; Russell 1975; Schultz 1975; Walker and Brodsky 1976.

10. For an example of pre-feminist thinking on the subject of victim responsibility, see Menachem Amir's (1971) *Patterns in Forcible Rape*, especially the definition of "victim precipitated forcible rape" at 495. For a detailed discussion of pre-feminist British Common Law and U.S. legal thinking on rape that contrasts traditional and feminist views see Cuklanz (1996), *Rape on Trial*, chap. 2.

11. See Benedict 1992; Connell and Wilson 1974; Cuklanz 1996b.

12. Benedict 1992; Buchwold, Fletcher, and Roth 1993; Meyers 1996; Projanski 1995.

13. Police/detective dramas that aired just one rape episode in the late 1980s include *Spenser: For Hire*, *Crime Story*, *Simon and Simon*, *McClain's Law*, *Matt Houston*, *MacGruder and Loud*, *Tales of the Gold Monkey*, and *Quincy*.

Chapter 2

14. See Bourque 1989, Cuklanz 1996b, Hursch 1977.

15. See Benedict 1992, chap. 1; Cuklanz 1996, chap. 2.

16. For an excellent and detailed reading of a number of *L.A. Law* rape episodes, see Projanski's (1995) dissertation, "Working on Feminism: Film and Television Rape Narratives and Postfeminist Culture," chap. 3.

17. The eight false accusation plots discussed here are (1) *Gibbsville*, "The Price of Everything" (1976); (2) *Big Hawaii*, "The Trouble with Tina" (1977); (3) *Welcome Back, Kotter* (no title — 1978); (4) *Dallas*, "Lessons" (1978); (5) *Hill Street Blues*, "Invasion of the Third World Mutant Body Snatchers" (1982); (6) *21 Jump Street*, "Higher Education" (1987); (7) *The Bronx Zoo*, "Behind Closed Doors" (1987); and (8) *In the Heat of the Night*, "Accused" (1989). The *Tales of the Gold Monkey* episode ("Sultan of Swat," 1982) also features a false accusation against a protagonist male, but since the victim has been killed, it is caused by a mistaken impression rather than by victim psychology.

Chapter 3

18. Only two episodes in the entire collection deal with the rape of a male victim. Both episodes, *Kaz*'s "A Day in Court" (1978) and *Cagney and Lacey*'s "Violation" (1985) are discussed along with other unusual episodes in Chapter 5.

19. References to other explanations of rape are discussed in Chapter 4.

20. *L.A. Law*, as noted elsewhere in this book, ran numerous episodes closely examining various aspects of rape and its legal ramifications ("Broth-

ers Grim," 1986, "Hey, Lick Me Over," 1988, "Belle of the Bald," 1988, "Romancing the Drone," 1988, "Good Human Bar," 1990, "Noah's Bark," 1990). Since this book covers only the period through 1990, readers may remember specific *L.A. Law* episodes that are not covered here because they were aired between 1991 and 1993.

21. Victims, and the *L.A. Law* programs in general, are covered in detail in Chapter 4.

Chapter 4

22. Husbands are seldom mentioned in these episodes, and many scripts strongly imply that the victim is single. Some victims live alone, others have female roommates or are college students living in dormitories, and others are divorced. In the few episodes that feature married victims, the husband usually becomes an important character (as discussed in Chapter 3).

23. In contrast, one of only two episodes that has a male victim (*Kaz*, "A Day in Court," 1978), features a man who is discouraged from testifying in court by his brother, who warns that he will be destroyed in court. The victim rejects his brother's warning, saying that he has to testify. This episode is discussed in Chapter 5.

References

Amir, Menachim. 1971. *Patterns in Forcible Rape*. Chicago: University of Chicago Press.

Baron, Larry and Murray Strauss. 1989. *Four Theories of Rape in American Society: A State Level Analysis*. New Haven, Conn.: Yale University Press.

Bechhofer, Laurie and Andrea Parrot. 1991. "What Is Acquaintance Rape?" In *Acquaintance Rape: The Hidden Crime*, ed. Andrea Parrot and Laurie Bechhofer. New York: John Wiley and Sons, 9–25.

Benedict, Helen. 1992. *Virgin or Vamp: How the Press Covers Sex Crimes*. New York: Oxford University Press.

Beneke, Timothy. 1982. *Men on Rape*. New York: St. Martin's Press.

Berger, Arthur Asa. 1995. *Manufacturing Desire: Media, Popular Culture, and Everyday Life*. New Brunswick, N.J.: Transaction Press.

———. 1992. *Popular Culture Genres: Theories and Texts*. Newbury Park, Calif.: Sage.

Berger, Ronald J., Patricia Searles, and W. Lawrence Neuman. 1995. "Rape-Law Reform: Its Nature, Origins, and Impact." In *Rape and Society: Readings on the Problem of Sexual Assault*, ed. Patricia Searles and Ronald J. Berger. Boulder, Colo.: Westview Press, 223–32.

Berman, Ronald. 1987. *How Television Sees Its Audience: A Look at the Looking Glass*. Newbury Park, Calif.: Sage.

Bobo, Jacqueline and Ellen Seiter. 1997. "Black Feminism and Media Criticism: 'The Women of Brewster Place.'" In *Feminist Television Criticism: A Reader*, ed. Charlotte Brundson, Julie D'Acci, and Lynn Spigel. Oxford: Clarendon Press.

Bourque, Linda Brookover. 1989. *Defining Rape*. Durham, N.C.: Duke University Press.

Bumiller, Kristin. 1991. "Fallen Angels: The Representation of Violence Against Women in Legal Culture." In *At the Boundaries of Law*, ed. Martha Albertson Fineman and Nancy Sweet Thomadsen. New York: Routledge, 95–111.

Brinson, Susan. 1990. "TV Rape: The Representation of Rape in Prime-

Time Television Dramas." Unpublished doctoral dissertation, University of Missouri-Columbia.

———. 1992. "The Use and Opposition of Rape Myths in Prime-Time Television Dramas." *Sex Roles* 27, 7–8: 359–75.

Brooks, Tim, and Earle Marsh. 1995. *The Complete Directory to Prime Time Network and Cable TV Shows, 1946–Present.* 6th ed. New York: Ballantine Books.

Brownmiller, Susan. 1975. *Against Our Will: Men, Women, and Rape.* New York: Simon and Schuster.

Buchwald, Emily, Pamela Fletcher, and Martha Roth, eds. 1993. *Transforming a Rape Culture.* Minneapolis: Milkweed Editions.

Burgess, Ann Wolbert. 1995. "Rape Trauma Syndrome." In *Rape and Society: Readings on the Problem of Sexual Assault,* ed. Patricia Searles and Ronald J. Berger. Boulder, Colo.: Westview Press, 239–45.

Burgess, Ann Wolbert and Linda Lytle Holmstrom. 1974a. "Rape Trauma Syndrome." *American Journal of Psychiatry* 131: 981–86.

———. 1974b. *Rape: Victims of Crisis.* Bowie, Md.: Robert J. Brady.

Buxton, David. 1990. *From the Avengers to Miami Vice: Form and Ideology in Television Series.* New York: Manchester University Press.

Byars, Jackie. 1987. "Reading Feminine Discourse: Prime-Time Television in the U.S." *Communication* 9: 289–303.

Cantor, Muriel. 1990. "Prime-Time Fathers: A Study in Continuity and Change." *Critical Studies in Mass Communication* 7: 275–85.

Campbell, Sandra. 1993. "Creating Redemptive Imagery: A Challenge of Resistance and Creativity." In *Transforming a Rape Culture,* ed. Emily Buchwald, Pamela Fletcher, and Martha Roth. Minneapolis: Milkweed Editions, 139–52.

Clark, Danae. 1990. "*Cagney and Lacey*: Feminist Strategies of Detection." In *Television and Women's Culture: The Politics of the Popular,* ed. Mary Ellen Brown. Newbury Park, Calif.: Sage, 117–33.

Cloud, Dana. 1992. "The Limits of Interpretation: Ambivalence and the Stereotype in *Spenser: For Hire.*" *Critical Studies in Mass Communication* 9: 311–24.

Connell, Nancy and Cassandra Wilson, eds. 1974. *Rape: The First Sourcebook for Women.* New York: New American Library.

"Corroborating Charges of Rape." 1967. *Columbia Law Review* 67: 1137–48.

Craik, Elizabeth. 1984. *Marriage and Property.* London: Aberdeen Press.

Cuklanz, Lisa. 1998. "The Masculine Ideal: Rape on Prime Time Television, 1976–1978." *Critical Studies in Mass Communication* 15: 423–48.

———. 1996a. "Mainstream News Frames the Hill/Thomas Hearings." In *Outsiders Looking In: A Communication Perspective on the Hill/Thomas Hearing,* ed. Paul Siegel. Communication and Law Series. New York: Hampton Press, 167–182.

———. 1996b. *Rape on Trial: How the Mass Media Construct Legal Reform and Social Change.* Philadelphia: University of Pennsylvania Press.

———. 1995a. "News Coverage of Ethnic and Gender Issues in the Big Dan's Rape Case." In *Feminism, Multiculturalism, and the Media: Global Diversities,* ed. Angharad N. Valdivia. London: Sage Publications, 145–62.

———. 1995b. "Opposing Verdicts in the Webb-Dotson Rape Case: Legal Versus News Constructions." *Communication Studies* 46: 45–56.

———. 1995c "Public Expressions of 'Progress' in Discourses of the Big Dan's Rape." *Women and Language* 27, 1: 1–11.

———. 1993. "Truth in Transition: Discursive Constructions of Character in the Rideout Rape in Marriage Case." *Women's Studies in Communication* 16, 1: 74–101.

Cuklanz, Lisa and Kathryn Cirksena. 1992. "Male is to Female as ——— is to ———. "A Guided Tour of Five Feminist Frameworks for Communication Studies." In *Women Making Meaning: New Feminist Directions in Communication*, ed. Lana Rakow. New York: Routledge, Chapman and Hall, 18–44.

D'Acci, Julie. 1994. *Defining Women: Television and the Case of Cagney and Lacey*. Chapel Hill: University of North Carolina Press.

———. 1987. "The Case of Cagney and Lacey." In *Boxed In: Women and Television*, edited by H. Baehr and G. Dyer. London: Routledge and Kegan Paul, 203–26.

Davis, Flora. 1991. *Moving the Mountain: The Women's Movement in America Since 1960*. New York: Touchstone.

D'Emelio, John and Estelle B. Freedman. 1988. *Intimate Matters: A History of Sexuality in America*. New York: Harper and Row.

de Lauretis, Teresa. 1997. "The Violence of Rhetoric." In *The Gender/Sexuality Reader: Culture, History, Political Economy*, ed. Roger N. Lancaster and Micaela di Leonardo. New York: Routledge, 265–78. Originally published in *Semiotica* 54, 1/2: 11–31.

di Leonardo, Micaela. 1997. "White Lies, Black Myths." In *The Gender/Sexuality Reader: Culture, History, Political Economy*, ed. Roger N. Lancaster and Micaela di Leonardo. New York: Routledge, 53–68.

Dow, Bonnie J. 1996. *Prime-Time Feminism: Television, Culture, and the Women's Movement Since 1970*. Philadelphia: University of Pennsylvania Press.

Dworkin, Andrea. 1974. *Woman Hating*. New York: E. P. Dutton.

Eaton, Mary. 1995. "A Fair Cop? Viewing the Effects of the Canteen Culture in *Prime Suspect* and *Between the Lines*." In *Crime and the Media: The Post-Modern Spectacle*, ed. David Kidd-Hewitt and Richard Osborne. London: Pluto Press, 164–84.

Ehrenreich, Barbara. 1983. *The Hearts of Men: American Dreams and the Flight from Commitment*. New York: Doubleday.

Estrich, Susan. 1987. *Real Rape: How the Legal System Victimizes Women Who Say No*. Cambridge, Mass.: Harvard University Press.

Evans, Sara M. 1980. *Personal Politics: The Roots of Women's Liberation in the Civil Rights Movement and the New Left*. New York: Vintage Books.

Evans, William A. 1990. "The Interpretive Turn in Media Research: Innovation, Iteration, or Illusion?" *Critical Studies in Mass Communication* 7: 147–68.

Fairstein, Linda A. 1993. *Sexual Violence: Our War Against Rape*. New York: William Morrow.

Faludi, Susan. 1991. *Backlash: The Undeclared War Against American Women*. New York: Crown.

Famighetti, Robert, ed. 1993. "Crimes in the U.S., 1973–1992." *World Almanac and Book of Facts, 1994.* Mahwah, N.J.: Funk & Wagnalls, 964.

Fawal, Joseph. 1976. "Questioning the Marital Privilege: A Medieval Philosophy in a Modern World." *Cumberland Law Review* 7: 307–22.

Ferguson, Marjorie. 1983. "Images of Power and the Feminist Fallacy." *Critical Studies in Mass Communication* 7: 215–30.

Feuer, Jane. 1995. *Seeing Through the Eighties: TV and Reaganism.* Durham, N.C.: Duke University Press.

Feuer, Jane, Paul Kerr, and Tise Vahimagi, eds. 1984. *MTM: "Quality" Television.* London: British Film Institute.

Field, Hubert S. and Leigh B. Bienen. 1980. *Jurors and Rape: A Study in Psychology and Law.* Lexington, Ky.: Lexington Books.

Fiske, John. 1989. *Reading the Popular.* Boston: Unwin Hyman.

———. 1987. *Television Culture.* New York: Methuen.

Flexner, Eleanor. 1973. *Century of Struggle: The Woman's Rights Movement in the United States.* New York: Atheneum.

Freeman, Jo. 1975. *The Politics of Women's Liberation: A Case Study of an Emerging Social Movement and Its Relation to the Policy Process.* New York: David McKay.

Friedan, Betty. 1974 [1963]. *The Feminine Mystique.* New York: Dell.

Gager, Nancy and Cathleen Schurr. 1976. *Sexual Assault: Confronting Rape in America.* New York: Grossett and Dunlap.

Gamman, Lorraine. 1988. "Watching the Detectives: The Enigma of the Female Gaze." In *The Female Gaze: Women as Viewers of Popular Culture,* ed. Lorraine Gamman and Margaret Marshment. London: Women's Press, 16–28.

Gitlin, Todd. 1985 [1983]. *Inside Prime Time.* 2nd ed. New York: Pantheon.

Goodwin, Andrew and Garry Whannel, eds. 1990. *Understanding Television.* New York: Routledge.

Griffin, Susan. 1979. *Rape: The Power of Consciousness.* San Francisco: Harper and Row.

Hale, Sir Matthew. 1847 [1650]. *History of Please to the Crown.* Philadelphia: Robert H. Small.

Hanke, Robert. 1992. "Redesigning Men: Hegemonic Masculinity in Transition." In *Men, Masculinity, and the Media,* edited by Steve Craig. Newbury Park, Calif.: Sage.

Hilberman, Elaine. 1976. *The Rape Victim.* New York: Basic Books.

Holland, Heidi, ed. 1992. *Television Programming Source Book, 1992–93.* Philadelphia: North American Publishing Company.

Holmstrom, Lynda Lytle, and Ann Wolbert Burgess. 1978. *The Victim of Rape: Institutional Reactions.* New York: John Wiley and Sons.

hooks, bell. 1989. *Talking Back: Thinking Feminist, Thinking Black.* Boston: South End Press.

Horos, Carol V. 1974. *Rape.* New Canaan, Conn.: Tobey Publishing.

Hursch, Carolyn. 1977. *The Trouble with Rape.* Chicago: Nelson-Hall.

Joyrich, Lynne. 1996. *Re-Viewing Reception: Television, Gender, and Postmodern Culture.* Bloomington: Indiana University Press.

———. 1990. "Critical and Textual Hypermasculinity." In *Logics of Television:*

Essays in Cultural Criticism, ed. Patricia Mellencamp. Bloomington: Indiana University Press, 156–72.

Kaplan, E. Ann. 1987. "Feminist Criticism and Television." In *Channels of Discourse*, ed. Robert C. Allen. Chapel Hill: University of North Carolina Press, 211–53.

Katz, Sedelle and Mary Ann Mazur. 1979. *Understanding the Rape Victim*. New York: John Wiley and Sons.

Kelly, P. T., ed. 1996. *Television Violence: A Guide to the Literature*. New York: NOVA Science Publishers, Inc.

Kidd-Hewitt, David. 1995. "Crime and the Media: A Criminological Perspective." In *Crime and the Media: The Post-Modern Spectacle*, ed. David Kidd-Hewitt and Richard Osborne. London: Pluto Press, 1–24.

Koss, Mary P. 1992. "Defending Date Rape." *Journal of Interpersonal Violence* 7, 1: 122–26.

———. 1988. "Hidden Rape: Sexual Aggression and Victimization in a National Sample of Students in Higher Education." In *Rape and Sexual Assault II*, ed. Ann Wolbert Burgess. New York: Garland, 3–25.

LaFree, Gary. 1992. *Rape and Criminal Justice: The Social Construction of Sexual Assault*. Belmont, Calif.: Wadsworth Publishing Company.

Laqueur, Thomas. 1990. *Making Sex: Body and Gender from the Greeks to Freud*. Cambridge, Mass.: Harvard University Press.

Levinson, Richard and William Link. 1981. *Stay Tuned: An Inside Look at the Making of Prime Time Television*. New York: Saint Martin's Press.

Lichter, S. Robert, Linda S. Lichter, and Stanley Rothman. 1994. *Prime Time: How TV Portrays American Culture*. Washington, D.C.: Regnery Publishers.

MacKellar, Jean. 1975. *Rape: The Bait and Trap*. New York: Crown.

MacKinnon, Catharine A. 1995. "Sex and Violence: A Perspective." In *Rape and Society: Readings on the Problem of Sexual Assault*, ed. Patricia Searles and Ronald J. Berger. Boulder, Colo.: Westview Press, 99–106.

Madigan, Lee and Nancy Gamble. 1989. *The Second Rape: Society's Continued Betrayal of the Victim*. New York: Lexington Books.

Malamuth, Neil. 1981. "Rape Proclivity Among Males." *Journal of Social Issues* 37, 4: 138–57.

Marsh, Jeanne C., Alison Geist, and Nathan Caplan. 1982. *Rape and the Limits of Law Reform*. Boston: Auburn House.

Martindale, David. 1991. *Television Detective Shows of the 1970s: Credits, Storylines, and Episode Guides for 109 Series*. Jefferson, N.C.: McFarland.

Matoesian, Gregory M. 1993. *Reproducing Rape: Domination Through Talk in the Courtroom*. Chicago: Polity Press.

Matthews, Nancy A. 1994. *Confronting Rape: The Feminist Anti-Rape Movement and the State*. New York: Routledge.

Mayne, Judith. 1997. "*L.A. Law* and Prime-Time Feminism." In *Feminist Television Criticism: A Reader*, ed. Charlotte Brundson, Julie D'Acci, and Lynn Spiegel. Oxford: Clarendon Press.

McNeil, Alex. 1984. *Total Television: A Comprehensive Guide to Programming from 1948 to the Present*. New York: Penguin.

Medea, Andra and Kathleen Thompson 1974. *Against Rape*. New York: Farrar, Straus and Giroux.

Meyers, Marian. 1997. *News Coverage of Violence Against Women: Engendering Blame.* Thousand Oaks, Calif.: Sage.

———. 1996. "Advocating Change: News Coverage of Violence Against Women." Symposium conducted at the annual meeting of the International Communication Association, Chicago.

Millett, Kate. 1970. *Sexual Politics.* Garden City, N.Y.: Doubleday.

Montgomery, Kathryn. 1989. *Target, Prime Time: Advocacy Groups and the Struggle over Entertainment Television.* New York: Oxford University Press.

Moorti, Sujata. 1995. "Screening Sexuality: Democratic Sphere and Television Representation of Rape." Unpublished doctoral dissertation, University of Maryland.

Myrdal, Gunnar. 1944. *An American Dilemma: The Negro Problem in Modern Democracy.* New York: Harper and Row.

O'Sullivan, Chris. 1991. "Acquaintance and Gang Rape on Campuses." In *Acquaintance Rape: The Hidden Crime*, ed. Andrea Parrot and Laurie Bechhofer. New York: John Wiley and Sons, 140–56.

Pines, Jim. 1995. "Black Cops and Black Villains in Film and TV Crime Fiction." In *Crime and the Media: The Post-Modern Spectacle*, ed. David Kidd-Hewitt and Richard Osborne. London: Pluto Press, 67–77.

Pleck, Elizabeth. 1983. "Feminist Responses to 'Crimes Against Women,' 1868–1896." *Signs* 8, 3: 451–70.

Porter, Roy. 1986. "Rape: Does It Have a Historical Meaning?" In *Rape*, ed. Sylvana Tomaselli and Roy Porter. London: Blackwell, 216–36.

Press, Andrea. 1991. *Women Watching Television: Class, Gender, and Generation in the American Television Experience.* Philadelphia: University of Pennsylvania Press.

Projanski, Sara. 1995. "Working on Feminism: Film and Television Rape Narratives and Postfeminist Culture." Unpublished doctoral dissertation, University of Iowa.

Rapping, Elayne. 1992. *The Movie of the Week: Private Stories, Public Events.* American Culture 6. Minneapolis: University of Minnesota Press.

Rhode, Deborah L. 1995. "Media Images, Feminist Issues." *Signs: Journal of Women in Culture and Society* 20: 685–710.

Rowland, W. D. 1983. *The Politics of TV Violence: Policy Uses of Communication Research.* Beverly Hills, Calif.: Sage.

Russell, Dianna E. H. 1975. *The Politics of Rape.* New York: Stein and Day.

———. 1982. *Rape in Marriage.* New York: Macmillan.

Sanday, Peggy Reeves 1996. *A Woman Scorned: Acquaintance Rape on Trial.* New York: Doubleday.

———. 1990. *Fraternity Gang Rape: Sex, Brotherhood, and Privilege on Campus.* New York: New York University Press.

Sanders, William B. 1980. *Rape and Women's Identity.* Sage Library of Social Research 106. Beverly Hills, Calif.: Sage.

Schlesinger, Philip., R. Emerson Dobash, Russell P. Dobash, and C. K. Weaver. 1992. *Women Viewing Violence.* London: British Film Institute.

Schultz, Leroy G., ed. 1975. *Rape Victimology.* Springfield, Ill.: Charles C. Thomas.

Scully, Diana and Joseph Marolla. 1995. " 'Riding the Bull at Gilley's': Convicted Rapists Describe the Rewards of Rape." In *Rape and Society: Readings on the Problem of Sexual Assault,* ed. Patricia Searles and Ronald J. Berger. Boulder, Colo.: Westview Press, 58–73.

Searles, Patricia and Ronald Berger, eds. 1995. *Rape and Society: Readings on the Problem of Sexual Assault.* Boulder, Colo.: Westview Press.

Spigel, Lynn. 1992. *Make Room for TV: Television and the Family Ideal in Postwar America.* Chicago: University of Chicago Press.

Storaska, Frederick. 1975. *How to Say No to a Rapist and Survive.* New York: Random House.

Taylor, Ella. 1989. *Prime-Time Families: Television Culture in Postwar America.* Berkeley: University of California Press.

Thompson, E., Joseph H. Pleck, and D. Ferrera. 1992. "Men and Masculinities: Scales for Masculinity Ideology and Masculine-Related Constructs." *Sex Roles* 27, 11–12: 573–607.

Thompson, Mildred. 1990. *Ida B. Wells-Barnett: An Exploratory Study of an American Black Woman, 1893–1930.* Brooklyn, N.Y.: Carlson Publishing Company.

Verna, Tony. 1987. *Live TV: An Inside Look at Directing and Producing.* Boston: Focal Press.

Walker, Marcia J. and Stanley L. Brodsky. 1976. *Sexual Assault: The Victim and the Rapist.* Lexington, Mass: D.C. Heath.

Warshaw, Robin. 1988. *I Never Called It Rape: The Ms. Report on Recognizing, Fighting, and Surviving Date and Acquaintance Rape.* New York: Harper and Row.

Wober, Mallory and Barrie Gunter. 1988. *Television and Social Control.* Sydney: Avebury.

Wriggins, Jennifer. 1983. "Rape, Racism, and the Law." *Harvard Women's Law Journal* 6: 103–41.

Index

acquaintance rape, 3, 4, 11, 17, 25, 27, 28–32, 36–43, 54, 69, 73–76, 97, 154, 170; *In the Heat of the Night* example, 94–96; *21 Jump Street* example, 136–39; television victims of, 116–19, 135. *See also* date gang rape; date rape; gang rape

African Americans 11, 41 (Hoffs), 46–47, 49, 106, 110–11, 116, 121–26, 143–46, 150–52. See also *Different World*; *In the Heat of the Night*

alcohol, 10, 12, 138

All in the Family, 128, 129, 139–41

Amir, Menachim, 11, 174

Annenberg Television Script Archive, 4, 173

anti-rape movement. *See* rape reform movement

attempted rape: *All in the Family* example, 139–41; *Facts of Life* example, 141–43

Asians, 52, 138

Barbeau, Adrienne, 107

Baretta, 5, 33, 35, 55–57, 77–78, 79, 80, 100, 102, 104, 106, 115, 121

Barnaby Jones, 32–33, 71, 106, 111, 70, 71, 72, 104, 111

Barney Miller, 5, 128, 129–32

basic rape plot, 6–7, 17, 27, 28–29, 31, 32–36, 96, 99, 123–24, 133, 141;

Baretta "Shoes" example, 55–57; masculinity in, 68–73; rape in, 32–36; victims in, 101–5; *Rockford Files* example, 119–21. *See also* stranger rape

Benedict, Helen, 15, 75, 145, 174

Big Dan's tavern case, 170

Big Hawaii, 48–49, 51, 52, 174

Brinson, Susan, 16, 36, 51

boyfriends of rape victims, 22, 62, 83, 86–87, 91–94. *See also* male relatives of rape victims

British common law. *See* common law

Bronx Zoo, The, 46, 53–54, 174

brothers of rape victims, 62, 132, 136–37. *See also* male relatives of rape victims

Brownmiller, Susan (*Against Our Will*), 8, 9, 11

Burgess, Ann Wolbert. *See* rape trauma syndrome

Cagney and Lacey, 21, 23, 42, 111–14, 117–18, 119–27, 128, 132–35, 173, 174

causes of rape, 7. *See also* feminist structural analysis of rape; rapist psychology

Central Park jogger case, 74–75, 136, 170

Charlie's Angels, 105, 113, 114

chastity, 11, 30–33. *See also* victim reputation

child rape, 73, 91–94. *See also* false
  accusation; *Little House on the Prairie*;
  statutory rape
Coker v. Georgia, 44, 170
college, 40–41, 89, 116–17, 135–38. See
  also *Different World*; fraternity gang
  rape; *21 Jump Street*
common law, 10, 16, 30–32, 130–31,
  158, 174
Collins, Anne, 107
consent, 10, 12, 35–39, 43, 51–53, 57,
  59–60, 65, 76, 97, 102, 129–31, 135,
  155, 157. *See also* acquaintance rape;
  date rape
contempt of court, 125
conviction (for rape): rates/statistics,
  8–9, 43; on television, 25, 106, 107,
  120–22, 151
cop genre. *See* detective genre
cop victims, 101, 111–15
corroboration, 10, 25, 37, 44, 118, 126
Crime Story, 29, 36, 74, 174
crisis counseling. *See* rape crisis
Cuklanz, Lisa M., 5; *Rape on Trial*, 43,
  130, 145, 155–56

Dallas, 46, 51, 63–65
D'Acci, Julie, 112, 114, 121–22
date gang rape, 136
date rape, 4, 25, 27, 28–32, 36–43, 54,
  69, 73–76, 97, 108, 154, 170; *Facts of
  Life* example; *Miami Vice* example,
  55–60; *21 Jump Street* example, 41–42,
  116, 141; victims of, 116–19. *See also*
  acquaintance rape; date gang rape;
  simple rape
daughters of rape victims, 104, 140–41
Davis, Flora, 8
decoys, women police officers as, 111–
  15
defense attorney, 75–76
Depp, Johnny, 41, 138
Dennehy, Brian, 63–65
Designing Women, 1
detective genre on TV, 19–25, 159. *See
  also* detective as nurturer; detective
  violence; hegemonic masculinity;
  individual program titles

detective as nurturer, 22–23, 54, 77–
  90
detective violence, 6, 17, 22, 50, 56–58,
  78–82
Different World, 29, 42–43, 85, 116–17
district attorney, 48, 107, 108, 121, 131
Dog and Cat, 34, 35, 69, 80, 101
domestic violence, 130
Dow, Bonnie J., 14, 129
drug dealers, 73
drug use, 10, 12, 21, 73, 134, 135, 159

English common law. *See* common law
Equalizer, The, 23, 63–69, 88
Estrich, Susan, 11–12, 25
ethnicity, 17, 143

Facts of Life, 5, 82, 108, 128, 129, 141,
  152
false accusation, 29–30, 43–55, 92–93,
  118, 157, 158
fantasy, 74, 146
fathers of rape victims, 43–55, 62, 86,
  88–94, 133–34. *See also* male relatives
  of rape victims
felons, 106
feminist activism and ideas, 7–12, 18,
  22, 30–32, 37, 51–55
feminist ideas and characters on TV, 14,
  36, 42, 75–77, 82, 100–101, 105–10,
  119, 122, 127. See also *Cagney and
  Lacey*
feminist structural analysis of rape, 12,
  82, 139
Fiske, John, 12, 13, 18, 19–21, 76, 122
Fox, 40
fraternity rape , 41; *21 Jump Street* example, 135–39

gang rape, 34, 38, 41, 43, 71–72, 74–75,
  79, 82, 102, 113, 128–29, 153, 154,
  157; *Cagney and Lacey* example, 121–
  26; *Rockford Files* example, 119–21; *21
  Jump Street* example, 135–39
gangsters, 57–60
Gibbsville, 46
Gitlin, Todd (*Inside Prime Time*), 13–15
Griffin, Susan, 9, 170, 174

Hale, Sir Matthew, 43
Hanke, Robert, 18, 76
Hawaii Five-O, 35, 71, 89
hegemonic masculinity, 1–2, 18–23, 44,
    57, 62–98, 138, 147
hegemony, 12–13
high school, 23, 26, 41, 45–49, 51–54,
    75, 90–96, 117, 128, 133–34; See also
    Facts of Life; *The Bronx Zoo*; *21 Jump
    Street*; *Welcome Back Kotter*
Hill Street Blues, 13, 21, 22, 23, 33, 34, 50,
    51, 72, 79, 81, 110
Hispanics, 26, 70–71, 110, 148–49
Holmstrom, Lynda Lytle. *See* rape
    trauma syndrome
homosexual rape. *See* male victims of
    rape
homosexuality, 132, 134, 135
hospital scenes, 6, 83, 84, 95, 103, 106,
    108
Hotel, 103
husbands of rape victims, 22, 62, 63–65,
    84, 86–88, 94–96, 130–32. *See also*
    male relatives of rape victims

intra-racial rape, 10, 110–11, 116
In the Heat of the Night, 23, 36, 39, 49,
    52, 80, 90, 91–94, 97, 110, 114, 117,
    143

Johnson, Don, 58
jury, 9, 10, 43, 48, 107, 147–49; jury
    instructions in rape trials, 43
justice, 6, 8, 65, 77, 79, 124, 150

kidnapping, 34–36, 70, 79, 82–83, 89,
    119–21
Kaz, 128

L.A. Law, 23, 42, 75, 76, 81, 117, 118,
    128, 146–52
LaFree, Gary, 10
law, 27, 84–85, 146–52. *See also* rape law
    reform; common law; *L.A. Law*
Law and Order, 159
Lear, Norman, 139
Little House on the Prairie, 5, 33, 90, 91–
    94, 141

limited variability, 6–7, 44–45
Lou Grant, 33, 71, 78, 81, 108, 110

"MO," 6, 32, 36
MacGruder and Loud, 29, 33, 39, 69, 84,
    110, 114
"macho" victims, 101, 111–15
made-for-TV movies, 15, 159, 173
male-female colleague relationships,
    78, 82–85, 155
male relatives of rape victims, 86–90. *See
    also* boyfriends; brothers; fathers; hus-
    bands; sons
male socialization, 77
male victims of rape, 31, 128, 132–35
marital rape, 5, 25, 128, 129–32, 155,
    157
marital rape exemption, 129
masculine gendered programming, 19
Matt Houston, 33, 70, 111
Maude, 1
Mayne, Judith, 146
McClain's Law, 33, 83, 102
mental handicap, 104
Mexicans, 70–71
Miami Vice, 23, 24, 57–60, 80, 97, 110,
    128, 146, 150–52, 154
Michigan (rape reform) Statute of
    1974, 3, 31, 201
Millett, Kate, 170
minority victims, 110–11
Mississippi, The, 71
mistaken identity, 43–55, 66–68
Moorti, Sujata, 15
motorcycle gangs, 34, 102, 119–21
murder, 11, 35, 36, 55–58, 59, 66–67,
    73–78, 115, 148–50

National Guard, 67
New York Radical Feminists, 8
news media, 15
nonconsent. *See* consent
NYPD Blue, 159

Oregon Trail, 5

patriarchy, 36
police genre. *See* detective genre

pregnancy, 37, 43, 46, 51–53, 92–93
prison rape, 122; *Cagney and Lacey*
    example, 133–35. *See also* homosex-
    ual rape; male victims of rape
Projanski, Sara, 42, 148
professional women as rape victims,
    101–2, 111–15
Puerto Ricans, 110
"pulling train," 135. *See also* fraternity
    rape; gang rape

Quest, The, 5
Quincy, 5, 33, 70, 78, 106

race, 17, 25–26, 41, 49–51, 74–75,
    80–81, 107, 110–11, 122–26, 134,
    143–46, 146–49, 152–53, 157, 158,
    159
racism, 11, 26, 41, 49, 70–72, 110–11,
    138, 143–46, 146–49, 152–53, 155,
    156, 157–58
Rafferty, 33, 114, 115
rape as "special crime," 10
rape crisis centers/hotlines/counsel-
    ing, 2, 11, 25, 31–32, 38, 57, 85, 88,
    98, 101, 106–10, 116, 155, 156, 157
rape law reform, 22, 84, 85, 108, 109,
    129, 155, 160; blaming the victim, 71,
    88, 91–94, 134–36, 149, 156, 158. *See
    also* feminist ideas and characters on
    TV; feminist activism and ideas; rape
    reform movement
rape myths, 8–11, 15–17, 44. *See also*
    traditional views on rape; false
    accusation
rape reform (anti-rape) movement, 7–
    12, 25, 32; on TV, 105–10, 127
rape trauma syndrome, 95, 99–102,
    114, 170. *See also* victims of rape
rape trials. *See* trials
rapist character, 35–36, 61, 68–76, 97,
    155
rapist psychology, 6, 21, 59, 66–76
Rapping, Elayne, 159
"real rape." *See* stranger rape
Reasonable Doubts, 159
revenge, alleged motive for false accusa-
    tion, 10

Rideout case, 79–81, 115, 120, 129–30,
    131
Rockford Files, 5, 59, 70, 102, 119–21,
    136
Russell, Dianna E. H., 11

St. Elsewhere, 13, 33, 38, 87, 105, 108,
    109–10
Sanday, Peggy Reeves, 3, 8, 11, 37, 44,
    135–36
serial rape, 6, 31, 35, 56, 66–67, 69, 71–
    72, 111
sexism, 6, 7, 21, 65, 70–72, 74–76, 79,
    97, 110, 121, 135–36, 155
Serpico, 72, 113, 137–38
sexual history of victim, 43
Shannon, 35, 83, 102, 104, 106
Simon and Simon, 39, 80, 109, 117
simple rape, 11–12, 40–43. *See also*
    acquaintance rape; date rape
situation comedy, 5, 14, 47, 82, 129–32,
    139–43, 152. See also *All in the Family*;
    Barney Miller; *Facts of Life*; *Welcome
    Back Kotter*
sons of rape victims, 39, 80, 109. *See also*
    male relatives of rape victims
Speak Out on Rape (1971), 8
Spenser: For Hire, 5, 40, 82–83, 88–89
Starsky and Hutch, 5, 21, 32, 35, 71, 89,
    102, 104
state rape statutes, 129
statutory rape, 51–52, 91–94
stranger rape, 11, 17, 27, 28, 30–37, 69–
    76, 90–94, 99, 128, 132–36, 139–43.
    See also gang rape
Strike Force, 23, 33, 34, 69, 71, 79, 86,
    101–15. *See also* basic plot
suicide, 107, 125, 148–49

Tales of the Gold Monkey, 34, 70, 79, 89
talk shows, 15
Taylor, Ella, 13
TJ Hooker, 23, 33, 69, 71, 79, 83, 84, 85,
    87, 103, 109, 115
torture, 32, 34, 59, 72, 79
traditional views on rape, 9–12, 30–
    32, 43–55, 76–77. *See also* rape
    myths

trials, 9, 15, 30, 31, 42, 43, 48, 75, 85, 99,
    104, 106, 107, 109, 118, 123–26, 128,
    132–33, 146–52, 155–58
21 Jump Street, 21, 26, 40–42, 46, 51, 74–
    75, 81, 82, 85, 116, 128, 135–39, 143–
    46, 154

unfounded rape cases, 30
utmost resistance standard, 10–11, 12

Vegas, 34, 107, 108, 109, 136
victims of rape on TV, 99–127; of date/
    acquaintance rape, 116–19; identity
    of, 101, 103; post-rape condition, 6,

17, 34–36, 119–21, 133. *See also* cop
    victims; "macho" victims
victim reputation, 30–31, 44
Vietnam, 78
virginity, 12, 103

Walking Tall, 34, 70
Warshaw, Robin, 37
Welcome Back, Kotter, 5, 45, 47–48, 51
women detectives on prime time, 51–
    53, 57–60, 74, 82–85, 104, 111–15,
    121–26, 145, 150–52. *See also Cagney
    and Lacey*; *Charlie's Angels*; "macho"
    victims

Acknowledgments

The research for this project would not have been possible without the invaluable input and assistance of friends, family, and colleagues over the several years that this work has been in progress. In particular, special thanks are due to the staff of the Boston College Audiovisual Department for their patient help with off-air episode taping, without which the project could not have been completed. Research assistance grants from Boston College provided much needed time and resources for conducting the initial research. Marlene Fine, Val Fabj, Lynn Obrien-Hallstein, Mary Marcel, and Anne Mattina, members of my writing group in Boston, have given consistent support as well as critical comments on the final draft. Dale Herbeck's consistently active assistance and encouragement of my academic work at Boston College has earned a debt of gratitude. Diane Waldman was generous with her time in providing helpful critical comments on the manuscript. I am grateful to Hong Kong colleagues Wendy S.Y. Wong and Bernie Anderson for their support and friendship during my year at Hong Kong Baptist University. My teaching assistant, Eileen Turo devoted long hours to the preparation of the index. Finally, my parents Harlan and Joyce Cuklanz have always provided unqualified and profoundly appreciated faith and encouragement.